Contents

Introduction

Thinking about History

Before exploring this book, take a few minutes to think about these questions.

- What do you think history is?
- What have you learned in History lessons before? Did you enjoy the lessons or not? Think about why that is.
- Have you read any books about things that happened a long time ago? Have you watched any television programmes, films or plays about past events? Which ones?

So what is history?

History is about what happened in the past. It's about people in the past, what they did and why they did it, what they thought, and what they felt. To enjoy history you need to have a good imagination. You need to be able to imagine what life was like long ago, or what it may have been like to be involved in past events.

What about my History lessons?

Your History lessons are designed to get you thinking very carefully about Britain's past and its place in the wider world. For example, in the year this book starts (1901) the British controlled the largest empire the world had ever known. Britain's queen (Victoria) proudly called herself 'Empress of India' and Britain's factories, businesses and banks made more money than those of any other nation. But after taking part in two devastating world wars, a weaker and poorer Britain gave up most of its empire and its global power was greatly reduced.

This book covers some lasting and amazing changes. And you must be wondering how things changed, and when, and why. This book will take you on that journey of discovery… and hopefully turn you into a top historian on the way!

How does this book fit in?

This book will get you thinking. You will be asked to look at different pieces of evidence and to try to work things out for yourself. Sometimes, two pieces of evidence about the same event won't agree with each other. You might be asked to think of reasons why that is. Your answers might not be the same as your friend's or even your teacher's answers. The important thing is to give **reasons** for your thoughts and ideas. This book will challenge you to think critically, weigh up evidence, ask questions, sift through arguments and develop your own thoughts and opinions. It will help you understand the complex nature of people's lives and the diverse world we live in.

How to use this book

Features of the *Student Book*, are explained here and on the opposite page.

Key to icons

Source bank

Film

Worksheet

History skills activity

Literacy

Numeracy

Depth Study

In each book, there is a mini depth study that focuses on a significant event or concept. These sections give you the chance to extend and deepen your understanding of key moments in history.

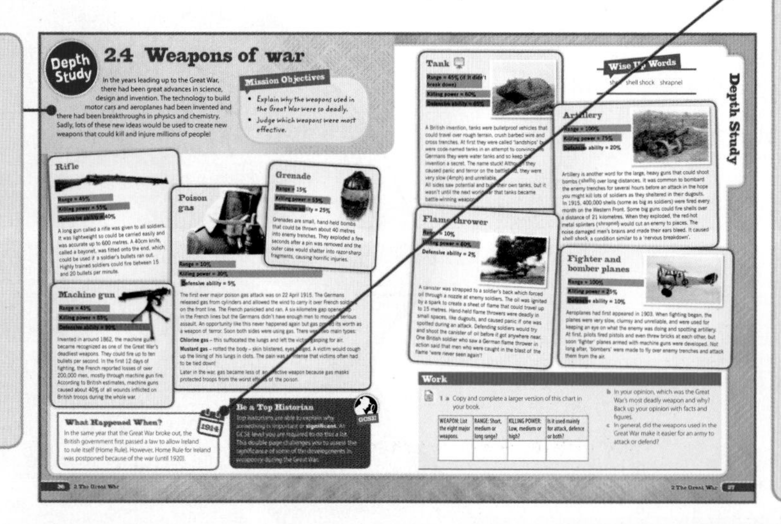

History skills

Be a Top Historian – GCSE

Sometimes the tasks, ideas and sources will challenge you to think and act like a top historian. Some of you might want to study History at GCSE level and should look out for opportunities to stretch your skills and abilities.

What Happened When?

This gives you an idea of what else is going on in the world (perhaps in another country on a different continent) at the same sort of time as the period you are studying in the lesson. It could also focus on a specific topic and make links across time, showing how things are connected.

KS3 HISTORY

Third Edition

Technology, War and Independence

1901–Present Day

Aaron Wilkes

OXFORD

Contents

Mission Objectives

All lessons in this book start by setting you 'Mission Objectives'. These are your key aims that set out your learning targets for the work ahead. At the end of the each lesson you should review these objectives and assess how well you've done.

Wise Up Words

Wise Up Words are the really important key words and terms that are vital to help you understand the topics. You can spot them easily because they are in **bold red** type. Look up their meanings in a dictionary or use the glossary at the back of the book. The glossary is a list of these words and their meanings.

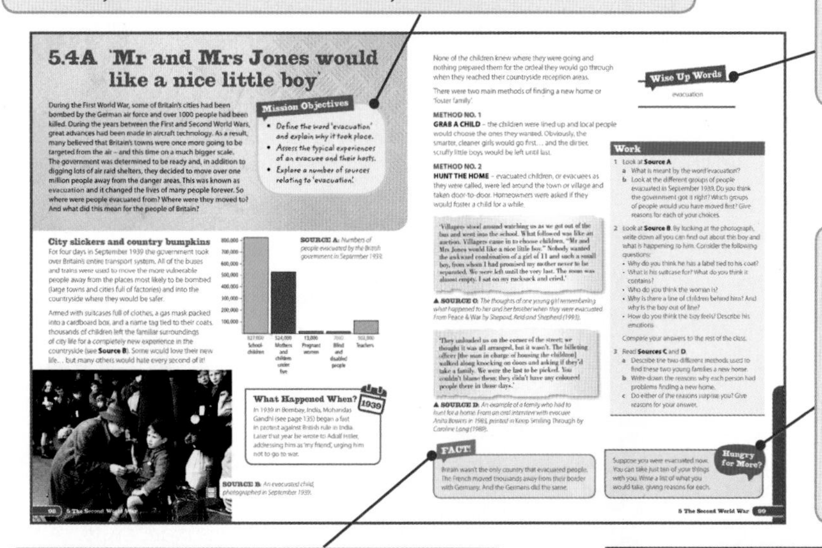

Hungry for More?

You might be asked to extend your knowledge and research beyond the classroom. This is a time to take responsibility for your own learning. You might be asked to research something in the library or on the Internet, work on a presentation, or design and make something. Can you meet the challenge?

Fact!

These are the funny, fascinating and amazing little bits of history that you don't usually get to hear about! But in this series, we think they're just as important – they give you insights into topics that you'll easily remember.

History Mystery

These sections give you an opportunity to pull all your skills together and investigate a controversial, challenging or intriguing aspect of the period, such as whether Emily Davison meant to kill herself or whether man really landed on the moon.

Work

Work sections are your opportunity to demonstrate your knowledge and understanding. You might be asked to:

- identify significant events
- make connections, draw contrasts and analyse trends over time
- work out why two people have different views about the same event
- discover what triggered an event… and uncover the consequences.

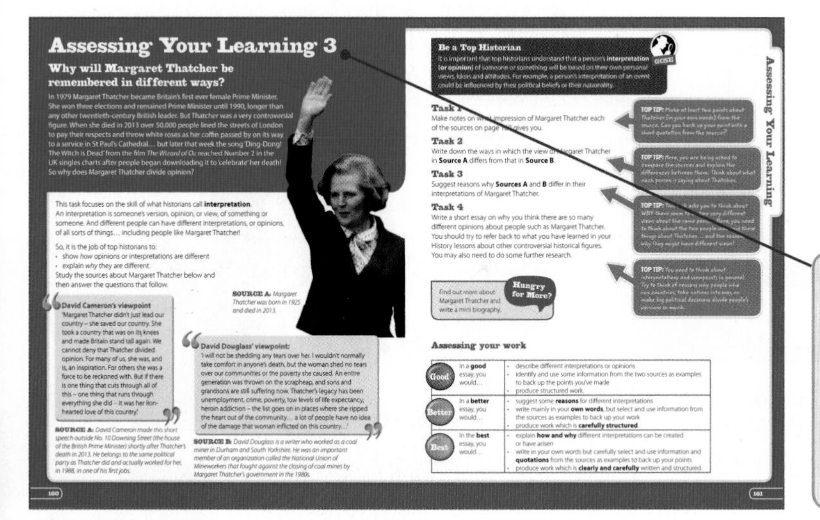

Assessing Your Learning

In the book, there are three extended assessments. These are opportunities for you to showcase what you have learned about the topic and to put your research and analysis skills to the test. These will focus on extended writing or looking at sources.

A journey into the modern world

At the beginning of the twentieth century Victoria was in her sixty-third year as Britain's queen. Despite increasing competition from other countries, the British controlled the largest empire the world had ever known, covering one fifth of all the land on the planet… and Britain's factories, businesses, shipyards and banks made more money than those of any other nation! Telephones and cars had been invented, but were very rare, and television didn't exist! Most British men could vote, but women couldn't, and the average person could expect to live to about 48 years of age. As the century progressed, things changed beyond all recognition!

This book covers this period of change, not only in Britain, but in the world as a whole.
The timeline on these pages gives you an idea of some of the key events, ideas, and discoveries that have happened since the dawn of the twentieth century.

1901

Death of Queen Victoria; succeeded by her son, Edward VII

1906

A new law introduces free school meals for Britain's poorer children

1947

British controlled India gains independence and is partitioned (split) into the nations of India and Pakistan

1948

Start of National Health Service

1952

Elizabeth II becomes queen of the UK

1957

Russia launches the world's first ever satellite into space: *Sputnik I.*

1979

Margaret Thatcher becomes Britain's first female Prime Minister

1989

British computer scientist, Tim Berners-Lee, invents the World Wide Web; the first website was launched in 1991

1998

'Good Friday Agreement' ends 30 years of conflict in Northern Ireland and a National Assembly (type of parliament) is set up

1999

Scottish Parliament and Welsh Assembly set up

THE Sun
DAY THAT CHANGED THE WORLD
SPECIAL EDITION

2001

Terror attacks in US lead to US-led forces entering Afghanistan to hunt for terrorists

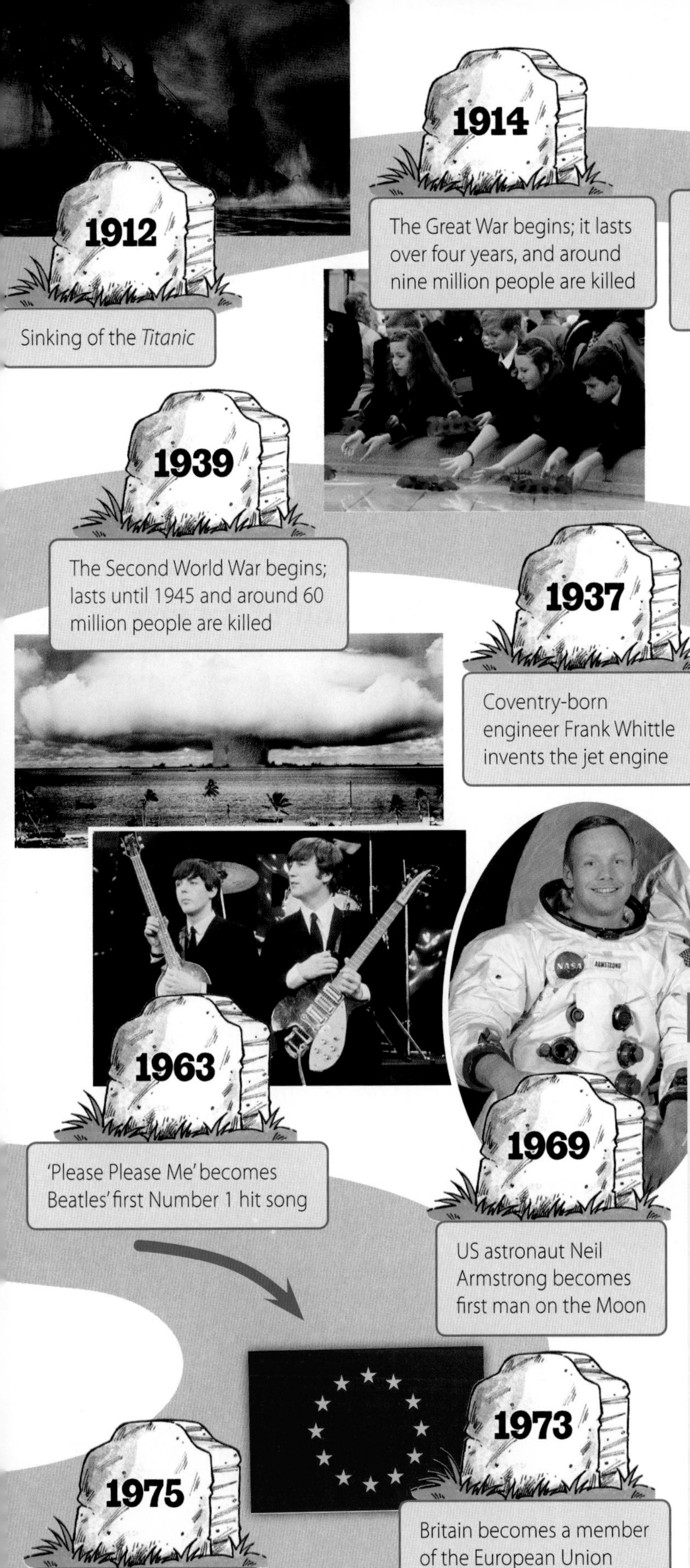

1912

Sinking of the *Titanic*

1914

The Great War begins; it lasts over four years, and around nine million people are killed

1918

Vote given to British women over 30 if they own a home or are married to someone who does; all women get the vote in 1928

1928

Scotsman Alexander Fleming discovers penicillin

1929

World financial crisis begins; many banks, businesses and individuals are ruined

1933

Adolf Hitler becomes leader of Germany

1937

Coventry-born engineer Frank Whittle invents the jet engine

1939

The Second World War begins; lasts until 1945 and around 60 million people are killed

1963

'Please Please Me' becomes Beatles' first Number 1 hit song

1969

US astronaut Neil Armstrong becomes first man on the Moon

1973

Britain becomes a member of the European Union (then known as the European Community)

1975

Equal Opportunities Act introduced in UK, making discrimination against women illegal

Work

1 Make a list of:
   a as many different historical periods as you can. You will have studied many during your time in school, for example, the Victorian period.
   b In the future, what might be a suitable name for the period of history we live in today? You could discuss this with a partner or as a group before explaining your choice.

2 a Look at each of the events, inventions, laws and changes on the timeline. Try to fit each into one of the following categories:
   - Politics
   - Technology
   - Exploration
   - Daily life

   b Could you fit them all in? If not, can you suggest other category titles?

3 Look at some of the inventions on the timeline. Pick out a few that you think have made the greatest impact or change. Explain your reasons.

1.1A Britain and the world in 1901

Mission Objectives

- Judge Britain's place in the world at the turn of the twentieth century.
- Explain how and why other countries were catching up with Britain in terms of industry, trade and empire.

In 1901 the British people had every reason to be proud. For a start, most Brits were better fed, better clothed, healthier and more educated than many people in other nations around the world. Cities were full of shops that contained a wide range of goods, either made in British factories or brought in from parts of their Empire. In 1901, Britain controlled over a quarter of the world (about 400 million people) and was the largest empire the world had ever seen.

The world in 1901

Britain had been the first country in the world to have an industrial revolution. As a result, Britain became a great industrial power and, by 1901, was the richest country in the world. Yet Britain's status in the world was under serious threat. The USA was now making more goods than Britain, and Germany and Japan were quickly catching up. How long could Britain hold onto its position as the country that did more trade (and made more money) than any other?

And there were some serious rivals on the military front too. Despite Britain having more battleships than any other two countries added together, several other nations were increasing the size of their armies and navies. By 1901 France had a big army and Germany's was one of the largest and best-trained that Europe had ever seen. Japan, Germany, Russia, and the USA greatly increased the number of battleships they had in the years around 1901 too. And these countries were just as proud and patriotic as the British were. So could this rivalry lead to war?

The end of an era

Queen Victoria died on the evening of Tuesday 22 January 1901. She had been queen for 63 years. Her son, Edward, became King Edward VII. Through her marriage to Albert, and the marriages of her children, Britain's royal family was directly connected to the rulers of Russia, Germany, Spain, Norway, Denmark, Sweden, Greece, and Romania. Indeed, before the end of her reign, some people had started to call Queen Victoria the 'Grandmother of Europe'.

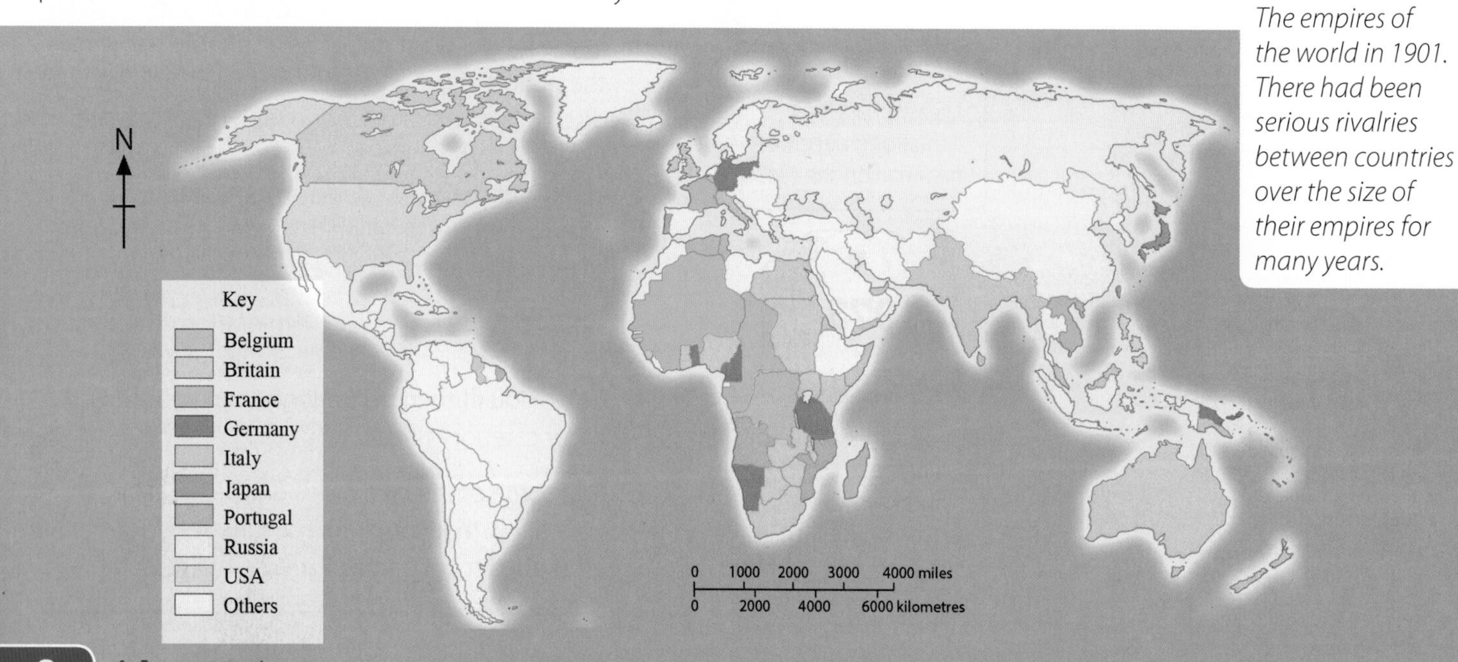

SOURCE A: *The empires of the world in 1901. There had been serious rivalries between countries over the size of their empires for many years.*

What was Britain like?

Britain itself, in 1901, was a very mixed nation. One writer even went so far as to claim that the lives led by the rich and poor were so different that Britain was like two nations – a poor one and a rich one. About 3 per cent were very rich (the upper class), 25 per cent were relatively wealthy (the middle class – bankers, doctors, accountants, managers, and so on) and the rest, the working class, were poor – with some being very, very poor!

The richer side of Britain enjoyed a life of luxury and ease. They owned land, homes and many didn't even have to work at all because they made so much money out of investments and rents. On the other side, the vast majority of poor people lived miserable lives – some earning only enough money to get by, others earning nowhere near enough to feed their families. There was no state sick pay, pensions or unemployment benefit. The injured and sick paid for their own medical care.

Wise Up Words

assembly line   mass-produce

Work

1 a Why do you think many British people were proud of their nation in 1901?

b For what reasons might some British people have been worried about their nation's status by 1901?

2 Look at **Source B**.

a Write a sentence or two describing each of the photographs.

b What details in the photographs helped you to decide which area was rich and which was poor?

SOURCE B: *These two photographs highlight the contrast between rich and poor at the start of the twentieth century. The poor slum area is vastly different from the rich Park Lane region of London. How can you tell which one is poor and which is rich?*

SOURCE C: *Shopping habits were beginning to change in the early 1900s. Instead of shopkeepers selling just a few similar items, they would sell a wide range of different items in separate departments – the department store was born. This early photograph of a John Lewis department store on Oxford Street, London was taken in November 1936. By 1910 the store would be able to sell Coca-Cola (which arrived from the USA in 1900), Heinz Baked Beans (1901), Marmite (1902), Gillette razors (1905), Hoover vacuum cleaners (1908), and Persil washing powder (1909).*

1.1B Britain and the world in 1901

What were the latest inventions?

The start of the twentieth century saw major developments in three particular areas of discovery and invention. This new technology was to have a major impact on life after 1901.

Transport

In 1885 Karl Benz, a German, made the first successful petrol-driven vehicle. It had three wheels and could reach speeds of up to ten miles per hour. In 1886 Gottlieb Daimler, another German, made the first four-wheeled petrol-driven car.

SOURCE A: *An advert for the Ford Model T, one of the bestselling motor cars in history.*

By 1901 building cars had become a big moneymaking industry but they were still too expensive for most people. Then, in 1908, an American called Henry Ford began making what was to become one of the best-selling cars ever – the Ford Model T. Based in Detroit, USA, the Ford Motor Company had made over one million Model Ts by the end of 1915. Ford used state-of-the-art techniques in his factory to **mass-produce** the cars on an **assembly line**. They would pass in front of the workers on a conveyor belt and each person would have an individual job to do. The cars were made quickly… and cheaply. In fact, in 1908 a Model T cost $900 to buy, but by 1927 Ford was making them so efficiently that the price dropped to around $200.

FACT!

Along with the motor car came the motor driving offence. In 1896, Walter Arnold from Kent became the first British driver to be fined for speeding. He was caught doing eight miles per hour in a two miles per hour zone.

On 17 December 1903, in North Carolina, USA, Orville Wright made the first manned powered flight. It lasted 12 seconds and he flew a distance of 37 metres. He had built the aeroplane with his brother, Wilbur. By 1905, the brothers had made over 150 flights, some lasting nearly 40 minutes. Flying became the latest craze and, in 1909, a Frenchman, Louis Bleriot, flew over the English Channel. By 1910 some countries were investigating the possibility of attaching bombs to planes so they could be dropped on an enemy!

SOURCE B: *The Wright Brothers' 'Baby Grand' plane.*

Communications

The telephone (invented in 1876) and the radio became very popular after 1901 and by the 1920s would be two of the most popular household items. These inventions sped up the spread of news and enabled business to be done more quickly.

Consumer goods

Other new inventions, such as vacuum cleaners and electric irons, were based on the growing use of electricity. Other consumer goods, such as wristwatches, gramophones (ask your grandparents!) and cameras, became widespread after 1901, each helping to turn the old way of life upside down.

How did people amuse themselves?

Sport remained a popular activity, as it had been in the previous century. Football, cricket, rugby, tennis, and golf continued to attract thousands of spectators and participants. Going to the pub was as popular as ever, too! The early 1900s also saw the growth of the cinema and 'movie stars' such as Charlie Chaplin, Laurel and Hardy and Buster Keaton, who became household names. It wouldn't be long before people were familiar with the likes of Mickey Mouse, Donald Duck and Pluto as well.

SOURCE C: *A film poster for a famous Charlie Chaplin comedy.*

Be a Top Historian

GCSE

Top historians are able to **pull lots of information together** to produce organized, well structured pieces of work in order to answer specific questions. At GCSE level you will be asked to do this and more!

Work

1. a Design a poster that describes Britain and the world at the start of the twentieth century. Your poster should:
   - be aimed at a Year 6 pupil who has never studied Britain in the early 1900s
   - include no more than 50 words
   - mention the rich/poor divide, shopping, the media, sport, and transport developments.

   b Using the same guidelines, design another poster that describes Britain and the world today.

   c In what areas and categories are the two posters similar and how are they different?

What Happened When?

1908

In the same year that Henry Ford started making cars, the Coal Mines Act limited the length of a miner's working day to eight hours.

1.2 How was poverty attacked?

When Queen Victoria died in 1901, Britain was a very divided nation. The gap between rich and poor was huge. A tiny minority of people enjoyed fine food, large houses and long holidays… but many millions of people were very poor. One estimate is that 13 per cent of the population owned 92 per cent of the wealth at the time! But for the poor of the country, life was really, really tough. So just how poor were Britain's poorest? And who chose to help them… and why?

Mission Objectives

- Outline key events and significant people in the attempt to help the poor in the early twentieth century.
- Assess the impact of the Liberal Reforms.

Poverty hits the headlines

In 1902 and 1903 a man named Charles Booth published his final report on the poor people of London. Over a period of 17 years Booth collected information from all over the city… and his findings shocked people. He discovered that nearly one third of Londoners were so poor that they didn't have enough money to eat properly, despite having full-time jobs! But the problems weren't just in London. Up in York, Seebohm Rowntree (of the sweet-making family) found that 28 per cent of the city's wage-earners didn't earn enough to eat healthily, and 40 per cent of children suffered illness and stunted growth from lack of food (see **Source A**)!

'If there's anything extra to buy, such as a pair of boots for one of the children, me and the children go without dinner – or maybe only 'as a cuppa tea and a bit of bread, but Jack 'ollers [shouts] to take his dinner to work and I give it to 'im as usual. He never knows we go without and I never tells 'im.'

▲ **SOURCE A:** *Taken from an interview in* Poverty: A Study of Town Life *by S. Rowntree (1901).* **Poverty** *is a situation where someone is so poor that they cannot live properly.*

Booth and Rowntree's investigations caused quite a stir – and famous politicians like David Lloyd George and a young Winston Churchill felt that governments should try harder to look after people who couldn't help themselves. Army leaders soon became worried too. Nearly one third of all men who volunteered to join the army failed their medical examination because they were too small, too thin, too ill, or had poor eyesight. Unless something was done about the health of the nation's young men, how was Britain going to fight its wars in the future?

Children were hit hardest

Millions of youngsters were not getting the good diet they needed because their parents couldn't afford it – and they didn't know anything about healthy eating. Also, calling a doctor cost money in the early 1900s, so parents rarely did unless they were desperate. By 1901 15 out of every 100 born died before their fifth birthday. Further, a poor child was, on average, 9cm shorter than a rich child of the same age!

Change at last?

In 1906 the general election was won by a political party (group) called the Liberal Party. They were committed to trying to wipe out poverty in Britain, and decided to start with the children. One of the first moves they made was to introduce free school meals for the poorest children (see **Source B**).

▼ **SOURCE B:** *A typical week of free school meals. The poorest children could eat for free, but other children could buy a meal for a small charge. By 1914 over 158,000 children were having free meals once a day, every day.*

THIS WEEK'S MENU

Monday: Tomato soup ~ currant roly-poly pudding

Tuesday: Meat pudding ~ rice pudding

Wednesday: Yorkshire pudding, gravy, peas ~ rice pudding and sultanas

Thursday: Vegetable soup ~ currant pastry or fruit tart

Friday: Stewed fish, parsley sauce, peas, mashed potatoes ~ blancmange

Other measures were introduced too – free medical checks and treatment, for example (see **Source D**). A Children's Charter was also introduced, which made law many of the things that still protect young people today.

- Children are 'protected persons' – parents can be prosecuted if they neglect or are cruel to them.
- Inspectors are to regularly visit any children who have been neglected in the past.
- All children's homes are to be regularly inspected.
- Youth courts and young offenders' homes are to keep young criminals away from older ones.
- Children under 14 are not allowed in pubs.
- Shopkeepers cannot sell cigarettes to children under 16.

▲ **SOURCE C:** *The Children's Charter (or the Children's Act), 1908. As you can see, many of these reforms are still in place today.*

SOURCE D: *An anxious mother watches the doctor examine her son in one of Britain's first free medical checks.*

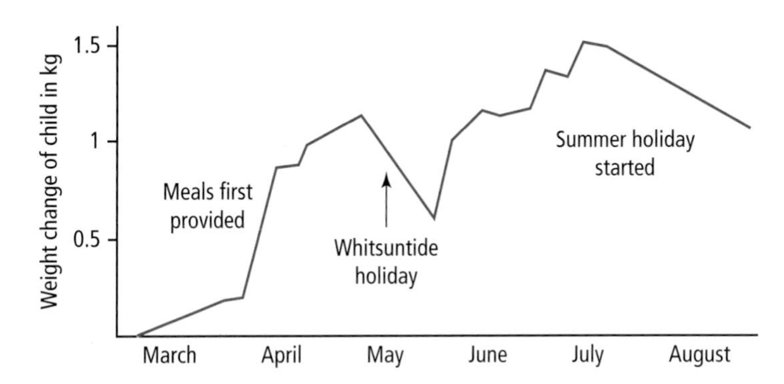

SOURCE E: *This graph shows how children gained and lost weight during part of the year.*

After helping children, the new Liberal government moved on to help other vulnerable sections of society. They introduced unemployment benefit (the 'dole'), sickness benefit and old age pensions. They even built Britain's first job centres. It seemed that, at last, politicians were focusing more on helping ordinary people.

Wise Up Words

poverty

FACT!

In Victorian times, there were two main political parties – the Conservatives and the Liberals. In 1900 a new political party was formed – the Labour Party – to attract the votes of workers. Some say the Liberal Party's focus on helping ordinary, working people and children after 1906 was an attempt to pull voters away from the New Labour Party!

Work

1. **a** Who were i) Charles Booth and ii) Seebohm Rowntree?
   b Why do you think their reports shocked so many people?
2. Why do you think army leaders were so worried about the health of Britain's young men in the early 1900s?
3. Look at **Source B**.
   a Why were school meals introduced?
   b Choose any day from the source and write a few sentences comparing it to the meal you ate for dinner on the same day of the week. You might wish to make a judgement on which was the healthier meal.
4. Look at **Source E**.
   a Draw **Source E** in your book. Remember to label it carefully.
   b What was the result of introducing school meals? Try to use numbers from the graph in your answer.
   c Why do you think children lost weight in May and July?
5. **a** Apart from the introduction of school meals, how else were children helped in the early 1900s?
   b Why do you think that helping children was seen as one of the main priorities of the new Liberal government?

1.3 Why is the *Titanic* so famous?

If you were to ask somebody to name a famous shipping disaster, they would probably answer: 'the *Titanic*'. In fact, they would probably struggle to name another one! The *Titanic* is famous all over the world – and not just because of the Hollywood film that focused on its sinking. So just why is the *Titanic* so famous? What makes it different from the thousands of other shipping tragedies? And what does the disaster tell us about how poor people were treated in the early twentieth century?

Mission Objectives

- Explain why the *Titanic* is such a famous ship.
- Decide if women and children really were rescued first.

Titanic technology!

One of the most impressive – and staggering – things about the *Titanic* was its sheer size. At more than three football pitches long, weighing 46,000 tons and being taller than a 17-storey building, it was the biggest moving object ever built. Its **hull** was made from 16 watertight compartments – which led many to believe that the ship was 'unsinkable'! On top of all that, it was widely tipped to beat the **transatlantic** speed record. What could possibly go wrong?

Passengers – posh and poor

When the *Titanic* set sail on 10 April 1912, some of the richest people in the world were on board. To keep them comfortable, the first-class cabins were fitted out like rooms in a five-star hotel. To keep them entertained, there was a state-of-the-art gymnasium, a swimming pool, a tennis court, and a Parisian café. As you can imagine, a first-class ticket was very expensive. In fact, a top-priced ticket from Southampton to New York would have cost £870 – about £27,000 in today's money! But the rich passengers were in the minority (there were only 322 in first class). The vast majority of passengers (709) were poor people who had bought a one-way ticket to a new life in the USA. They weren't just British and Irish working-class people: Russians, Italians, Swedes, Germans, Spaniards, French, and many other nationalities were on board too. Some had paid as little as £3 (about £95 today) for a space in a basic third-class compartment deep inside the ship.

SOURCE A: *The first class passengers enjoyed luxury similar to a five-star hotel.*

The icy end?

Just four days into its **maiden** voyage, on the evening of Sunday 14 April, the *Titanic* moved into the freezing waters in the middle of the Atlantic. As the temperature dropped below zero degrees Celsius, hitting one of the giant, silent icebergs in the inky-black night became a real possibility. Just before midnight, one of the lookouts spotted the outline of an iceberg 'dead ahead'. Despite desperately turning to avoid it and putting the engines in full reverse, the *Titanic* struck the iceberg at speed and was damaged below the waterline. Six of the watertight compartments had been ripped open and water flooded in. The ship could stay afloat if only four compartments filled with water and so, less than three hours later, the *Titanic* sank beneath the waves. The order had been given for women and children to get in the lifeboats first, but of the 2206 people on board, only 704 were rescued from the icy waters.

hull maiden transatlantic

First class 

	On board	Rescued	% Rescued
Men	173	58	34
Women	144	139	97
Children	5	5	100
Total	**322**	**202**	**63**

Second class

	On board	Rescued	% Rescued
Men	160	13	8
Women	93	78	84
Children	24	24	100
Total	**277**	**115**	**42**

Third class

	On board	Rescued	% Rescued
Men	454	55	12
Women	179	98	55
Children	76	23	30
Total	**709**	**176**	**25**

Total passengers and crew

	On board	Rescued	% Rescued
Men	1662	315	19
Women	439	338	77
Children	105	51	49
Total	**2206**	**704**	**32**

SOURCE B: *Casualty figures issued shortly after the sinking.*

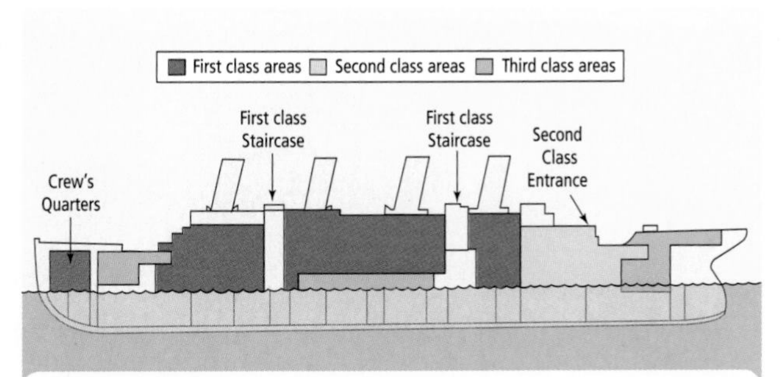

SOURCE C: *This cross-section diagram of the ship shows where the first-, second- and third-class areas were.*

'When anyone asks me to describe my career at sea, I just say – uneventful. Of course there have been winter gales, storms and fog, but in all my years, I have never been in an accident. I've only seen one ship in trouble in all my years at sea. I've never seen a wreck, have never been wrecked, and I have never been in a situation that threatened to end in disaster.'

▲ **SOURCE D:** *The ship's captain, E. J. Smith, said this in an interview in 1910. The captain was a very well-respected sailor who'd had a successful and accident-free career.*

Work

1. There are a number of factors that explain why the *Titanic*'s sinking is such a famous event. Put the following factors in order of how important you think they were:
   - It was the *Titanic*'s maiden voyage.
   - People said it was practically unsinkable.
   - It was the biggest ship in the world.
   - There is a very successful film called *Titanic*.
   - Many people died.
2. Look at **Source B**.
   - **a** Draw three separate bar charts to show the percentage of men, women and children rescued from each class of passengers.
   - **b** Which class of passengers suffered the most?
   - **c** Do you think the order for women and children to get on the lifeboats first was followed? Explain your answer carefully.
   - **d** What does this evidence tell you about the attitude that rich people had towards poor people in 1912?
   - **e** Do you think the same thing would happen today?
3. Write a fact file on the *Titanic*, including your top ten facts about the ship and the sinking. Why not use a computer to design your fact file, including any pictures you can find on the Internet?

1.4 Who or what was to blame for the *Titanic* disaster?

The sinking of the *Titanic* caused a sensation on both sides of the Atlantic. Over 1500 people had lost their lives in the freezing waters and it wasn't just their grieving relatives who wanted to know who was to blame. Your task is to conduct an enquiry into the disaster and write a report for the US and British governments. Your report should be entitled 'The *Titanic* Disaster Enquiry' and you must come to a conclusion as to who was most to blame. Your job is to look through all the evidence (**A** to **E**) and complete the Work section on page 17. Good luck!

Mission Objectives

- Explain how several factors led to the sinking of the Titanic and the enormous loss of life.
- Judge who or what was most to blame for the tragedy.

EVIDENCE A

Was it Captain Smith's fault?

Captain Smith was due to retire after the *Titanic's* maiden voyage. Did he want to set a transatlantic speed record on his last ever trip? He ignored at least seven warnings from other nearby ships and the *Titanic* was travelling at 20 knots per hour – close to top speed – when it struck the iceberg. If the ship had been going slower, could it have turned out of the iceberg's way in time? Perhaps Captain Smith thought an iceberg couldn't sink a modern ship. He once said, 'I can't imagine anything causing a modern ship to sink. Shipbuilding has gone beyond that.'

EVIDENCE C

The original plans for the *Titanic* had more lifeboats than the completed ship eventually had.

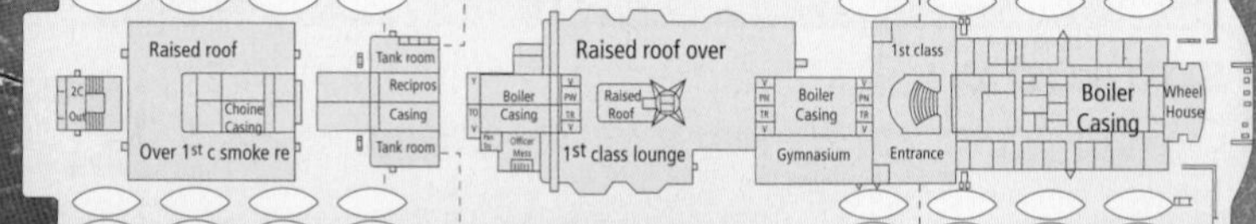

EVIDENCE B

Was it Harland and Wolff's fault?

The *Titanic* was built at the Harland and Wolff shipyard in Belfast, Northern Ireland. About three million rivets were used to hold the ship together. When the wreck of the *Titanic* was finally discovered in 1985, some of the rivets were brought to the surface and analysed. The investigations showed that the rivets were made from poor-quality iron. When the ship struck the iceberg, the heads of rivets snapped off and sections of the ship were torn wide open. If the rivets had been made of more expensive, higher-quality iron, perhaps the hole in the *Titanic*'s side would have been smaller – and maybe the ship wouldn't have sunk at all. Further tests showed that the cheap rivets became **brittle** in extremely low temperatures – just like on the night of 14 April 1912.

EVIDENCE D

Was it Thomas Andrews' fault?

Thomas Andrews was the naval architect who designed the *Titanic*. The ship was thought to be unsinkable by many because of the 16 watertight compartments in the hull that Andrews had designed. However, the compartments didn't reach as high as they should have done. Andrews had reduced their height to make more space for first-class cabins. If just two of the watertight compartments had reached all the way to the top, there is a chance that the *Titanic* wouldn't have sunk.

EVIDENCE E

Was it Stanley Lord's fault?

Stanley Lord was the captain of a ship called the *Californian*, which was only 30 kilometres away from the *Titanic* when it struck the iceberg. Despite being aware of icebergs in the area, Lord allowed his radio operator to go to bed at around 11:15pm. At around midnight, members of the *Californian*'s crew saw rockets being fired into the sky on the horizon. They woke Captain Lord and told him, but he decided not to sail towards the fireworks – he assumed it was just another ship having a cocktail party! Should Lord have made the *Californian* race towards the scene? Should he at least have insisted that the radio be turned on so they could have heard the *Titanic*'s **SOS** signals? How many more people would have survived if the *Californian* had been there to pull them from the icy waters?

Was it Bruce Ismay's fault?

Bruce Ismay was the man in charge of the White Star Line – the owners of the *Titanic*. He was also one of the first-class passengers on board the ship and managed to secure a place on one of the lifeboats before it went down. Ismay was eager to prove the *Titanic* was not only the biggest and most luxurious ocean liner, but also the fastest. Did he put pressure on Captain Smith to maintain top speed despite sailing through icebergs? Was he hoping that the *Titanic* would make a record crossing? One witness claimed she heard Ismay and Smith arguing on the evening of 13 April – was it over the ship's speed? Also, was Ismay responsible for more deaths than there should have been? The original design for the *Titanic* equipped it with 32 lifeboats – enough for everyone on board. The finished ship had only 20 – enough for just 1178 of the 2206 people on board. The White Star Line decided to remove some of the lifeboats to make room for more first-class cabins.

Wise Up Words

brittle SOS

Work

So who was to blame for the huge loss of life on-board the *Titanic*? Start to work on your theory.

Step 1: Analyse the evidence

Under the following headings, write a sentence or two outlining how each may have contributed to the sinking.
i) Captain Smith ii) The shipbuilders
iii) Thomas Andrews iv) Captain Lord
v) Bruce Ismay

Step 2: Prioritize the evidence

In your opinion, is one person more at fault than any other? Can you put your list in order of responsibility? Did one person's actions contribute more to the sinking than any other's? Write a paragraph or two explaining why you made your decision. Did some people have nothing at all to do with the sinking? If so, say who, and how you arrived at this conclusion.

Step 3: Deliver your verdict

Time to write up your report and present your findings on who was most to blame to the US and British governments. Your report should be structured under a series of headings:

- Start your report with a brief introduction to the disaster.
- Outline the role in the sinking of each person under investigation.
- Write a conclusion – is one person to blame or several, or a combination of all?
- Remember, if you don't blame one person, it doesn't mean your investigation has failed! There is often more than one factor to consider in most investigations.

1.5A Who were the suffragettes?

Mission Objectives

- Analyse a variety of posters.
- Compare suffragettes and suffragists.
- Evaluate what finally won the vote for women.

In 1901 no woman in Britain (around half of the population) had the right to vote. The nation was completely ruled by men in Parliament and women were expected to keep out of the way. It was widely believed (by men, and some women, including Queen Victoria) that a woman's place was in the home, looking after her children and husband. If a woman had a job, they were always paid less than men and they were only allowed jobs that were deemed suitable by men, such as nurses, cleaners, nannies, teachers, and factory workers. Some women obviously thought this was terribly unfair and decided to do something about it. So how did these women try and win the vote? What tactics did they use? And what finally won the vote for women?

A WOMAN'S MIND MAGNIFIED

SOURCE A: *What point is this poster from 1905 trying to make?*

Time for change?

Look at **Source A**. This postcard appeared in 1905 and demonstrates what many men thought about a woman's mental abilities. The men who produced this poster would clearly never accept that women should be allowed to vote!

However, by 1897 many women no longer accepted the way they were treated and a group formed that campaigned for women to be allowed the right to vote. They thought that if women could vote, they might be able to elect politicians who promised to improve their lives (make sure women were paid the same as men, for example). This group was known as the **suffragists** ('suffrage' is another word for 'vote') and they held meetings, wrote letters to Parliament, went on protest marches, and produced posters of their own (see **Source B**).

SOURCE B: *This poster is from around 1912. What point is it trying to make?*

New tactics

Unfortunately, the suffragists were not particularly successful, and in 1903 some of the group's members decided to form their own group and after a couple of years they changed tactics. Known as **suffragettes**, and led by Emmeline Pankhurst and her daughters, the motto of these women became 'deeds not words'!

Spectacular suffragettes!

The Pankhursts decided that the best way to highlight their cause was to commit spectacular stunts that would guarantee an appearance in the newspapers. They disrupted political meetings, chained themselves to railings in Downing Street, pelted politicians with eggs and flour, and smashed Parliament's windows with stones (see **Source C**). They also set fire to churches and railway stations and some poured acid on golf courses. When they were arrested and fined, they refused to pay and were sent to prison. Soon, they were refusing all food in prison (hunger strike). This gave the government a terrible choice – free the suffragettes or let them starve to death! At first, they released all hunger strikers, but soon decided to force-feed them instead (see **Source D**). All this guaranteed that the suffragettes were front page news!

Wise Up Words

munitions suffragette suffragist

SOURCE C: *This photograph shows a suffragette being arrested outside Buckingham Palace.*

'What good did all this violent campaigning do us? For one thing our campaign made women's suffrage a matter of news – it had never been that before. Now the newspapers are full of us.'

▲ **SOURCE E:** *Written by Emmeline Pankhurst in* My Own Story *(1914).*

'The activities of the suffragettes had reached a stage at which nothing was safe from their attacks. Churches were burned, buildings and houses were destroyed, bombs were exploded, the police assaulted and meetings broken up. The feeling in the House [of Commons] caused by the actions of the suffragettes hardened opposition to their demands. The result was a defeat of their Bill by 47 votes, which the Government had previously promised to support.'

▲ **SOURCE F:** *The Speaker of the House of Commons writing in 1925 about the events of 1913. Many MPs sympathized with the cause of votes for women, but didn't want to look as if they had given in to the suffragettes' demands.*

SOURCE D: *Hunger strikers were force-fed meat and lime juice. The suffragettes tried to use this harsh treatment to gain sympathy for their cause.*

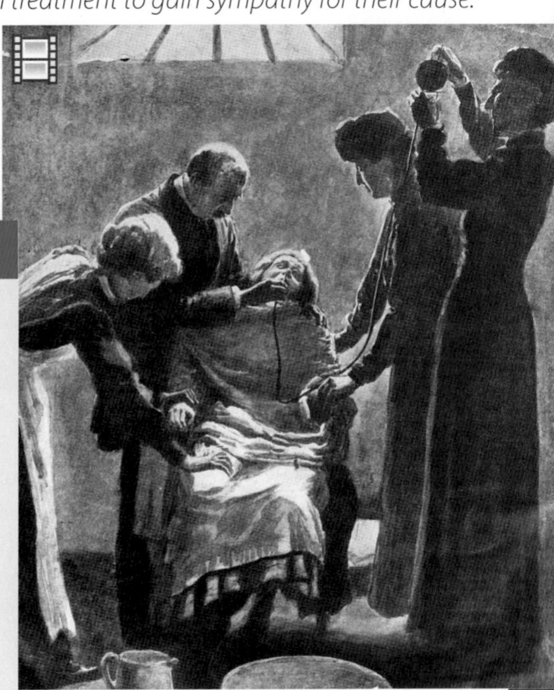

Work

1. Look at **Source A**.
   a. Explain what is meant by the term 'sexist'.
   b. In what ways is **Source A** sexist?
2. Look at **Source B**. What is the message of this poster?
3. a. Explain the difference between a suffragist and a suffragette.
   b. Why do you think the suffragettes chose the motto, 'deeds not words'?
4. Read **Source E**. How did the suffragettes intend to win women's right to vote?
5. Read **Source F**. How may the actions of the suffragettes have damaged support for their cause?

1.5B Who were the suffragettes?

SOURCE A: *Women working in a munitions factory during the Great War. This was a very dangerous job that could leave women very ill because of the toxic chemicals in the explosives.*

An unexpected opportunity

By 1914 women had still not won the right to vote. When the Great War started that year the suffragettes called off their campaign of violence and asked their supporters to help the war effort as much as possible instead. In fact, the war brought women an unexpected opportunity! With more and more men leaving their jobs to become soldiers, women got the chance to 'fill in' for the men and do jobs they had never done before. They became bus drivers, police officers, car mechanics, and road menders. Thousands of women worked in **munitions** factories (which were very unhealthy and dangerous – see **Source A**) or became nurses or ambulance drivers near the battlefields in France and Belgium.

The impact of women

The work done by women during the war was vital (see **Sources B** and **C**). By the end of the war, many people felt that women had earned the right to vote – and many politicians didn't want the suffragettes to start their violent campaign again! In 1918 Parliament changed the voting laws and gave all men over the age of 21 and all women over the age of 30 the right to vote (as long as they owned their own land or were married to a man who did). Some people argued that this wasn't enough, while others said it was a move in the right direction. Eventually, in 1928, Parliament reduced the voting age for women to 21, regardless of whether they owned a house or were married. Finally, women had the same voting rights as men!

Be a Top Historian

GCSE

Top historians can recognise that countries can be very **diverse**. This means that people's lives are varied and different even though they live in the same country in the same period of history. And its not just about differences between rich and poor – the lives of men and women can be just as diverse.

'It is true that women cannot fight with rifles, but they have aided in the most effective way in the war. What is more, when the war comes to an end, don't women have a special claim to be heard on the many questions that affect their interests? I cannot deny that claim.'

SOURCE B: *Prime Minister Herbert Asquith, speaking in August 1916. What do you think he means by women's 'special claim'?*

Quality

Metal – women's work better than men's
Aircraft woodwork – women equal to men
Bullet making – women equal to men
Shell making – women's work poorer than men's

Quantity

Metal – women's production equal to men's
Aircraft woodwork – women's production equal to men's
Bullet making – women's production equal to men's; in some cases, women produce 20 per cent more than men
Shell making – women's production behind men

▲ **SOURCE C:** *A comparison of the quality and output in factories of men and women in 1918. It is little wonder that Herbert Asquith said, 'How could we carry on the war without women? There is hardly a service in which women have not been at least as active as men.'*

SOURCE D: *The suffragette campaign to gain women the vote is commemorated in this 50p coin from 2003. It features a suffragette chained to a railing and a WSPU banner (the Women's Social and Political Union was the official name of the suffragettes). The WSPU was formed in 1903.*

Hungry for More?

What about the contribution of women in the Second World War? Did they do the same sort of jobs or were there new things for them to do? Research their contribution.

Work

1 What impact did the Great War have on:
   i) the suffragette movement?
   ii) the roles of women?

2 Look at **Sources B** and **C**. In your own words, assess the impact that women had during the Great War.

3 Which of these two factors do you think was the most important for winning women's right to vote?
   - Women proved they were equal with war work.
   - The suffragettes' campaign highlighted the cause of 'votes for women'.

   Now write a paragraph explaining your choice.

4 Look at **Source D**.
   a Do you think the suffragette movement deserves to be commemorated on a 50p coin in this way? Give reasons for your answer.
   b Design your own coin commemorating the story of how women won the right to vote.

History Mystery

1.6 Did Emily Davison mean to kill herself?

The Derby is one of the best-known horse races in the world. Every year, thousands of people – including the Royal Family – flock to Epsom Downs racecourse to watch the best horses and riders in the world battle it out for the famous trophy. It always gets plenty of coverage in the newspapers, which is why a suffragette named Emily Davison thought it would make the ideal opportunity for the suffragettes' next publicity stunt. Historians cannot agree over what happened next. What we do know is that Davison was knocked down and killed by the king's horse, Anmer, and that over 20,000 people attended her funeral. But did Davison deliberately kill herself for the suffragettes' cause or did she misjudge the speed of the horses and die in a tragic accident? And what does the evidence say?

Read through the following pieces of evidence before explaining your conclusions in the Work section.

EVIDENCE A: *Part of Emily Davison's prison record. She was a very militant suffragette who believed in 'deeds not words'.*

March 1909	One month in prison for obstruction (blocking a road)
September 1909	Two months for stone throwing
November 1910	One month for breaking windows
January 1912	Six months for setting fire to postboxes
November 1912	Ten days for assaulting a vicar whom she mistook for a Member of Parliament

EVIDENCE B: *From a book by G. Colmore,* The Life of Emily Davison *(1913). The Suffragette Summer Festival was a week-long meeting of hundreds of suffragettes.*

'She was able to go to the [Suffragette Summer] Festival on the opening day, Tuesday 3 June. Emily was never brighter than on that day. She stayed long at the fair and said she should come every day, "except tomorrow. I am going to the Derby tomorrow".
"What are you going to do?"
"Ah ha!"
It was her usual answer… when she had planned something. "Look in the evening paper," she added, "and you will see something".'

EVIDENCE C: *From an eyewitness, John Ervine, who stood near to Emily Davison on the day.*

'The King's horse, Anmer, came up and Ms Davison went towards it. She put up her hand, but whether it was to catch hold of the reins or protect herself, I don't know. It was all over in a few seconds. The horse knocked her over with great force and then stumbled and fell, throwing the jockey violently onto the ground. Both he and Ms Davison were bleeding a lot. I feel sure that Ms Davison meant to stop the horse and that she didn't go onto the course thinking the race was over.'

EVIDENCE D: *From an Internet website, written by a modern historian.*

'Some believed that Davison was trying to cross the racecourse and had failed to see that not all the horses had cleared the course. Other spectators claimed that they heard her shout "Votes for women" before leaping out in front of the King's horse. A crude black and white film was taken that caught the event "live"… and it shows clearly that Davison stopped in front of Anmer (therefore she did not want to simply cross the course) and it appears that she tried to make a grab for the reins of the horse.'

EVIDENCE E: *From Sylvia Pankhurst's* The Suffragette Movement: An Intimate Account of Persons and Ideals *(1931).*

'Her friend declared that she would not have died without writing a farewell message to her mother. Yet she sewed the [suffragette] flags inside her coat as though to make sure that no mistake could be

EVIDENCE F: *The front page of a newspaper published the day after the Derby and before Davison had died of her injuries. Look closely at the photograph. Why do you think there were so few reliable witnesses despite the thousands of people who attended the race?*

DAILY SKETCH.

ONE HALFPENNY.

HISTORY'S MOST WONDERFUL DERBY: FIRST HORSE DISQUALIFIED: A 100 TO 1 CHANCE WINS: SUFFRAGETTE NEARLY KILLED BY THE KING'S COLT.

EVIDENCE G: *Part of the official report surrounding Davison's death. She had asked for the flags a few days before the race meeting.*

FOUND ON THE BODY OF EMILY DAVISON

OFFICIAL POLICE REPORT

2 large suffragette flags (green, white and purple stripes) pinned inside the back of her coat; 1 purse (containing three shillings, eight pence and three farthings); 8 postage stamps; 1 key; 1 helper pass for the Suffragette Summer Festival, Kensington, London; 1 notebook; 1 handkerchief; some envelopes and writing paper; 1 race card; 1 return railway ticket.

EVIDENCE H: *Adapted from the writings of Emily Davison herself. These events occurred in Holloway Prison, two weeks before her release from a six-month sentence for arson.*

'As soon as I got the chance I threw myself over the prison railings. The idea in my mind was that one big tragedy would save many others; but the netting prevented any injury. Then I threw myself down on an iron staircase, a distance of 10 to 13 metres, but the netting caught me again. I felt I had only one chance left, so I hurled myself head first down the staircase, a distance of three metres. I landed on my head with a mighty thud and was knocked out. When I recovered I was in agony.'

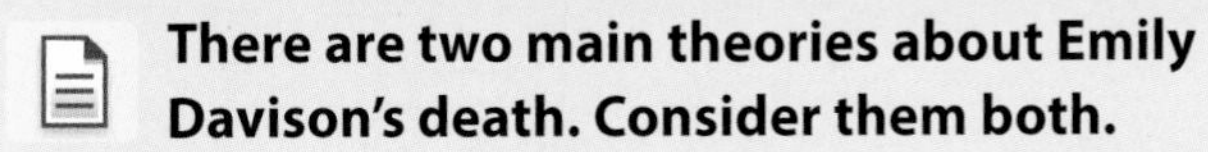

Wise Up Words

martyr

Work

There are two main theories about Emily Davison's death. Consider them both.

1. She tried to kill herself for the cause of 'votes for women', hoping to turn herself into a **martyr** in the process.
2. She wanted to make a protest by stopping the king's horse but it went badly wrong and she died in a tragic accident.

Now reread the evidence on these pages and consider:

- why she had two flags
- why she didn't tell anyone what she planned to do
- why she chose the king's horse – or did she step in front of Anmer by chance?

Step 1 Make sure you fully understand all the evidence.

Step 2 Find any evidence that Davison was trying to kill herself.

Step 3 Find any evidence to show that Davison did *not* plan to kill herself.

Step 4 Deliver your verdict in the form of a report.

Imagine you are part of a government enquiry team that has been that given the job of investigating the death in order to arrive at a conclusion.

Give a basic outline of Davison's death. You might include details of Davison herself and the events before she was killed.

Do you think Emily Davison planned to make a protest or did she plan to die as well? Back up any of your conclusions with evidence. Best of luck!

Depth Study

2.1A Why did the Great War start?

You can go to almost any town or village in Britain and see the names of dead soldiers, sailors and air crew carved on stone memorials like the one in **Source A**. This one was built to commemorate 60 ex-students of Castle High School, Dudley in the West Midlands, who died during the Great War of 1914–1918. It is outside the school's library. Many schools, factories, sports clubs, and town councils built memorials like this to record the names of young men who had died fighting for their country. So what caused this war? Why was it called the 'Great War'? And why were so many men so keen to join up to fight?

Mission Objectives

- *Define and identify short- and long-term causes of the Great War.*
- *Explain how an assassination led to the outbreak of war.*

What was so 'great'?

The Great War wasn't 'great' because men enjoyed themselves and had a great time; it was called the Great War because the world had never experienced such a big war before. Millions and millions of men, split into two sides (or **alliances**), spent over four years killing each other. To help them in their task, they used the deadliest weapons the world had ever seen. In total, around nine million people were killed – that's over 5000 deaths every day, seven days a week, 365 days a year, for over four years. Such was the horror felt at this enormous **death toll** that many called it 'the war to end all wars'. So just how did the Great War start?

Long-term causes

Wars usually have a number of different causes that build up over time. Some causes go back a very long time indeed, perhaps years or decades. But some causes may have happened only recently, in the last few days, weeks or months. Historians like to divide the reasons why something happened into **long-term** and **short-term causes**. The cartoons, maps and explanations on page 25 outline the long-term causes of the Great War.

SOURCE A: *As well as ex-pupils, the memorial includes the name of a teacher who joined up to fight in September 1914. He was killed in action in France two years later, aged 31.*

Wise Up Words

alliance arms race assassinate death toll long-term cause short-term cause Triple Alliance Triple Entente

Hungry for More?

Where is the nearest Great War memorial to you? Is it close enough for you to walk to it? Maybe your school has a memorial like Castle High School, Dudley. If so, why not go and visit it and read through the list of names? Are there any names that are the same as yours or your friends'? You can research some of the names and details of how they died on www.cwgc.org.

What could so many countries fall out about? And why did so many young men volunteer to join the slaughter?

Nationalism

At the beginning of the twentieth century, people started to take great pride in their countries. This is called 'nationalism' – thinking that your nation is better than others. Unfortunately, for many leaders of Europe, the best way to prove they were the best was to have a war with their rivals.

Militarism

People took great pride in their armies and navies. To make sure that theirs were the best, countries spent more and more money on bigger and bigger armies (known as 'militarism'). Nobody wanted the smallest army, so countries got caught up in an **arms race**. To many, there was no point in having a big, expensive army if you weren't going to use it, and whenever countries fell out the temptation to use those weapons was always there.

Imperialism

Britain had conquered lots of land all over the world by 1914 and had a huge empire. But other nations wanted big empires too – a desire known as 'imperialism' (from the word 'empire'). The race to gain control of other nations, particularly in Africa, led to tension and fierce rivalries among European countries. They began to see each other as a threat to their overseas possessions and thought war was the only way to remove this threat permanently.

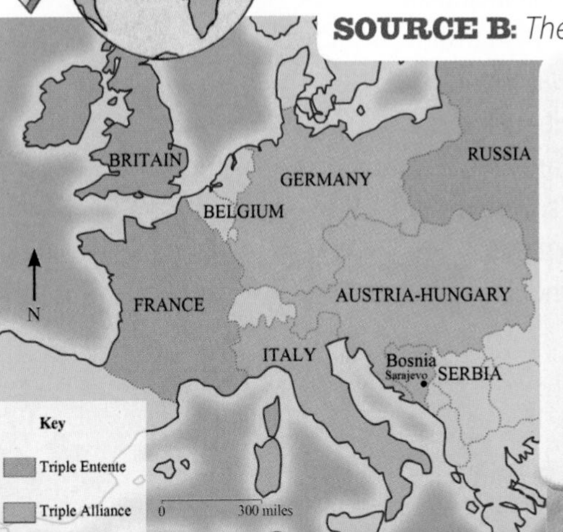

SOURCE B: *The Alliance System.*

Alliances

As each country began to feel threatened, they looked for friends to back them up in a war – known as allies. Europe split into two alliances. Britain, France and Russia formed the **Triple Entente**, and Germany, Austria-Hungary and Italy formed the **Triple Alliance**. The idea was to put people off starting a war as it would mean fighting against three nations instead of one. Although this made them feel more secure, it meant it would only take one small disagreement between any two nations involved and all of Europe would be dragged into a war.

Work

1 a Write a sentence that defines the following terms: • arms race • allies.

b Copy the terms from **List A** into your book and match them to the correct definitions from **List B**.

List A

• militarism • alliances
• imperialism • nationalism

List B

– Groups of nations that agree to back each other up in a war.
– To love your country and think it is superior to others.
– To take great pride in your country's armed forces.
– To gain control of land and people around the world and build an empire.

2 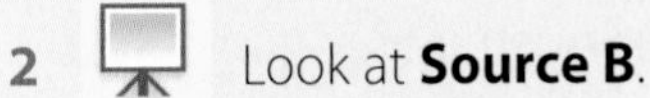 Look at **Source B**.

a Make a list of the countries in i) the Triple Alliance ii) the Triple Entente.

b If the Triple Alliance attacked France, how could Russia's friendship help France?

c If Austria-Hungary attacked Russia, how could France's friendship help Russia?

d If Russia attacked Germany, how could Austria-Hungary's friendship help Germany?

3 Some historians have compared Europe in 1914 to two groups of mountain climbers, all tied together with one rope.

– If one of the climbers slipped and fell, what's the best thing that could happen?
– If one of the climbers slipped and fell, what's the worst thing that could happen?

Depth Study

2.1B Why did the Great War start?

The short-term reason

Some historians have compared Europe in 1914 to a barrel of gunpowder in that it only needed a spark to make the whole thing explode. On 28 June 1914 the spark arrived. All it took was the murder of one man and his wife and all of the major nations of Europe were plunged into war. So who was this man? How was he murdered and why? And how did his death lead to the Great War?

'Unhappy anniversary'

On 28 June 1914, the heir to the kingdom of Austria-Hungary – Archduke Franz Ferdinand – arrived in the Bosnian city of Sarajevo. It was his wedding anniversary, so he was joined on the visit by his wife, Sophie. Bosnia was part of Austria-Hungary – but only since 1908 when it had been annexed. Many Bosnians were still deeply unhappy about this. They wanted to join with their neighbours, Serbia, and many Serbians wanted Bosnia to join with them. One gang of Serbians, known as the 'Black Hand', decided to take drastic action to highlight their cause – they planned to **assassinate** the Archduke. His visit to Sarajevo was the perfect opportunity.

1 Archduke Franz Ferdinand and his wife arrived at Sarajevo train station at 9:28am. They were driven towards the Town Hall to meet the Mayor. Crowds lined the streets and the car drove slowly so that the royal couple could wave to the people.

2 Six Black Hand assassins waited for the car by the Cumurja Bridge. As the open-topped car passed, one of the Serbians threw a bomb at the royal couple. The bomb ended up beneath the car behind and blew up, injuring several people. The Archduke's car sped off to the Town Hall with a terrified Ferdinand inside.

3 The Archduke cancelled the rest of his visit, but decided to visit those injured by the bomb before he went home. At 11:00am, he again got into the chauffeur-driven car – but it drove a lot faster this time! As they passed Schiller's café, the driver was informed that he'd taken a wrong turn. He stopped to turn around.

4 After the bomb attack, the assassins had split up and run into the crowds. By coincidence, one of the gang – 19-year-old Gavrilo Princip – was standing outside the café. He took out a pistol, walked towards the car and fired two shots. Ferdinand was hit in the throat; his wife Sophie was shot in the stomach. Both were killed.

SOURCE A: *Princip is thought to have been terminally ill with tuberculosis when he murdered Franz Ferdinand. He survived another four years – long enough to see the terrible consequences of his actions.*

How did this murder lead to war?

Although the assassination was a terrible event, you might be wondering how this started a war. Read **Source B** carefully and you will discover that the murder started a countdown to the biggest war the world had ever known.

28 July: Austria-Hungary blames Serbia for killing the Archduke and attacks Serbia.

29 July: Russia, which has promised to protect Serbia against attack, gets its army ready to attack Austria-Hungary.

1 August: Germany, which supports Austria-Hungary, hears about Russian preparations for war. Germany declares war on Russia.

2 August: Britain prepares its warships.

3 August: Germany, which is more worried about the French army than about the Russians, decides to attack France first. It declares war on France, hoping to defeat the French quickly, and then on to face the Russians!

2 August: Germany asks Belgium to allow German soldiers to march through Belgium to attack France. Belgium says 'no'. Germany marches in anyway two days later. Britain, which has a deal to protect Belgium from attack (dating back to 1839), declares war on Germany.

6 August: Austria-Hungary declares war on Russia.

12 August: Britain and France declare war on Austria-Hungary.

▲ **SOURCE B:** *Timeline of events.*

As **Source B** shows, the murder in Sarajevo on that Sunday morning in June 1914 started a whole chain of events that threw Europe into war – a war in which millions would die.

FACT!

Italy didn't stick to the agreements it had made before the murder. Instead it joined Britain, France and Russia's side in 1915. In total, 32 countries joined the war and the major ones lined up like this:

ALLIES: Britain and its Empire • France • Belgium • Italy (from 1915) • Serbia • Romania (from 1916) • Portugal (from 1916) • Russia (until 1917) • USA (from 1917) • Japan

VERSUS CENTRAL POWERS: Germany • Austria-Hungary • Turkey • Bulgaria (from 1915)

Work

1 Imagine you were Franz Ferdinand's chauffeur on the day of the assassination. You have been called in as a witness by the police. Using the information from the cartoons, copy and complete this writing frame:

Crime:
Date:
Witness:
The Archduke, Franz Ferdinand, was dressed in ……
His wife was wearing ……
As I approached the Cumurja Bridge ……
The Archduke was furious so ……
Shortly after 11:00am I drove past Schiller's café, when I ……
It was just as I was reversing that ……
I did my best to help, but ……

2 Look at **Source B**. Why did:
- **a** Austria-Hungary attack Serbia?
- **b** Russia attack Austria-Hungary?
- **c** Germany invade Belgium?
- **d** Britain declare war on Germany?

3 Did Gavrilo Princip start the Great War? Explain your answer carefully – you may want to discuss it and/or plan your answer with a partner first.

Depth Study

2.2A Joining up

When Britain declared war on 4 August 1914, the government asked for volunteers aged between 19 and 30 to join the armed forces. At first, there was a great rush to 'join up' as a wave of **patriotism** and excitement swept the country. By Christmas 1914, over a million men had enlisted to 'do their bit for king and country'. It soon became clear that this number of men wasn't going to be enough and the enthusiasm of 1914 didn't last long. So how did the government encourage more men to join the war? What reasons did these men give for joining up? And how did the government finally solve the shortage of fighting men?

Mission Objectives

- Outline the reasons why men chose to fight.
- Define 'propaganda' and explain how the government used propaganda to attract more volunteers.

The power of propaganda

When war broke out the government knew that it needed people to support the war… and lots of men to fight in it! So a huge **propaganda** campaign was started throughout the country. This meant that the government controlled all information about the war and sent out only the messages they wanted people to hear. So, in newspapers the government only allowed news of victories in battle to be printed, while defeats were hardly mentioned. British soldiers were always made to look like heroes, while any Germans were made to look like cruel savages. The government hoped that if people loved Britain (and hated Germany and its people), they were more likely to support the war and even join up to fight. Most famously of all, the government printed millions of propaganda posters aimed at making men either love their country and their king, feel guilty about not joining up, or hate the enemy! Look through the posters on these pages and think about how they were designed to make people feel and act.

SOURCE A: *This is one of the most famous recruitment posters of all time. It shows Lord Horatio Kitchener, the man in charge of getting enough men to fight, asking for volunteers to join the army. Wherever you stand, Kitchener always seems to be staring and pointing directly at YOU.*

SOURCE B: *This poster shows a German nurse pouring water on the floor in front of a thirsty, injured British soldier. Two Germans laugh in the background. How do you think this was meant to make British men feel?*

TO THE
YOUNG WOMEN
OF LONDON

Is your "Best Boy" wearing Khaki? If not don't YOU THINK he should be?

If he does not think that you and your country are worth fighting for—do you think he is WORTHY of you?

Don't pity the girl who is alone—her young man is probably a soldier—fighting for her and her country—and for YOU.

If your young man neglects his duty to his King and Country, the time may come when he will NEGLECT YOU.

Think it over—then ask him to

JOIN THE ARMY TO-DAY

SOURCE C: *What did the designer of this poster hope young women would do after they had read it?*

The push and pull of propaganda

The propaganda campaign had a remarkable effect, and by January 1916 a total of 2.5 million men had agreed to fight. Some felt 'pushed' or pressured into joining up while others felt the 'pull' of the excitement of war and serving their king and country.

Wise Up Words

called up conscientious objector conscription pals battalion patriotism propaganda

Work

1 Write a sentence explaining the meaning of:
- patriotism
- propaganda

2 Study all the recruitment posters carefully. For each one, write a sentence explaining:
- who the poster was appealing to
- how it was trying to appeal to them
- how successful you think it might have been.

3 Why not design your own Great War recruitment poster? Use the posters on these pages for inspiration.

SOURCE D: *This poster attempts to show an example of life after the war. Why do you think the father looks so guilty?*

FACT!

Think of propaganda like advertising in newspapers and on television. However, with advertising, *companies* try to make you think a certain way and believe certain things about their product. With propaganda, *governments and politicians* try to get people to believe different things.

HOW THE HUN HATES!

THE HUNS CAPTURED SOME OF OUR FISHERMEN IN THE NORTH SEA AND TOOK THEM TO SENNELAGER. THEY CHARGED THEM WITHOUT A SHRED OF EVIDENCE WITH BEING "MINE LAYERS". THEY ORDERED THEM TO BE PUNISHED WITHOUT A TRIAL.
THAT PUNISHMENT CONSISTED IN SHAVING ALL THE HAIR OFF ONE SIDE OF THE HEAD AND FACE.
THE HUNS THEN MARCHED THEIR VICTIMS THROUGH THE STREETS AND EXPOSED THEM TO THE JEERS OF THE GERMAN POPULACE.
BRITISH SAILORS! LOOK! READ! AND REMEMBER!

SOURCE E: *This poster claims that innocent British fishermen were captured and humiliated by the Germans. How would this make British people feel about Germans?*

YOUR COUNTRY'S CALL

Isn't this worth fighting for?
ENLIST NOW

SOURCE F: *This poster shows a romantic version of Britain's countryside and asks people if it isn't worth fighting for. What kind of feelings would this create in young men?*

Depth Study

2.2B Joining up

Millions join up

Millions of men had joined up to fight within the first 18 months of the war. How many different reasons for joining the Great War can you find in **Sources A**, **B**, **D**, **E,** and **F**?

Stay together, die together

The British government used another method to get men to join the armed forces. They thought that fighting alongside friends and neighbours rather than strangers would encourage people to join up – and they were right. Rival towns competed with each other to prove how patriotic they were and formed '**pals battalions**'. Brothers, cousins, friends, and workmates enlisted together. There was a footballer's battalion in London, alongside battalions of bankers, railway workers and even former public school boys. Although they were very successful, there were tragic consequences. Of the 720 Accrington Pals who fought, 584 were killed, wounded or missing during one attack. The Leeds Pals lost 750 of their 900 men and both the Grimsby Chums and the Sheffield City Battalion lost half of their men. This robbed entire communities of many of their young men, and no new pals battalions were created after 1916.

'I hate the thought of missing out. It's my chance to do something, you know, to contribute to the war effort. I might even get a gong if I'm lucky... and the girls; they love a man in uniform, don't they?'

▲ **SOURCE A:** *Part of a letter written by a young soldier to his mum, Christmas 1914. A 'gong' is a nickname for a medal.*

'I was walking down Camden High Street when two young ladies said, "Why aren't you in the army with the boys?" I said, "I'm sorry, I'm only 17" and one of them said, "Oh we've heard that one before." Then she pulled out a feather and pushed it up my nose. Then a sergeant came out of one of the shops and said, "Did she just call you a coward? Come across the road to the Drill Hall and prove that you aren't a coward." I told him I was 17 and he said, "What did you say, 19?" To my amazement, I found I was soon being called Private S. C. Lang.'

▲ **SOURCE B:** *S. C. Lang joined up in 1915. White feathers were used to represent cowardice. From* Forgotten Voices of the Great War *by Max Arthur (2002).*

ACCRINGTON. BATT" E.L.R. B Co No 1 PLATOON.

◀ **SOURCE C:** *A pals battalion of friends from Accrington, Lancashire, who all joined up together in 1914. One of the men, who is lying down on the right, survived the war, despite being wounded on three occasions. Sadly, there is no record of who else survived.*

'It was seeing the picture of Kitchener and his finger pointing at you – any position that you took up the finger was always pointing to you – it was a wonderful poster really... My mother was very hurt when I told her that I had to report to the army the next morning. I was 16 in the June.'

▲ **SOURCE D:** *Thomas McIndoe joined the Middlesex Regiment in 1914. From* Forgotten Voices of the Great War *by Max Arthur.*

'I said to the boss, "I want to join the army, I want to be released from my job." He said, "Here in the steelworks, you're doing just as much for the country as if you're in the army." Well, I couldn't see myself going to work every day and going home every evening while my pals were suffering – and probably dying somewhere – they were serving their country. I said, "I've made up my mind – I must go."'

▲ **SOURCE E:** *F. B. Vaughan of the Yorks and Lancs Regiment. From* Forgotten Voices of the Great War *by Max Arthur.*

'A girl would come towards you with a delightful smile all over her face and you would think, "My word, she must know me." When she got about five paces away she would freeze up and walk past you with a look of utter contempt – as if she could have spat. It made you curl up and there was no replying as she had walked on. I was only 16 but went round the recruiting offices with extra zeal.'

▲ **SOURCE F:** *Norman Demuth of the London Rifle Brigade. From* Forgotten Voices of the Great War *by Max Arthur.*

FACT!

Around 1.4 million men from India, Pakistan and Bangladesh decided to help Britain in the struggle against Germany, convinced by posters that promised an 'easy life', 'good pay' and 'very little danger'. Up to 64,000 of them died and another 65,000 were injured. Twelve were awarded the Victoria Cross – Britain's highest award for bravery.

Conscription and 'conchies'

By the summer of 1916, the flood of volunteers had slowed down to a trickle. With thousands dead and many more returning home disabled, war didn't seem like such an exciting adventure. Unfortunately for the government, they still needed more men to join the war. The solution they came up with was **conscription**. This meant that any man aged between 18 and 41 could be forced to join the army and an extra 2.5 million people were **called up** – but not without problems. Some men believed that war was wrong under any circumstances and refused to join up – they became known as **conscientious objectors**.

There were around 16,000 conscientious objectors or 'conchies'. Most refused to fight because of political or religious beliefs – but joined in the war effort by working in factories or mines or carrying stretchers on the battlefields. Around 1500 people refused to have anything at all to do with the war and were sent to prison. Conditions were made very hard for them and 69 of them died in prison.

Work

1 a Read through **Sources A**, **B** and **D** to **F**. Separate them into soldiers who felt pushed into joining the war and those who felt the pull of doing 'the right thing'.

Push	Pull

b Imagine that you've just enlisted in the army. Write a diary entry for the day you joined, explaining how you feel and why you did it.

2 Groups of friends who joined up together were kept together in 'pals battalions'. What were the advantages and disadvantages of this?

3 a What is conscription?

b Why was conscription needed?

4 Do you think 'conchies' were brave or cowards? Give reasons for your answer. Why not discuss it with a partner?

SOURCE G: *Soldiers from every part of the Empire fought in Britain's armed forces. Here a group of Indian soldiers are photographed in a Belgian town.*

Depth Study

2.3A Fighting in the war

The Great War was fought mainly in Europe. The areas where the armies fought each other were called 'fronts'. The longest was the **Western Front** (in Belgium and France) where French, Belgian and British soldiers tried to stop the Germans advancing to the coastline of northern France. But how did they do this? And what was it like fighting under these conditions?

Mission Objectives

- *Describe the typical experience of a soldier in the trenches.*
- *Identify the main areas of conflict and the main features of trench warfare.*

Digging in

As enemy soldiers faced each other they dug holes in the ground to protect themselves. These soon turned into deep trenches as they dug deeper. Soon, long lines of trenches stretched for over 640 kilometres between the English Channel and Switzerland (see **Source A**).

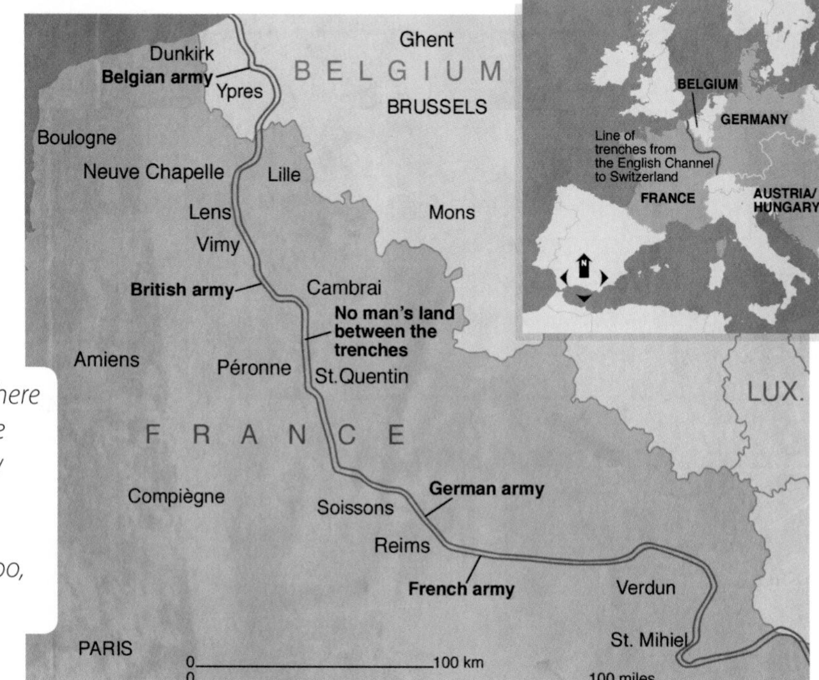

SOURCE A: *This map shows the Western Front. There was fighting in the east too (the Eastern Front), where Russians faced Germans and Austrians, and in Turkey (Turkey was on Germany's side). Italy (which joined Britain's side) fought Austria-Hungary on the Italian border and the war spread to Africa and the Pacific too, as Germany's colonies were attacked by Allied forces.*

SOURCE B: *These British soldiers are in a German trench, which was dug into the earth to give protection against enemy fire.*

Trench warfare

Most of the fighting was done by foot soldiers (**infantry**), who spent their days in the trenches they had built in the earth to protect themselves (see **Source B**). The trenches were protected with sandbags and barbed wire. They were defended by men with rifles, **bayonets**, machine guns, and **hand grenades**. A few hundred metres away, the enemy did the same. In between was an area called **no man's land**, a dead world full of bomb craters and rotting human remains.

Attack!

Occasionally, the soldiers would try to capture each other's trenches. The attackers would run across no man's land towards the enemy trenches and the defenders would try to pick them off with rifle fire and machine guns. For the loss of 50,000 men (yes, 50,000 human beings!), one side might move forward for a week or two and gain a few hundred metres of muddy, useless ground (see **Sources C** and **D**). A week later, for the loss of even more men, they might be pushed back to their original trenches. Unbelievably, despite the loss of millions of men, the Western Front didn't move more than a few miles either way in over four years of war! This was **stalemate** – a complete inability to move forward and a solid determination not to be pushed back. In 1914 Lord Kitchener summed up the stalemate when he said, 'I don't know what is to be done… but this isn't war'.

Wise Up Words

bayonet censor hand grenade infantry no man's land stalemate trench foot Western Front

> 'At noon we went over the top. After less than 100 yards we came up against an almost concrete wall of whistling and whining machine gun bullets. The company commander had his face shot away; another man yelling and whimpering held his hands to his belly and, through his fingers, his stomach protruded [stuck out]. A young boy cried for his mother, bright red blood pouring out from his face.'

▲ **SOURCE C:** *A German soldier's description of a British attack. 'Over the top' was the expression used when soldiers left their trenches and ran towards the enemy.*

SOURCE D: *This painting shows Canadian soldiers (who were fighting on Britain's side) taking part in the Battle of Ypres on 8 May 1915. Look for: i) the different weapons used; ii) the Germans charging across no man's land; iii) the commanding officer shouting orders; iv) the dead or wounded soldiers lying on the ground.*

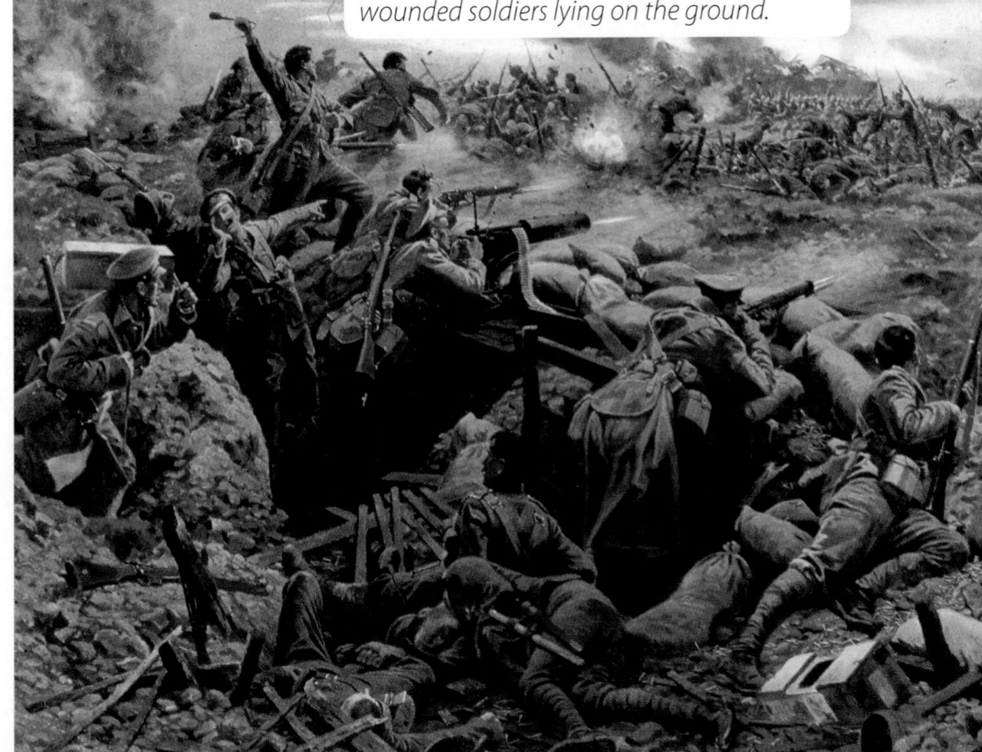

Depth Study

Work

1 Work out which of the following sentences are true and which are false. Copy out all the sentences, correcting each false one as you write.
  - **a** A 'front' is an area where fighting takes place.
  - **b** All the fighting took place in Europe.
  - **c** The longest front was the Eastern Front.
  - **d** The Western Front stretched for 300 kilometres through France and Belgium from the English Channel to Swaziland.
  - **e** 'Stalemate' is the word used to describe the situation for many soldiers during the Great War – neither side could move forwards and neither side wanted to retreat.

2 Look at **Source D**.
  - **a** Write a paragraph to describe this painting. You must write more than 20 words, but do not use more than 100 words.
  - **b** Use this painting and your own knowledge to explain why trench warfare made it difficult for either side to advance.

2.3B Fighting in the war

Depth Study

On the front line

A soldier's basic training did nothing to prepare him for what he found on the front line. The deadly fire of the machine guns forced entire armies to live almost underground for months on end. As well as the mud, the cold and the wet, they lived with the knowledge that they could lose their lives at any moment. Look at these pages and see how the Great War soldiers fought, lived and died.

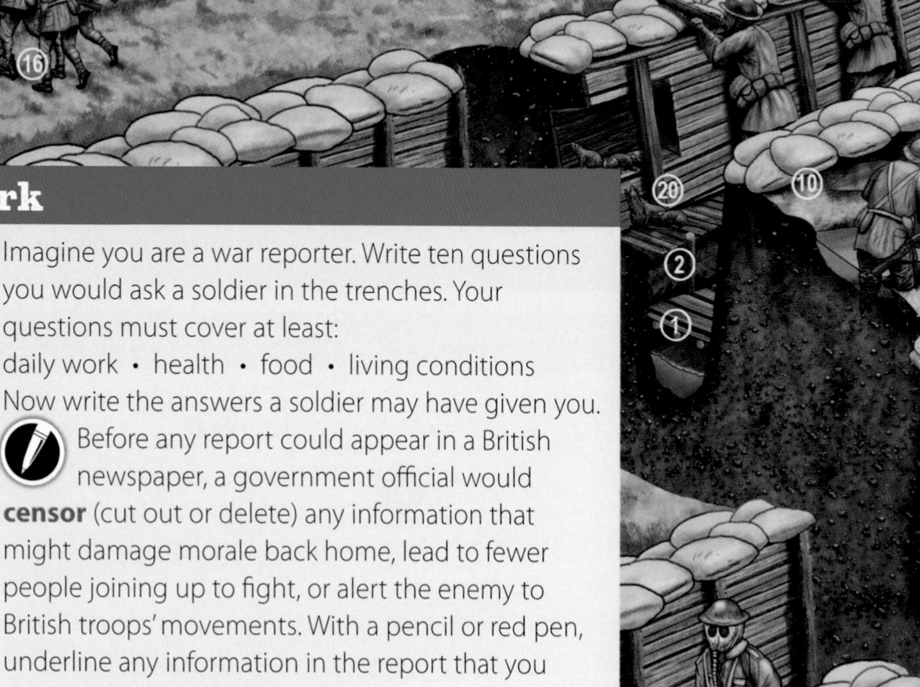

Work

1 a Imagine you are a war reporter. Write ten questions you would ask a soldier in the trenches. Your questions must cover at least:
daily work • health • food • living conditions

b Now write the answers a soldier may have given you.

c Before any report could appear in a British newspaper, a government official would **censor** (cut out or delete) any information that might damage morale back home, lead to fewer people joining up to fight, or alert the enemy to British troops' movements. With a pencil or red pen, underline any information in the report that you think the censor would not allow.

d In what ways has 'censorship', as this was known, changed your report?

1: Duckboards: These were placed on the ground to stop troops sinking in the mud
2: Fire step: Soldiers stood on these to look and fire 'over the top'
3: Dugouts: Rooms dug out of the back wall of trenches. Orders received by telephone here
4: Periscope: Enabled troops to see 'over the top' without risk of being shot
5: Barbed wire: Slowed down attacking troops; millions of miles of barbed wire were used
6: Machine gun: Rapid-firing gun that mowed down attacking troops
7: Concrete bunker: Reinforced underground bunker
8: Artillery: Huge guns that fired enormous explosive or poisonous shells for miles
9: Machine gun nest: Protected the machine-gunner from enemy fire
10: Sandbags: Reinforced the walls, muffled explosions and soaked up moisture
11: Aeroplanes: Helped spot targets for artillery, dropped bombs on the enemy and shot down enemy planes
12: Communication trench: Linked the front line trench to the reserve trenches
13: Reserve trenches: Soldiers went here to rest or to wait to go to the front line
14: Gas bell: Would be rung to tell troops to put on gas masks
15: No man's land: a muddy wasteland between the two lines of trenches; around 50 to 200 metres wide
16: Soldiers split their time between facing the enemy on the front line and recovering in the reserve trenches behind the main ones
17: Soldiers didn't fight all the time; as well as guard duty, they collected food, wrote letters, cooked, cleaned their weapons, and repaired the trenches
18: The soldiers would be boiling hot in the summer… and freezing cold and wet in winter; many suffered ill health – ulcers, boils, pneumonia, dysentery, and bronchitis
19: Spending days knee deep in water could lead to **trench foot**, a painful condition where the foot swells up and develops open sores – it can even rot away
20: Keeping clean was tough, so soldiers were infested with lice, and rats roamed the trenches!
21: Food was basic – stew, bread and hard biscuits; bacon, cheese and jam were treats but the water tasted of chlorine (used in swimming pools), which killed germs

Be a Top Historian

GCSE

Top historians realize that their History studies are full of new words, phrases and ideas. The term 'censor' is an example of this. The spellings and meanings of these words will have to be learned as there is every chance you will use them again when studying history at a higher level.

Depth Study

2.4 Weapons of war

In the years leading up to the Great War, there had been great advances in science, design and invention. The technology to build motor cars and aeroplanes had been invented and there had been breakthroughs in physics and chemistry. Sadly, lots of these new ideas would be used to create new weapons that could kill and injure millions of people!

Mission Objectives

- *Explain why the weapons used in the Great War were so deadly.*
- *Judge which weapons were most effective.*

Rifle

Range = 45%

Killing power = 55%

Defensive ability = 40%

A long gun called a rifle was given to all soldiers. It was lightweight so could be carried easily and was accurate up to 600 metres. A 40cm knife, called a bayonet, was fitted onto the end, which could be used if a soldier's bullets ran out. Highly trained soldiers could fire between 15 and 20 bullets per minute.

Grenade

Range = 15%

Killing power = 55%

Defensive ability = 25%

Grenades are small, hand-held bombs that could be thrown about 40 metres into enemy trenches. They exploded a few seconds after a pin was removed and the outer case would shatter into razor-sharp fragments, causing horrific injuries.

Poison gas

Range = 10%

Killing power = 30%

Defensive ability = 5%

The first ever major poison gas attack was on 22 April 1915. The Germans released gas from cylinders and allowed the wind to carry it over French soldiers on the front line. The French panicked and ran. A six-kilometre gap opened up in the French lines but the Germans didn't have enough men to mount a serious assault. An opportunity like this never happened again but gas proved its worth as a weapon of terror. Soon both sides were using gas. There were two main types:

Chlorine gas – this suffocated the lungs and left the victim gasping for air.

Mustard gas – rotted the body – skin blistered, eyes bulged. A victim would cough up the lining of his lungs in clots. The pain was so intense that victims often had to be tied down!

Later in the war, gas became less of an effective weapon because gas masks protected troops from the worst effects of the poison.

Machine gun

Range = 45%

Killing power = 85%

Defensive ability = 90%

Invented in around 1862, the machine gun became recognized as one of the Great War's deadliest weapons. They could fire up to ten bullets per second. In the first 12 days of fighting, the French reported losses of over 200,000 men, mostly through machine gun fire. According to British estimates, machine guns caused about 40% of all wounds inflicted on British troops during the whole war.

What Happened When?

1914

In the same year that the Great War broke out, the British government first passed a law to allow Ireland to rule itself (Home Rule). However, Home Rule for Ireland was postponed because of the war (until 1920).

Be a Top Historian

Top historians are able to explain why something is important or **significant**. At GCSE level you are required to do this a lot. This double page challenges you to assess the significance of some of the developments in weaponry during the Great War.

Tank 

Range = 45% (if it didn't break down)

Killing power = 60%

Defensive ability = 65%

A British invention, tanks were bulletproof vehicles that could travel over rough terrain, crush barbed wire and cross trenches. At first they were called 'landships' but were code-named tanks in an attempt to convince the Germans they were water tanks and so keep the invention a secret. The name stuck! Although they caused panic and terror on the battlefield, they were very slow (4mph) and unreliable.
All sides saw potential and built their own tanks, but it wasn't until the next world war that tanks became battle-winning weapons.

Wise Up Words

shell shell shock shrapnel

Artillery

Range = 100%

Killing power = 75%

Defensive ability = 20%

Artillery is another word for the large, heavy guns that could shoot bombs (**shells**) over long distances. It was common to bombard the enemy trenches for several hours before an attack in the hope you might kill lots of soldiers as they sheltered in their dugouts. In 1915, 400,000 shells (some as big as soldiers) were fired every month on the Western Front. Some big guns could fire shells over a distance of 21 kilometres. When they exploded, the red-hot metal splinters (**shrapnel**) would cut an enemy to pieces. The noise damaged men's brains and made their ears bleed. It caused **shell shock**, a condition similar to a 'nervous breakdown'.

Flame thrower

Range = 10%

Killing power = 60%

Defensive ability = 2%

A canister was strapped to a soldier's back which forced oil through a nozzle at enemy soldiers. The oil was ignited by a spark to create a sheet of flame that could travel up to 15 metres. Hand-held flame throwers were deadly in small spaces, like dugouts, and caused panic if one was spotted during an attack. Defending soldiers would try and shoot the canister of oil before it got anywhere near. One British soldier who saw a German flame thrower in action said that men who were caught in the blast of the flame 'were never seen again'!

Fighter and bomber planes

Range = 100%

Killing power = 25%

Defensive ability = 10%

Aeroplanes had first appeared in 1903. When fighting began, the planes were very slow, clumsy and unreliable, and were used for keeping an eye on what the enemy was doing and spotting artillery. At first, pilots fired pistols and even threw bricks at each other, but soon 'fighter' planes armed with machine guns were developed. Not long after, 'bombers' were made to fly over enemy trenches and attack them from the air.

Work

1 a Copy and complete a larger version of this chart in your book.

WEAPON: List the eight major weapons.	RANGE: Short, medium or long range?	KILLING POWER: Low, medium or high?	Is it used mainly for attack, defence or both?

b In your opinion, which was the Great War's most deadly weapon and why? Back up your opinion with facts and figures.

c In general, did the weapons used in the Great War make it easier for an army to attack or defend?

Depth Study

2.5A Was it right to shoot Harry Farr?

The sheer horror of trench warfare was too much for some soldiers to cope with. The constant danger of death, the relentless noise of shelling and witnessing close friends being killed in terrible ways all took their toll on the men at the front line. More and more men were diagnosed with a condition called shell shock. Some shook uncontrollably, others became paralysed despite suffering no physical injury. Many had panic attacks, cried constantly or were unable to speak. The British soldier in **Source A** would lie perfectly still for hours on end – not responding to any visitors or questions. However, whenever he heard the word 'bomb', he would fly into a panic and hide. So how did the British army cope with this problem? What would shell shock be called today? And what were the consequences for Private Harry Farr?

Mission Objectives

- Define 'shell shock' and what it would be called today.
- Decide whether Harry Farr was a coward or the victim of cruel injustice.

A shocking diagnosis

Shell shock was first diagnosed as an illness in 1915, but doctors struggled to find a way to cure it. They tried rest, hypnosis, counselling, and even electric shocks through the brain. Many men just needed time away from the front line to recover. Unfortunately, when they did get better, they were often sent straight back to fight. Their symptoms soon returned and they sometimes ran away – unable to handle the situation any longer. Commanding officers were keen to maintain discipline, and when these men were caught they were charged with **desertion** or **cowardice**. These were just two of the 'crimes' that men could be shot for during the war (see **Source B**). In total, Britain shot 306 of its own soldiers for cowardice and desertion during the Great War. The French shot 600, but the Americans and Australians shot none of their own men. Official figures show that the Germans shot fewer than 50.

SOURCE A: *A shell shock victim.*

- Being a coward (cowardice)
- Leaving their trench or position (desertion)
- Disobeying orders
- Falling asleep on guard duty
- Going on strike
- Throwing away a weapon

SOURCE B: *The sort of 'crimes' for which British soldiers could go on trial (with the possibility of being shot).*

A step too Farr?

Your task over these four pages is to consider the case of Private Harry Farr (see **Source C**). He was put on trial (known as a **court martial** in the army) charged with cowardice, found guilty and shot dead at 6:00am on 18 October 1916. Was this verdict correct? Was he suffering from shell shock? Should he have been in hospital rather than looking down the barrels of a firing squad?

Farr's background

Private Harry Farr, who lived in London with his wife and baby daughter, had been a professional soldier in the army since 1908. He had been fighting in France for nearly two years and, in that time, he had reported sick with his 'nerves' three times. Each time he had been sent to hospital – once for five months – and he shook so violently that a nurse had to write his letters home to his wife. But, as he wasn't physically injured, he was returned to the front line each time he recovered. These adapted notes from his court martial tell the story of what happened on his final return to the trenches.

Wise Up Words

court martial cowardice desertion pardon

Depth Study

Court Martial at Ville-Sur-Ancre, 2 October 1916

Alleged Offender: No. 8871 Private Harry T FARR 1st Battalion – West Yorkshire Regiment.

Offence Charged: Section 4. (7) Army Act: Misbehaving before the enemy in such a manner as to show cowardice.

Plea: Not Guilty.

SOURCE C: *Private Harry Farr.*

THE PROSECUTION

1st Witness: Sergeant Major H. HAKING

'On 17 September, at about 9:00am, FARR reported to me well behind the lines. He said he was sick but had left his position without permission. He said he couldn't find his commanding officer. I told him to go to the dressing station [a trench hospital]. They sent him back saying he wasn't wounded. I sent him back to the front lines.

'At about 8:00pm, his commanding officer (Captain BOOTH) told me FARR was missing again. Later on I saw FARR back where I'd first seen him well behind the line. I asked him why he was there. He said, "I cannot stand it". I asked him what he meant and he repeated, "I cannot stand it". I told him to get back to the front line and he said, "I cannot go". I then told BOOTH and two other men to take him back by force. After going 500 metres, FARR began to scream and struggle. I told him that if he didn't go back he would be on trial for cowardice. He said, "I'm not fit to go to the trenches". I then said I'd take him to a doctor but he refused to go saying, "I will not go any further". I ordered the men to carry on but FARR again started struggling and screaming. I told the men to leave him alone and FARR jumped up and ran back to where I'd first seen him early in the day. He was then arrested.'

2nd Witness: Captain J. W. BOOTH

'On 17 September 1916 at 3:00pm I told FARR to get back up to his trench. Later that evening, I could see he was missing without having received permission. At about 9:00pm, I saw him well away from where he should have been. Sergeant Major HAKING ordered me to take him back to his trench under escort. After about 500 metres, FARR became violent and threatened the three of us. FARR was later arrested.'

3rd Witness: Private D. FARRAR (one of the soldiers ordered to take FARR back to his trench)

'On 17 September 1916, at about 11:30pm, I was ordered by Captain BOOTH to take FARR back to the trenches. After going 500 metres, he started struggling and saying he wanted to see a doctor. The Sergeant Major said he could see one later. FARR refused to go any further. I tried to pull him along. The Sergeant Major told me to let go and FARR ran off.'

4th Witness: Lance-Corporal W. FORM

Lance-Corporal FORM said exactly the same as Private FARRAR, the third witness.

Work

1 a Write a sentence or two to explain these terms:
- shell shock • desertion • cowardice • court martial

b How many people did the British shoot for cowardice and desertion during the Great War?

2 Up to this point, what is your impression of i) Sergeant Major Haking and ii) Private Harry Farr?

2.5B Was it right to shoot Harry Farr?

After the army presented its prosecution case, it was time for Harry Farr to try and defend his actions.

THE DEFENCE

Harry Farr was not given an opportunity to ask someone to help him with his defence. Instead, he defended himself.

First witness: The accused, Private H FARR

'On 16 September 1916, I started to feel sick. I tried to get permission to leave the trenches but couldn't because people were asleep or unavailable. Eventually, I found Sergeant Major HAKING on 17 September at 9:00am and he told me to go to the dressing station. They said I wasn't physically wounded and sent me back to my trench. I started to go but felt sick again so I told an ordinary officer where I was going and went back well behind the front line again.

'When I saw Sergeant Major HAKING, I told him I was sick again and couldn't stand it. He said, "You're a f****** coward and you'll go back to your trench. I give f*** all for my life and I'd give f*** all for yours so I'll get you f****** well shot". I was then escorted back to my trench. On the way, we met up with another group of soldiers and one asked where I'd been. Sergeant Major HAKING replied, "Ran away, same as he did last night". I said to HAKING that he'd got it in for me.

'I was then taken towards my trench but the men were shoving me. I told them I was sick enough already. Then Sergeant Major HAKING grabbed my rifle and said, "I'll blow your f****** brains out if you don't go". I called out for help but there was none. I was then tripped up so I started to struggle. Soon after, I was arrested. If no one had shoved me I'd have gone back to the trenches.'

Court question: Why haven't you been sick since you were arrested?

Answer by FARR: Because I feel much better when I'm away from the shell fire.

Second witness: Sergeant J. ANDREWS

'FARR has been sick with his nerves several times.'

Character witness: Lieutenant L. P. MARSHALL

'I have known FARR for six weeks. Three times he has asked for leave because he couldn't stand the noise of the guns. He was trembling and didn't appear in a fit state.'

Character Witness: Captain A. WILSON

'I cannot say what has destroyed this man's nerves, but on many occasions he has been unable to keep his nerves in action. He causes others to panic. Apart from his behaviour when fighting, his conduct and character are very good.'

What happened next?

The entire court martial took about 20 minutes. Soon after, the judging panel gave its verdict… GUILTY. They said, 'The charge of cowardice is clearly proved and the opinion of Sergeant Major HAKING is that FARR is bad. Even soldiers who know him say that FARR is no good.'

On 14 October 1916 Harry Farr's death sentence was confirmed by Sir Douglas Haig, the man in charge of the British Army. He was shot at dawn on 18 October 1916. He refused to be blindfolded. According to his death certificate, 'death was instant'. He has no known grave and doesn't appear on any war memorials. At first, his widow was told he had been killed in action, but was later told the truth when her war pension was stopped. Widows were not entitled to a pension if their husband had been shot for cowardice.

The Shot at Dawn campaign

In the years following the war, many relatives of the executed men campaigned to have their names and reputations cleared. They believed it was the army's lack of understanding about shell shock – not cowardice – that had led to many of the men's deaths. In June 2001, a memorial to the 306 British soldiers killed by their own side was unveiled by Mrs Gertrude Harris – the daughter of Private Harry Farr (see **Source B**). In 2006, the British government looked into the cases once more and decided to **pardon** all the men who had been 'shot at dawn'.

Hungry for More?

Why might Sir Douglas Haig, the man in charge of the British Army, think it was important to execute soldiers like Harry Farr? What do you think he was worried would happen if Farr had been allowed to go home unpunished? Why was it important to make an example out of 'deserters' and 'cowards'?

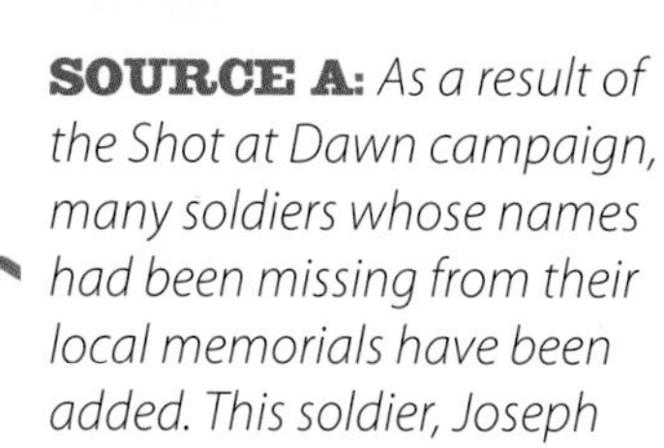

SOURCE A: *As a result of the Shot at Dawn campaign, many soldiers whose names had been missing from their local memorials have been added. This soldier, Joseph Bateman, who was 'shot at dawn' for desertion in 1917, was added to the memorial in his home town of Wordsley, West Midlands, in 2008.*

FACT!

In 1922 a British War Office committee announced that shell shock didn't exist and that it was a collection of already known illnesses. Today, it is recognized as a genuine condition and is called 'post-traumatic stress disorder'.

Work

1. a Write a definition of the word 'contradict'.
   b In what ways does Harry Farr's version of events on 17 September 1916 contradict Sergeant Major Haking's?
   c In what ways are the two versions similar?
   d Why do you think it is difficult for two versions of the same event to agree with each other all the time?
2. a In your opinion, was Harry Farr a coward or was he suffering from shell shock? You should include details from some of the witnesses in your answer.
   b Write two letters. The first should be from Sergeant Major Haking, one of Harry Farr's commanding officers. It was common practice for commanding officers to write home to the family of any dead soldiers in their 'care'. Imagine you are Haking and write a letter to Harry's widow informing her of the situation surrounding his death. The second letter should also be to Harry's widow but from one of Harry's friends, perhaps Captain Wilson.
   c In what ways are the letters similar and different? Give reasons for your answer.

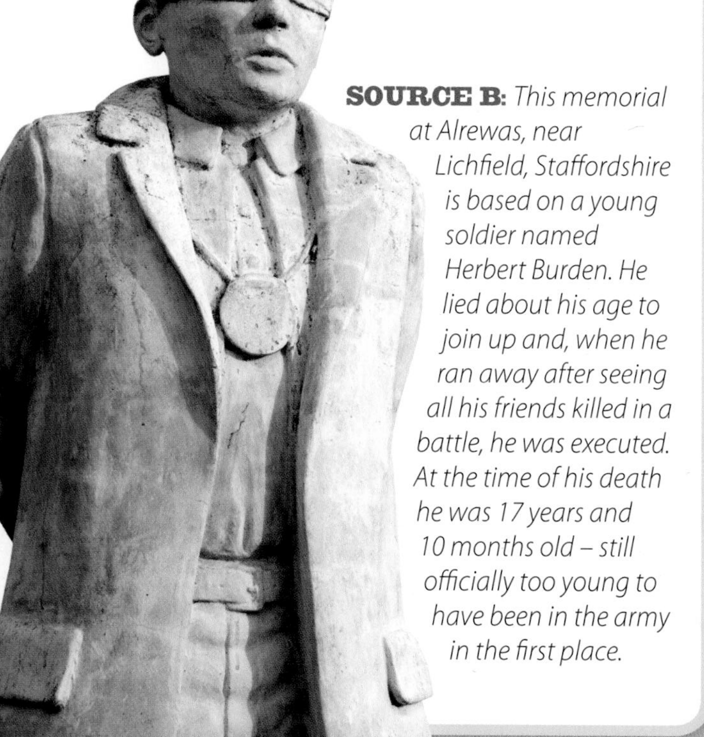

SOURCE B: *This memorial at Alrewas, near Lichfield, Staffordshire is based on a young soldier named Herbert Burden. He lied about his age to join up and, when he ran away after seeing all his friends killed in a battle, he was executed. At the time of his death he was 17 years and 10 months old – still officially too young to have been in the army in the first place.*

Depth Study

2.6 Soldiers of Empire

Meet a very brave man (see **Source A**). So courageous, in fact, that he was awarded Britain's top bravery medal, the Victoria Cross, during the Great War. His name was Khudadad Khan and he was one of millions of people who joined up to fight in Britain's army who weren't born in Britain… and had never even been there! So why did Khudadad Khan and millions of other people from India, Canada, Australia, and the West Indies risk their lives to fight for Britain? What made them join up? And did their contribution make any difference?

Mission Objectives

- Analyse why soldiers from the British Empire fought for Britain.
- Judge the contribution of these 'soldiers of Empire'.

Soldiers of Empire

When the Great War broke out in 1914, a great rush of young men in Britain volunteered to fight 'for king and country'. But there was also lots of enthusiasm in countries that were part of the British Empire (see **Source B**). The British Empire was a collection of countries that were ruled by Britain, and when the war started places such as Canada, Australia, New Zealand, India, the West Indies, South Africa, and other parts of Africa were all under British rule. These places were known as **colonies**. As a result, many thousands of people from these areas decided to join up to fight with the British (see **Source C**). In fact, this was lucky for Britain, because when war broke out there were ten times as many soldiers in the German Army as there were in the British. So the British Army had no choice but to use these 'soldiers of Empire'.

SOURCE A: *Khudadad Khan was born in what is now Pakistan. Khan won his Victoria Cross in October 1914 after he was wounded, fought off a German attack with his rifle, and managed to get back to the trenches after being left for dead.*

'Our father, the King-Emperor of India [King George V of England] needs us, and any of us who refuses to help him in his need should be counted among the most polluted sinners. It is our first duty to show loyalty to the British government.'

◀ **SOURCE B:** *A letter from a Sikh wounded in England, January 1915.*

'When Britain is at war, Canada is at war – there is no difference at all.'

▲ **SOURCE C:** *The Prime Minister of Canada in January 1915.*

SOURCE D: *A Great War recruitment poster, sent out to the colonies of the British Empire. Posters sent to India promised 'an easy life', 'good pay' and 'very little danger'! The posters clearly did the trick – by the autumn of 1914 one in every three soldiers fighting for Britain in France was from India. India also contributed almost £150 million in today's money to the war effort!*

SOURCE E: *The British West Indies Regiment in 1916. West Indian troops were usually used as ammunition carriers (a very dangerous job), rather than fighting soldiers. Some were unhappy with the 'lack of action' and many were treated badly while in France. One Trinidadian sergeant wrote: 'We are treated neither as Christians nor British citizens, but as West Indian "niggers", without anyone to be interested in or look after us.'*

Wise Up Words

colonial colony

Depth Study

'Two and a half million soldiers from the Empire fought in the First World War. They made a vital contribution to the British war effort and to eventual victory. More than a quarter of a million men made the ultimate sacrifice… [Before the war people had referred to] the colonies and dominions as "dependent" – during the war, Britain became dependent on them! Without them, without the 'soldiers of Empire', the British could not have won.'

▲ **SOURCE F:** *From a television programme presented by Ian Hislop, Channel 4,* Not Forgotten: 'Soldiers of Empire'.

How many?

The number of **colonial** soldiers fighting in the Great War was huge. For example, Canada sent nearly half a million men, Australia sent over 300,000 and New Zealand sent nearly 130,000 – about one tenth of its entire population. About 200,000 Irishmen served in the British forces too, and India sent around 1.4 million soldiers!

The ultimate sacrifice

At the end of the Great War, Britain's war dead numbered about 700,000 – and the rest of the Empire combined had lost over 200,000 men; India lost up to 64,000 soldiers, Australia and New Zealand lost 75,000 and Canada lost 56,000. And colonial troops were involved in some of the bloodiest campaigns and battles of the entire war – Ypres, the Somme, Gallipoli and Passchendaele. Colonial troops also won hundreds of medals during the war, including over 150 Victoria Crosses – the highest bravery award in the British Empire!

For more information on the Battle of the Somme, see **Assessing Your Learning 1** at the end of this chapter.

Work

1 a Who was Khudadad Khan?
  b What is meant by the term, 'soldier of Empire'?
  c Can you think of reasons why men like Khudadad Khan and other people from the British Empire might have joined up to fight?

2 Look at **Source D**. Write a sentence or two explaining:
- who the poster was meant to appeal to
- how it tried to do this
- how successful you think it was in getting men to join the British forces.

3 Look at **Source E** and read the caption carefully.
  a What sort of job did these men do in the war?
  b According to the sergeant quoted, how were they treated?
  c Can you think of reasons why they were treated in this way?

4 Many people today don't know about the contribution of troops from all over the British Empire in the Great War. Why do you think this is?

2.7 How did the war affect ordinary citizens?

The Great War didn't just involve soldiers, sailors and airmen. The armed forces may have been the ones who went off to fight the enemy on foreign soil, but the people left at home had their part to play too. So what impact did the war have on people in Britain on the **home front**?

Mission Objectives

- *Describe how the Great War affected everyday life in Britain.*
- *Explain how and why British civilians were at risk between 1914 and 1918.*

Study the cartoon, labels and sources carefully to assess how the Great War affected those who stayed at home.

In the early days of the war, women were encouraged to pin white feathers (a sign of cowardice) on young men who weren't in an army uniform. The idea was to shame them into 'doing their bit' in the war.

Around 70 million men fought in the Great War, with over eight million of these fighting for Britain and its Empire. Nearly one million of those were killed and twice as many were injured. By the end of the war, it was estimated that there were only 12 towns or villages in Britain that hadn't lost a young man in the fighting.

The Germans flew huge inflatable airships – called **Zeppelins** – over Britain and used them to bomb British towns. By the end of the war over 50 Zeppelin air raids had dropped over 5000 bombs, killing 557 people and injuring over 1300. German bomber planes attacked Britain too, and German battleships shelled seaside towns.

Work

1. What is meant by the term 'home front'?
2. What was DORA and why do you think the British government thought it was necessary?
3. How did the Great War change the role of women? Don't just think about jobs, think about their role in the family, too.
4. Imagine you were the older child pictured in the cartoon. Write a letter to your father, who is away fighting, telling him how the war has changed life in Britain and your family life at home. Remember to follow the coventions of a letter, including your address, the recipient's address, and the date.

Wise Up Words

civilian home front rationing Zeppelin

Depth Study

Britain was short of food during the war because German submarines and battleships were sinking the boats that brought it by sea. So the government introduced **rationing** to make sure that food was equally shared out. Each person was allowed a set amount of butter, sugar, bacon, ham, and so on.

The government issued posters showing people how to tell the difference between British and German aircraft – and warning them to take shelter if they spotted an enemy aircraft.

A week's worth of rations:

- 8oz of sugar (226g)
- 20oz of meat (567g)
- 2oz of lard (56g)
- 5oz of butter (141g)
- 8oz of bacon (226g)

During the war, some goods were in short supply – so prices went up. The government also had to borrow millions from the USA to pay for the war, so taxes went up to pay back the loans.

FACT!

When war broke out the government introduced a new law called the 'Defence of the Realm Act' or DORA. It gave the government the power to do whatever they felt was necessary to win the war. They could take over mines, railways and shipyards, and control newspapers and radio. To limit drunken behaviour, for example, they introduced strict pub opening hours… and even allowed beer to be watered down!

With so many men away fighting, women were needed to do their jobs. Before the war, no one would have dreamed of having female bus drivers, chimney sweeps or steel makers, but now Britain needed them! Thousands of women found work in shipyards, in weapons factories and with the ambulance service. And for the first time, the government recruited women into the police force!

2.8 How did 'Poppy Day' start?

Mission Objectives

- Outline the significance of the year 1917.
- Explain how and why 11 November is remembered today.

1917 was a significant year in the course of the war. Ordinary Russian people rebelled against their leaders (they eventually murdered their king and his entire family!) and stopped fighting the Germans. Germany now focused all of its soldiers, guns, gas, ships, and planes on the British and the French. By then, however, the USA had joined the war on Britain and France's side after German submarines had sunk American ships.

Final attack

The Germans now tried desperately to defeat the British and French before the fresh American soldiers arrived at the front line. But, despite an all-out attack, the Germans could not break through and started to **retreat**. Back in Germany, the civilians had reached breaking point – they were starving and there were riots in the streets, and German troops were exhausted too. Soon, the countries on Germany's side began to surrender. Eventually, Germany's king (Kaiser Wilhelm II) ran away to the Netherlands and the government that replaced him called for a ceasefire (also known as an **armistice**). At 11:00am on 11 November 1918, the Great War was over.

SOURCE A: *Some British celebrations lasted for three days – the police had to be sent to break them up!*

SOURCE B: *War deaths from 1914 to 1918. As you can see, it is little wonder that many people began calling it a world war. Soon after the end of the war, an outbreak of influenza (flu) swept across Europe and killed an estimated 25 million more people!*

Canada 56,000
USA 117,000
Cuba, Haiti, West Indies 1,200
Belgium 14,000
Great Britain 662,000
France 1,375,000
Portugal 7,200
Italy 650,000
Serbia 45,000
Germany 1,774,000
Austria-Hungary 1,200,000
Romania 336,000
Bulgaria 87,000
Turkish Empire 325,000
Greece 5,000
Russia 1,700,000
China 540
Japan 300
South Africa 6,900
Australia 58,000
New Zealand 16,0(

0 1000 2000 3000 4000 miles
0 2000 4000 6000 kilometres

Counting the cost

The war did terrible damage to the land on which it was fought. In France, where most of the fighting took place, an area the size of Wales was ruined. Buildings, roads, trees, and hedgerows were destroyed. Only one living thing seemed to flourish – the poppy. For many soldiers, the poppy had become a symbol of life and hope among all the fighting. The poppies continued to grow after the soldiers left the trenches in 1918.

Remembering the dead

In 1919 some of the poppies were collected and sold to raise money for war widows and injured soldiers. Soon, artificial ones were being made in a factory in London and sold all over Britain. In November 1919 the government received a letter from Sir Percy Fitzpatrick, whose son had been killed in France in 1917. Percy suggested that a period of silence be observed on the anniversary of the end of the war. King George V agreed. Today, the two-minute silence is held on the second Sunday in November. It is called Remembrance Sunday and poppies are distributed in return for donations to help people affected by any war. Some people call it 'Poppy Day'.

armistice commemorate retreat

FACT!

Some of the soldiers' bodies were never found, they just sank into the mud where they had died. Even today, French and Belgian farmers still find skeletons of dead soldiers when working in their fields.

SOURCE D: *Wearing a Remembrance Day poppy is a way of* **commemorating** *those who have fought and died for their country in the army, navy and air force. Every year over 35 million poppies are distributed. The Poppy Appeal raises almost £40 million a year, which goes to help members of the British Armed Forces, past and present, and their families.*

Work

1. **a** Why was 1917 such an important year in the war?
   b When exactly did the war end?
   c How do we remember the end of the Great War today?
2. Look at **Source B**.
   a Identify the main countries that fought in the war and turn these figures into either a bar chart or a pie chart.
   b Approximately how many people were killed in the Great War in total?
3.  Look at **Source D**.
   a Why did the poppy become a symbol of the Great War?
   b Have you ever bought a poppy? If not, say why not. If so, explain why you bought one – did you know how your money was used?

2.9 How did countries try to avoid any more wars?

When the Great War ended in November 1918, the British Prime Minister, David Lloyd George, made the following announcement to Parliament: 'At eleven o'clock this morning came to an end the cruellest and most terrible war that has ever been. I hope we may say that this is an end to all wars.' He wasn't alone in wanting this and, in January 1919, he met with the leaders of France, the USA, and other winning countries to talk about what to do with the world now that the war was over. It soon became clear that they had very different ideas about how to avoid more wars. So just what were these ideas? Who won the argument? And did their ideas work?

Mission Objectives

- Recall who the 'Big Three' were and how they dealt with the defeated countries.
- Decide whether the League of Nations was a success or a failure.

The 'Big Three'

In January 1919 politicians from the winning countries met at the Palace of Versailles, near Paris, to decide what was to happen to the beaten enemy.

The three most important politicians at the Paris Peace Conference were the leaders of France, Great Britain and the USA. They were nicknamed the 'Big Three' because they represented the three most powerful winning countries. Look at the boxes on the right of this page to see what they wanted. Germany was not allowed to send any politicians to put their viewpoint across, nor were the other defeated nations, Austria-Hungary, the Turkish Empire or Bulgaria.

So what did they decide?

In June 1919 the politicians announced their decision to the world. Germany's punishments, set out in a huge document called the Treaty of Versailles, were the first to be published. German politicians, sent over for the day, were told to sign the peace agreement… or face invasion! They signed (see **Source A**).

David Lloyd George – Prime Minister of Great Britain

Aims:

- Was elected by the British public to 'hang the Kaiser' and 'make Germany pay'. He wanted to keep Germany weak; however, he also wanted to avoid humiliating the Germans.
- Wanted to end the German threat to the British Empire and reduce Germany's navy so it was no longer a threat to Britain's navy!

Woodrow Wilson – President of the United States of America

Aims:

- The USA joined the war in 1917 and didn't suffer as much as Britain and France. He wanted to prevent Germany becoming aggressive again but didn't think it should be punished too much.
- Wanted different national groups to have the right to rule themselves – known as 'self-determination'.

Georges Clemenceau – Prime Minister of France

Aims:

- Around 1.4 million Frenchmen had been killed in the Great War and huge areas of France had been destroyed. He wanted revenge on Germany for all of this suffering.
- He wanted Germany to pay for all of the damage that the war had caused and wanted to weaken Germany's armed forces so they would never be able to attack France again.

Germany must pay for the war in money and goods. The figure was set at £6600 million. They must sign to agree that they had started the war too.

Germany to have no air force or submarines. Only a tiny army and navy. No tanks or submarines allowed. No German soldiers allowed anywhere near France.

Germany to hand over colonies to Britain and France.

League of Nations set up. The winning countries would join at first so they could talk about their problems rather than fight. The losing countries might be allowed to join later!

Parts of losing countries cut off to make new countries that wanted to run themselves.

Wise Up Words

treaty

SOURCE A: *The 'Big Three' argued for many months but, eventually, in June 1919, the Germans were summoned to the Palace of Versailles to sign a new* **treaty** *(a contract between countries). If they had refused, the war would have started again. The Treaty of Versailles (Germany's punishment) is the best known, but the other losing countries (Austria-Hungary, Turkey and Bulgaria) lost land and weapons, and were fined too.*

The League of Nations

After the defeated countries were punished, the victorious ones turned their attentions to trying to stop wars forever. As agreed in the treaty of Versailles, they set up a League of Nations, a kind of international club for settling problems peacefully. Its headquarters were established in Geneva, Switzerland. About 40 countries joined up straight away, hoping to solve any disputes by discussion rather than war. If one nation did end up declaring war on another, all of the other member nations would stop trading with the invading country until a lack of supplies would bring the fighting to an end.

The League would aim to help in other ways too. Countries would work together to fight diseases, stop drug smuggling and slavery, and improve working conditions. However, fewer than half the countries in the world joined – Germany wasn't allowed and politicians in the USA voted against it – and it didn't have its own army to handle disputes if necessary. Yet, for a few years, it seemed to work well.

Successes of the League:
- It freed 200,000 slaves.
- It helped 400,000 prisoners of war return home.
- It worked hard to defeat diseases such as leprosy, cholera and smallpox.
- It sorted out a dispute between Finland and Sweden in 1920.
- It sorted out a dispute between Greece and Bulgaria in 1925.

Failures of the League:
- The League never had its own armed forces.
- The USA never became a member, Japan and Italy eventually left, and Germany joined in 1926… then left in 1933!
- It couldn't stop Japan invading China in 1931.
- It couldn't stop Italy invading Abyssinia (Ethiopia) in 1935.
- It couldn't stop Germany expanding its territory in Europe between 1936 and 1939.

Work

1 a Who were the 'Big Three'?
  b Why do you think these men made most of the important decisions after the war had finished?

2 a Make a copy of **Source A**.
  b Overall, which of the 'Big Three' do you think would have been most happy with the Treaty of Versailles? Explain your answer very carefully.
  c Give three reasons why the Germans may have been unhappy with the Treaty of Versailles.

3 a How did the League of Nations try to stop wars?
  b What were its two main weaknesses?
  c In its early years, was the League of Nations a success or not? Give examples to go with your answer.

Assessing Your Learning 1

Were the 'lions' really led by 'donkeys'?

As top historians, you will be keen to develop your enquiry skills and your ability to use and interpret sources. This assessment task challenges you to do this – but it will also require you to use your very best literacy and communication skills, too.

The number of soldiers killed during the Great War is staggering. In total nearly nine million people were killed – which is over 5000 deaths *per day* for over four years. Nearly one million of those dead were from Britain and its Empire. Millions were wounded, too, scarred for life both physically and mentally.

In Britain some people have blamed British Army generals for the high number of British deaths. As a result, the generals (the men in charge of the army) have been called 'donkeys'. In fact, a common phrase to describe the British Army at this time is 'lions led by donkeys'. This means that the ordinary British soldiers who went into battle were brave (like lions) while the generals were incompetent, uncaring fools who were responsible for thousands of unnecessary deaths. Field Marshal Sir Douglas Haig, who was in charge of the army from 1915 to 1918, has been the subject of particular criticism. He has even been called a 'butcher' for allowing so many men to die. But is this criticism of Haig and his generals fair? Were they 'donkeys'… or just men trying to do their best to win a very difficult war?

Over to you

Your task is to sort through the following sources. Several of them focus on one of the most famous battles of the Great War – the Battle of the Somme. During this four-and-a-half-month battle, the British lost over 400,000 soldiers, the French lost 200,000 and the Germans lost around 450,000. The British and French viewed it as a victory (because they gained 15 kilometres of land)… but at a massive cost. Make sure you read the sources carefully and try to identify what they say about Haig and his generals. You should soon start to develop your own opinions.

▶ **SOURCE A:** *General Haig introduces Pertab Singh of Idar (an Indian army general serving with the British forces) to a French army general. Another British general looks on in the background.*

'The nation must be taught to bear losses. No amount of skill on the part of the commanders, no training, however good, no superiority of arms and ammunition, however great, will enable victories to be won without the sacrifice of men… The nation must be prepared to see heavy casualty lists… three years of war and the loss of one tenth of Britain's men is not too great a price to pay.'

▲ **SOURCE B:** *Haig wrote this just before the Battle of the Somme, 1916. He believed in a 'war of attrition'. 'Attrition' means wearing down.*

'You will be able to go over the top with a walking stick, you will not need rifles… you will find the Germans all dead, not even a rat will have survived.'

▲ **SOURCE C:** *Before the Battle of the Somme, the generals assured their troops that the shells would destroy the enemy before the men went into battle.*

'On that first day of the Battle of the Somme, 20,000 British soldiers were killed and 35,000 wounded, but this did not make General Haig want to change his methods. He ordered more attacks but the same tragic story was repeated each time. Against the advice of experts who said he did not have enough, he sent 50 tanks into the battle in September. Twenty-nine broke down before they even reached the battlefield and the rest soon got stuck in the mud. By the end of the battle, the British and French had lost 620,000 men and the Germans 450,000. The allies had advanced 15 kilometres at the furthest point.'

◀ **SOURCE D:** *From Josh Brooman's* The Great War *(1991).*

▼ **SOURCE E:** *Dead German soldiers at the Battle of the Somme. The British fired over a million shells at the German trenches for five days. Most escaped harm by digging very deep dugouts (German spy planes had seen men getting ready to attack) but this dugout suffered a direct hit.*

'The mud was terrible. When we tried to attack it was so slow and only the shortest gain was possible. I told General Haig that success was not possible or it would cost the lives of too many men. I asked him to stop the attack but he did not.'

▲ **SOURCE F:** *British General Sir Hubert Gough, writing about the Battle of Passchendaele, 1917.*

'We had heavy losses in men and material. As a result of the Somme we were completely exhausted on the Western Front.'

▲ **SOURCE G:** *This quotation is taken from the autobiography of the German general Erich Ludendorff,* My War Memories, 1914–1918 *(1919).*

▲ **SOURCE I:** *This cartoon appeared in the satirical magazine* Punch *in 1917. In the caption, the major-general in front of the group on the left is saying: 'There are three essential differences between a rehearsal and the real thing. First, the absence of the enemy. Now, what is the second difference?'. The sergeant-major replies, 'The absence of the general, sir.'*

'My God, did we really send men to fight in that?'

▲ **SOURCE H:** *One of Haig's generals said this about the area where the Battle of Passchendaele was fought. In it, Britain lost up to 400,000 men – many had drowned in a sea of stinking, liquid mud. As the bodies rotted, the generals in their headquarters could smell decaying flesh from ten kilometres away.*

▶ **SOURCE J:** *From an article by Dr Gary Sheffield, 3 October 2011, www.bbc.co.uk.*

'One undeniable fact is that Britain and its allies, not Germany, won the First World War. Moreover, Haig's army played the leading role in defeating the German forces…'

'Blaming Haig the individual for the failings of the British war effort is putting too much of a burden of guilt on one man. Haig was the product of his time, of his upbringing, education, training and previous, military experience. One argument goes that he was, ultimately, victorious and, even if he had been replaced, would there have been anyone better for the job? Even on the Somme a German officer called the battlefield "the muddy grave of the German army". This was the same battle in which Haig's numerous mistakes contributed to the half a million casualties suffered by the Allies.'

▲ **SOURCE K:** *From an article by S. Warburton in* Hindsight *magazine (1998).*

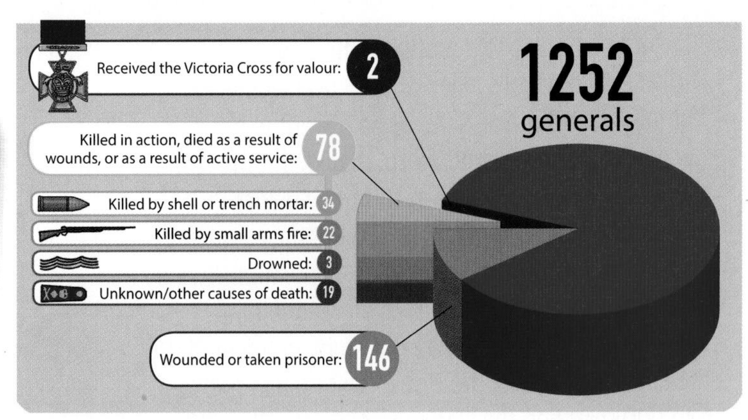

▲ **SOURCE L:** *This diagram explores the dangers of being a British general in the Great War. There is a belief that all generals sat well behind enemy lines, far from the fighting. This diagram goes some way to proving that theory wrong!*

'Was it stupid to fight at the Somme? Surely there can be only one opinion. If we had not attacked at the Somme, the Germans would have beaten the French at Verdun and the French and British alliance could have been broken.'

▲ **SOURCE M:** *Said by Haig, taken from a biography of him by Alfred Duff Cooper (1935).*

▶ **SOURCE N:** *Dan Snow, a historian, 25 February 2014, www.bbc.co.uk.*

'During the war more than 200 generals were killed, wounded or captured. Most visited the front lines every day. In battle they were considerably closer to the action than generals are today.

Naturally, some generals were not up to the job, but others were brilliant...

Within three years, the British had effectively invented a method of warfare still recognizable today. By the summer of 1918, the British Army was probably at its best ever and inflicted crushing defeats on the Germans.'

▼ **SOURCE P:** *The statue of Field Marshal Haig at Whitehall, London.*

'We say the statue should come down. It is a statement that will shock many people who regard the Field Marshal as a symbol of victory… Today, writing in *The Express*, the military historian Alan Clark records that "if the dead could march, side by side in continuous procession, it would take them four days to get past the statue". We believe that Haig, with his blinkered view of strategy and tactics, bears a heavy and perhaps unforgiveable responsibility for those deaths. We do not question his patriotism. But we doubt his judgement and his humanity.'

▲ **SOURCE O:** *'Time to pull down Haig's statue?',* The Express *newspaper, November 1998.*

'Nobody likes to see his father labelled as a butcher, and I think it's very important for the good of this country to set the record straight. I found the criticism really rather difficult and sad as his leadership was so important in winning the war. The country could not get anyone better than him and the Somme broke the backs of the Germans. It was a very, very close run thing and frontal attacks were the only way so deaths were inevitable. He was not a brute, he was a very kind, wonderful man and by God, I miss him.'

▲ **SOURCE Q:** *The son of General Haig, interviewed in 2006 for BBC News.*

Hungry for More?

General Haig was not a monarch or a politician. However, there is still a statue of him in London. What other people, who are not rulers or politicians, have been commemorated with statues in London? Can you find out who they are, what they did and why there are statues of them?

Task 1

Look at **Sources B** and **C**. What impression do these sources give of Field Marshal Haig and his generals? You could write two or three sentences to describe them. Start your first sentence: 'Source B makes me think Haig was…'

Task 2

Look at **Sources D**, **E** and **F**. Does your impression of Haig and his generals change after reading these sources? Give reasons for your answer.

Task 3

a What is meant by a 'war of attrition'?

b What evidence is there on these pages that Haig was a firm believer in this type of warfare?

c Is there any evidence in **Sources G** and **H** that Haig's plan to win the Battle of the Somme was successful?

Task 4

Look at **Source I**.

a What point is the cartoonist trying to make?

b Look at **Sources L** and **N**. How is the role played by the generals interpreted differently from **Source I**?

c Can you suggest reasons why opinions about the generals are so different?

Task 5

Read **Sources J**, **K**, **M**, **N**, **O**, and **Q**. Based on these sources – and the opinions you might have already formed about Haig (and his generals) – was Haig a 'butcher' and were the generals 'donkeys' for allowing thousands of men to die needlessly… or were they just trying to do their jobs and win the war?

Assessing your work

Look at the success criteria for this task to help you plan and evaluate your work.

Good	In a **good** extended answer, you would…	• show that you understand that people have different points of view about Haig and his generals – and demonstrate these views • identify and use some information from sources as examples to back up your points • produce work which shows some structure and organization, using dates and historical words correctly.
Better	In a **better** extended answer, you would…	• identify that there are different views about Haig and his generals and suggest **why** people have these different views • select and use information from a **variety of sources** as examples to back up your points • produce work which is **carefully structured and organized**, using the correct dates and historical words.
Best	In the **best** extended answer, you would…	• identify different views about Haig and his generals and suggest reasons why these views are different – and **explain why all of these opinions are important** • carefully **select the most appropriate information** from a variety of sources to reinforce your points • produce work which is **carefully and clearly structured**, using the correct historical terms and dates.

3.1A Was the Great War worth winning?

A few weeks after the Great War ended, Britain's Prime Minister (David Lloyd George) made a speech in which he promised to make the country 'fit for heroes to live in'. So how did he get on? What was Britain like in the years after the war? Did life improve? And was the Great War even worth winning?

Mission Objectives

- Examine the state of Britain in the decade after the Great War finished.
- Judge the extent to which Britain changed.

What changed?

After the war, life in Britain would definitely never be the same again! For a start, over half a million young British men were killed and a further two million were wounded. Wives lost their husbands and children lost their fathers (see **Source A**). Many communities, workplaces and even sports teams must have seemed empty. In addition, many of those who came back physically fit were unable to forget the horrors they had witnessed. However, for a short time, some things appeared to return to normal. People rushed out to buy the things they hadn't been able to get during the war and some businesses did very well. But this didn't last long!

'I wondered how ever I was going to get through the weary remainder of life! I was only at the beginning of my twenties – I might have another 40 or 50 years to live!'

SOURCE A: *Vera Brittain was a nurse during the Great War. Here, she tells of her sorrow after finding out about the death of her fiancé, Roland, who died during the war.*

Britain in decline

During the war, British factories and businesses had been totally dedicated to winning the war. They built guns, bombs and bullets, produced food and made ships. By the time the war ended, these factories were worn out, and other countries like Japan and the USA began to take a larger share of the world's trade (see **Source B**). In 1921, unemployment figures shot up to two million, which meant that one in five workers had no job (see **Source C**)! In 1922 a group of unemployed ex-soldiers marched through London on Remembrance Day with a banner that read: 'From the living victims to our dead comrades – you died in vain'.

SOURCE B: *An unemployed man on the streets of London. Part of his sign reads 'ex-soldiers starve'.*

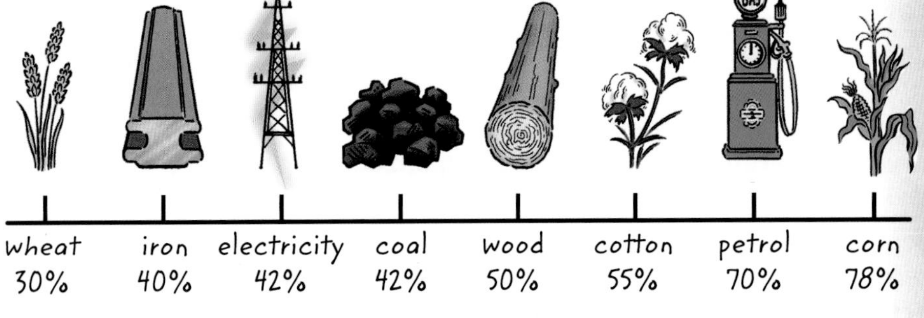

SOURCE C: *The percentage of the world's resources made in the USA by around 1920. By 1920 America was one of the world's leading producers and suppliers of raw materials.*

Did things improve at all?

The government *did* try to improve the lives of British people, though:

- Children under 14 were banned from working in mines, factories or on ships… and made to attend school!
- Old age pensions were increased.
- Great effort was put into finding work for ex-soldiers and those who were disabled in the fighting.
- Rules were changed which allowed more people than ever before to claim **dole** money if they lost their job.
- New laws protected tenants against large rent increases.
- The wages of teachers and farm workers were increased.
- A 'Ministry of Health' was set up to coordinate and improve healthcare across the country.
- Around 200,000 new homes were built that could be rented from local councils (see **Source D**). However, in some cases the rent was too high for the poorest people.

Wise Up Words

dole equality strike

SOURCE D: *Some of Britain's new 'council houses', built in the 1920s.*

SOURCE E: *The fashionable young ladies of the 1920s were known as 'flappers' (because of the way their arms moved when they danced!). They were generally middle- and upper-class girls who copied the styles and behaviour of American women of the time.*

What about the women? 

Perhaps the biggest (and most famous) change after the war was to the lives of women. Before the war, Britain was run by men, and women had very few rights. But during the war women took over a lot of the jobs left open when men went away to fight… and in 1918 women aged over 30 who owned property were given the right to vote. Soon, more jobs became open to women and they became lawyers and politicians, for example. And in 1928 all women over 21 were given the vote – just like men!

Along with this **equality** came a greater sense of freedom. Some women smoked and drank openly, drove motorbikes, had short hair, and wore shorter dresses and heavy make-up (see **Source E**).

Work

1. **a** What is meant by the term 'unemployed'?
   b Why did the amount of unemployed people increase in the early 1920s?
2. How did the British government try to improve the country in the years after the war?
3. Make a list of the ways in which the lives of women changed in the 1920s.

An American invasion?

In America in the 1920s, times were good for lots of people. American factories were busy and many Americans were making lots of money. This period of American history is sometimes called the 'Roaring Twenties'. For the first time, people in Britain began to copy American entertainment and fashions. Soon, American jazz music could be heard in British nightclubs as people danced the 'Charleston' and 'One Step' on packed dance floors. Hollywood films became popular too and by 1925 about half the population was going to the cinema twice a week. Film stars like Charlie Chaplin, Rudolph Valentino and Laurel and Hardy became household names (see **Source A**). A few years later, cartoon characters such as Mickey Mouse and Betty Boop (a flapper) prompted a whole generation of younger viewers to flock to their local cinemas.

SOURCE A: *Charlie Chaplain was one of the most famous silent film stars.*

SOURCE B: *A photograph of Blackpool seafront, one of Britain's most popular seaside resorts at this time. Can you see: i) key attractions – the pier, Blackpool Tower, 'big wheel'; ii) the very crowded beach with people paddling; iii) Punch and Judy show; iv) the bathing huts near the seas where people got changed.*

Good times?

While smoky dance halls and cinemas remained very popular throughout the 1920s, some people enjoyed spending time outdoors. Walking and camping holidays became common and trips to the seaside were as popular as ever. In the 1920s, for example, Blackpool attracted eight million visitors a year. The Boy Scout and Girl Guide Movements became very popular, too.

Hungry for More?

Find out why Blackpool was so popular at this time. What had attracted people to Blackpool in particular? How had Blackpool developed as a tourist destination over the years? And, for an extra challenge, identify the reasons for Blackpool's gradual decline as a tourist attraction during the twentieth century.

Be a Top Historian

GCSE

Top historians, whether studying History at KS3 or GCSE level, will sometimes have to study the **'big' questions.** These are challenging, thought-provoking questions that make you think critically about an event or issue. 'Was the Great War worth winning?' is one of these questions.

SOURCE C: *A volunteer driver during the General Strike protected by a police escort. Many middle-class British people helped out during the strike in order to fulfil their childhood dreams of being a train or bus driver!*

The BBC is born

A new form of entertainment entered many British homes in the 1920s – the radio. In 1922, the BBC was set up to 'educate, inform and entertain' and soon the radio became the 'must-have' home appliance; people listened to news, music, drama, children's shows, and sports events.

Bad times?

Despite some of the dramatic changes in society in the 1920s, there was still a large amount of unrest. Unemployment remained high throughout the decade and there were protests and **strikes** by shipbuilders, railway workers, engineers and even the police over pay and conditions. The situation was not helped by the fact that the government had massive debts as a result of the war, so huge cuts on what tax money was spent on had to be made.

A General Strike

In 1926 there was even a nine-day 'General Strike' when people with all kinds of jobs went on strike in support of coal miners who were about to have their pay *reduced* and their hours of work *increased*. On 4 May factories, docks and power stations all came to a standstill. Buses and trains stopped running and many newspapers weren't printed. The whole country ground to a halt! Volunteers drove buses and trains and unloaded ships (see **Source C**). But soon the strike pay fund ran out – strikers weren't receiving money any more – and so all workers (except the miners) went back to work. The miners fought on until November… and then returned to work for less pay and longer hours. In 1927 the government introduced a new law making general strikes illegal – a similar law is in force today.

Work

1. In what ways did America change Britain in the 1920s?
2. a What was the General Strike?
   b Why did the strike take place?
   c Why can't a general strike happen again?
3. a In your opinion, do you think the following people would think that all the sacrifices made during the Great War were worth it?
   i) a property-owning woman in 1918
   ii) an unemployed worker in 1922
   iii) someone living in a newly built council house.
   Give reasons for your opinions.
   b Why might people have different opinions as to whether the war was worth winning or not?

3.2 Independence in Ireland

Great Britain and Ireland have been closely linked for many hundreds of years. Sadly, for a large part of that time, relations between the two places weren't very good! There has frequently been bloodshed, violence and brutality. So what exactly is the history of the relationship between Britain and Ireland? How and why did this relationship become violent? And how did Ireland end up divided in two in the 1920s?

Mission Objectives

- Define a 'Nationalist' and a 'Unionist'.
- Analyse how and why Ireland was split in two in the 1920s.

Part of Britain

People from England and Scotland had been settling in (and helping rule) Ireland since the twelth century. In 1801, British politicians decided that the whole of Ireland should become part of Britain. Soon all the major decisions about Ireland were being taken by Parliament in London. There was even a new flag to symbolize this 'union' (see **Source A**).

A United Kingdom?

Many Irish people wanted more control over the country. They wanted Ireland to have its own Parliament and run itself. These people were mainly Catholics and became known as the '**Nationalists**' (because of their strong beliefs about their nation). However, there were other Irish people who wanted Ireland to stay a part of Britain. They were mainly Protestants and became known as '**Unionists**' (because they wanted to stay as part of the United Kingdom). The Unionists lived mainly in the northern part of Ireland, called Ulster.

SOURCE A: *The English and Scottish flags were joined after 1603 when the Scottish King James came to rule England after Queen Elizabeth I died. The Irish flag was added later to make the current Union Flag.*

SOURCE B: *British soldiers at a barricade on a street in Dublin during the Easter Rising.*

Easter Rising

For many years there was fierce debate in both Ireland and Britain about the future of Ireland. Sometimes there was violence too. During Easter 1916, a group of Nationalists took control of the city of Dublin (Ireland's capital) and declared independence from Britain (see **Source B**). The British sent in troops to sort out the rebels and within a week the Easter Rising (as it was known) had been stopped.

FACT!

Most Irish people didn't support the rebels at first, but when 15 of them were arrested by the British and executed by firing squad, opinions soon changed. The Easter Rising rebels became national heroes who had died for their beliefs and their country.

After the Easter Rising

In the 1918 British election, the leading Irish political party (called Sinn Féin) won 73 seats in the British Parliament. But the Irish politicians refused to go to London to sit in Parliament and set up their own Parliament (called the Dáil), based in Dublin. They then began ordering an armed group called the Irish Republican Army (**IRA**) to drive the British out of the country. The IRA attacked British police and government buildings. So, in 1920, the British sent in tough ex-soldiers known as 'Black and Tans' (because of their uniforms) to stop the fighting. Soon both sides were carrying out shootings and bombings… and the problems in Ireland seemed as bad as ever!

Stopping the bloodshed

Eventually, in 1921, a solution was found. The northern part of Ireland (where the majority of people were Protestant Unionists) would remain part of Britain, and be called Northern Ireland. And southern Ireland (mainly Catholic Nationalists) would become the Irish Free State and run its own affairs. But it would still remain part of Britain's empire (see **Source C**)!

Divided Ireland

Now Ireland was divided – and some people were happy… while others weren't. Some felt that all of Ireland should be united while others thought the split was a sensible compromise. The debate continues to this day!

Wise Up Words

IRA Nationalist Unionist

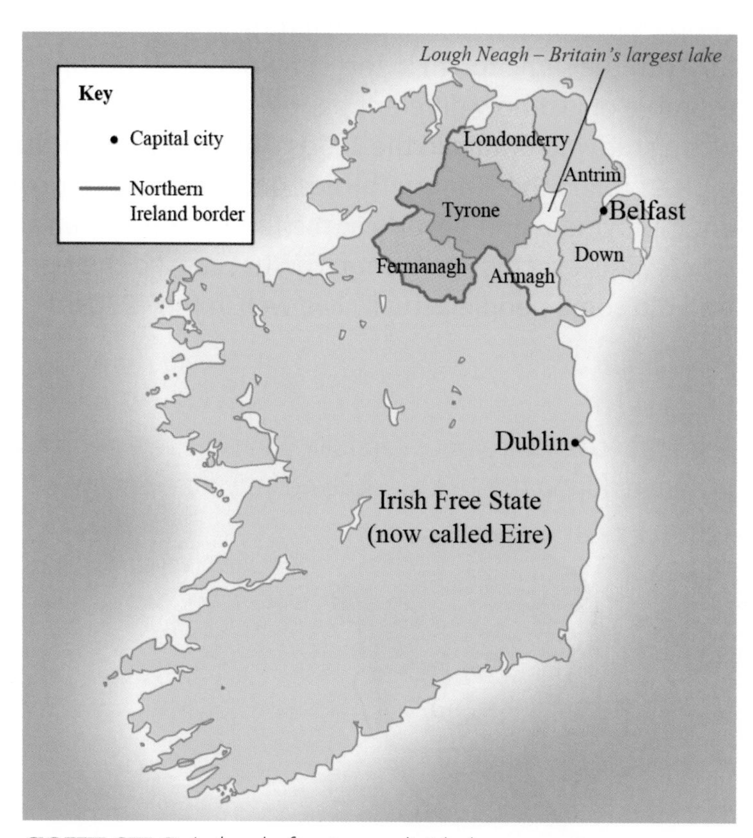

SOURCE C: *Ireland after it was divided.*

Work

1. a Create a diagram to explain the origins of the Union Flag.
   b Many people in Scotland and Ireland were not happy with the Union Flag when it was designed. Can you think of reasons for this?
2. What were the key differences between a Nationalist and a Unionist?
3. a What was the Easter Rising?
   b The Easter Rising is remembered with pride by many Irish people. Do you think it is mainly Nationalists or Unionists who remember it with pride? Explain your answer.
4. Explain why there are two countries within the island of Ireland.

3.3A The 'Hungry Thirties'

Today, if you asked two different people what their lives were like, you would almost certainly get two very different answers. People's lives are different, even if they live in the same country (or even the same town) in the same period of history. A great example of just how different people's lives can be can be found when studying Britain in the 1930s. This period in British history is often called the 'Hungry Thirties' because of the high levels of unemployment and poverty at the time. But is this an accurate label? Who, exactly, was 'hungry'? What caused their problems? And did some people actually live well in the 1930s?

Mission Objectives

- Define the term 'Hungry Thirties'.
- Assess the diverse range of experiences of ordinary British citizens in the 1930s.

Read the following stories carefully. Each of these people lived in Britain during the 1930s… but led very different lives!

An unemployed coal miner, 1935

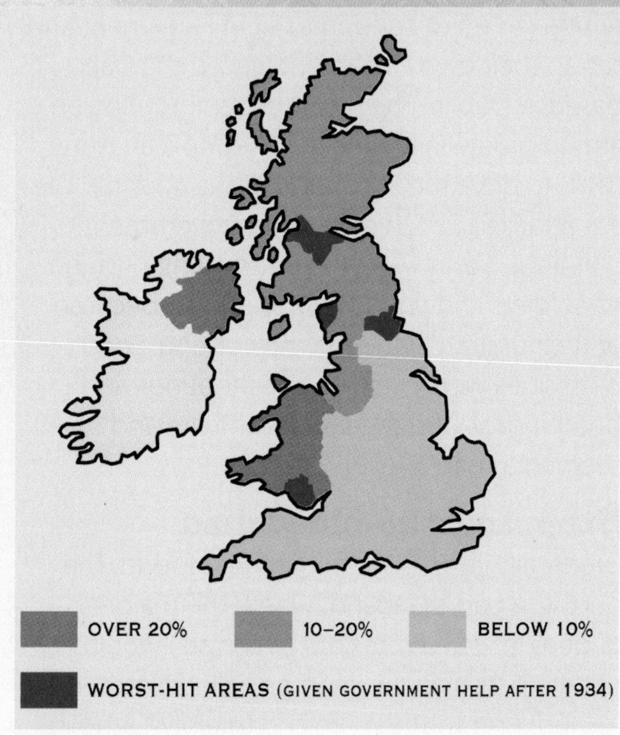

SOURCE A: *Percentage of workers unemployed in 1937.*

The wife of an unemployed shipbuilder, 1937

'If only he had work. Just imagine what it would be like. On the whole, my husband has worked about one year out of twelve and a half. His face was lovely when I married him, but now he's skin and bones. When I married, he was robust and had a good job. He was earning eight to ten pounds a week. He's a left-handed ship's riveter, a craft which could be earning him a lot of money.

He fell out of work about four months after I was married, so I've hardly known what a week's wage was. Through all the struggling I've still not lost my respectability… We don't waste nothing. And there's no enjoyment comes out of our money – no pictures, no papers, no sport. Everything's patched and mended in our house.'

▲ **SOURCE B:** *From a BBC radio interview, 1934.*

Wise Up Words

the Great Depression   Means Test   semi

The government is still paying for the Great War, so they have tried to save money by cutting unemployment benefit. They even introduced a **Means Test**, which meant that they sent officials to check if you had savings or any other money coming in. If you did, they cut your dole money even more! For example, my granddad lives with us and has a small pension coming in every week. But his pension counts as income… so we receive less dole money.

Unemployed young man, 1936

SOURCE D: *The 1930s saw many protest marches to London to draw attention to the plight of the unemployed. Perhaps the most famous was the 1936 'Jarrow March', when 200 unemployed people from Jarrow in the north-east (where two thirds of the workforce had no job) took a petition to Parliament demanding that new industry be introduced in the town.*

FACT!

The period in history when American banks, businesses and individuals hit hard times financially is known as **the Great Depression**. And when Americans no longer had money to buy goods from abroad, it meant that factories in other countries shut down too. Millions lost their jobs in France, Italy, Germany, Japan, and Britain.

Work

1  Look at **Source A**.
   a Which areas of Britain had the highest levels of unemployment in the 1930s?
   b Suggest reasons why these areas were hit harder than others.

2 Look at **Source B**.
   a How has unemployment changed this family?
   b Choose five words that might best describe how the woman interviewed here might feel.

3 Look at **Source D**.
   a Why did the Jarrow March take place?
   b Why do you think the protestors chose to walk to London?

3.3B The 'Hungry Thirties'

As you have seen on pages 60 and 61, times were hard for many people in Britain in the 1930s… but was it the same for everyone?

SOURCE A: *A photograph of car production in the 1930s. Some towns, such as Coventry, thrived during this time.*

A young female doctor, 1937

All women over the age of 21 gained the vote by 1928. We can now go to university (if we can afford it) and have careers that only men were allowed to have before the war – in politics, law or medicine, for example. However, we still get paid less than men for doing the same job, and some jobs, like banking, insist on employing unmarried women.

I hear things are bad in some areas of Britain, but I have had a steady job for years now! I work in the Midlands and make cars, which are becoming very popular and more affordable. My cousin in the south has a factory job, too – he makes radios. His wages have even gone up recently. Some industries are doing very well indeed at the moment, mainly new ones that make things like cars, plastics and electrical goods.

Midlands car factory worker, 1934

What Happened When?

1930s

In America, the 'Golden Age' of Hollywood really kicked off with the first full-colour films. More than 50 classic films were made in this decade, including *Gone With the Wind* and *The Wizard of Oz*.

'[In the 1930s] there were almost two Britains: the expanding, busy towns of the south-west and Midlands, with their towns of '**semis**', shops full of goods and almost full employment; and the run-down towns and cities of the north, Scotland, Wales and Northern Ireland, with slums, no money for improvements and unemployment blighting the lives of a quarter, a third or even half of the people.'

SOURCE B: *A modern historian.*

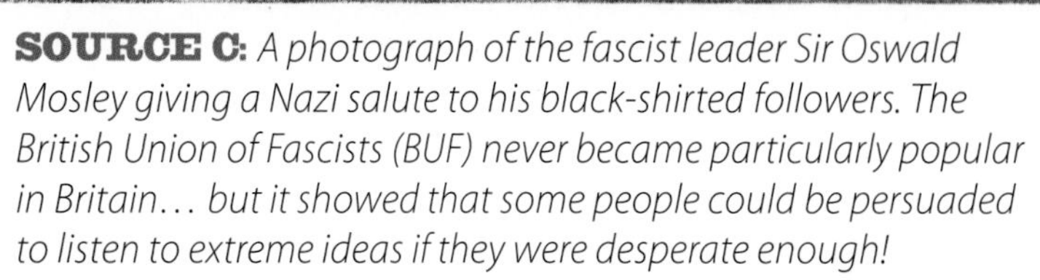

SOURCE C: *A photograph of the fascist leader Sir Oswald Mosley giving a Nazi salute to his black-shirted followers. The British Union of Fascists (BUF) never became particularly popular in Britain… but it showed that some people could be persuaded to listen to extreme ideas if they were desperate enough!*

A government official, 1938

A young unemployed man, 1936

Be a Top Historian

It is important that top historians, whether studying at KS3 or GCSE level, can identify how national history relates to (or fits into) world history. 'The Hungry Thirties' is a good example of this. At this time a depression that started in America spread all over the world… and affected Britain in a major way!

Work

1. Look at **Source A** and read the comments of the Midlands car factory worker. Can you suggest reasons why some industries, like car manufacturing, were doing better than others in the 1930s?
2. Read **Source B**.
   a. What do you think the writer means when he says that 'there were almost two Britains'?
   b. Do you agree with him? Explain your answer.
3. a. What areas of Britain were less affected by the depression of the Hungry Thirties?
   b. Why were these areas less affected?
4. a. What was the British Union of Fascists?
   b. Why do you think they became more popular at this time?

4.1 Different ways to run a country

No two countries in the world are run in exactly the same way. Britain has different laws and ways of doing things from France, which in turn is run differently from the USA. It's not just the laws that are different; there are also different punishments (some countries have the death penalty, for example), currencies, systems of education and healthcare – even the side of the road you must drive on! But despite these differences that have evolved over the centuries, it is possible to place most countries into one of two categories. So what are these categories? What are the main differences between the two? And which would you prefer to live in?

Mission Objectives

- Describe the differences between a democracy and a dictatorship.
- List the main features of each type of government.

Post-war problems

In the 1920s and 1930s, countries argued about the best way to organize themselves. These disagreements built up and eventually spilled over into another war. In order to fully understand the build up to the Second World War, it is important that you know the main features of, and differences between, a **democracy** and a **dictatorship**.

Type of government

DEMOCRACY

Origins Started in Ancient Greece. Developed gradually over hundreds of years, mainly in Europe and the USA.

Beliefs Ordinary people have a say in how their country is governed. They vote in regular elections in which there are several political parties to choose from. The people are represented by the organizations they elect – for example, Parliament or councils.

Rights The people have a number of 'freedoms' or rights:

- freedom of speech (the right to say what you think)
- freedom of information (the right to read, listen to and watch what you want)
- freedom of belief (the right to follow any religion)
- freedom in law (the right to a fair trial – if arrested, 'you have the right to remain silent' too!)
- freedom of association (the right to join or form a political party, join a trade union or any other organization).

Examples of democracies in the 1920s and 1930s
Britain, France and the USA

Wise Up Words

democracy dictatorship

Democracies to dominate?

As the Great War was won by democratic countries (Britain, France and the USA, for example), it was hoped that democracy would spread to most countries in the world. Unfortunately, many countries were in such a mess, and their people so desperate, that politicians were not able to discuss how to sort it out.

Extreme ideas

More and more people began to think that what they needed was a strong leader to take control and make all of the decisions rather than a group of politicians who might spend weeks, months or maybe years arguing about their actions. Incredibly, between 1919 and 1939 over 30 countries became dictatorships (a country with a dictator). And it was the rule of some dictators that brought about the Second World War.

Work

1 **a** Work with a partner. You must each choose to describe either a dictatorship or a democracy. Using only ten words each, explain to your partner the political system you have chosen. They must fully understand what a dictatorship or a democracy is by the end of your presentation.
- Use drawings to help you.
- Perhaps you could mime some of the features of your system.
- Which words will you use? Remember, you're only allowed to use ten words to describe your choice of democracy or dictatorship.
- Set aside some time to prepare!

b Now write up two descriptions, using a maximum of ten words to describe a democracy and ten words to describe a dictatorship.

2 What kind of country would you prefer to live in? Explain your answer very carefully, using a variety of sentence structures and interesting vocabulary.

Type of government

DICTATORSHIP

Origins For thousands of years, some people have tried to totally control others. The controllers are usually backed up by large numbers of supporters and lots of weapons.

Beliefs Ordinary people have no say in how their country is run. There are no regular elections because the country is run by one political party or one man – the dictator (usually helped by his 'friends' and his army).

Rights People have very few 'freedoms' or rights:
- there is no free speech (if they criticize their leaders, they are likely to be arrested)
- there is no freedom of information (the dictator controls the newspapers, books, magazines, films, and so on)
- not all religions are allowed – if any!
- there is no legal freedom (the police can arrest whom they want, when they want and keep them in prison without trial)
- people can only join groups or associations allowed by the dictatorship.

Examples of dictatorships from the 1920s and 1930s Italy, Spain, USSR (Russia), and Nazi Germany

4.2A Two types of dictatorship

Britain, France and the USA were the major victorious nations in the Great War. They were all democratic countries. It was hoped that other countries around the world would become democracies too. But many countries rejected democracy and turned to dictatorship instead! You might assume that all the dictatorships would gang up together against the democracies, but not all dictatorships are the same. So which countries became dictatorships? What were the two types of dictatorship called? And what are the differences between the two?

Mission Objectives

- Define both fascism and communism.
- Explain where and how these two extreme political beliefs took hold.

Theory of communism

Communism is a theory about how to run a country. It was dreamed up by Karl Marx, a German, in the 1840s. He wrote a book about his ideas… and it turned into a bestseller.

Marx believed that, one day, ordinary workers would rise up and get rid of the rich people (factory owners, landowners, bankers, etc.) because they were so unhappy. Then, he said, there would be no different classes – no very rich and no very poor. Money and goods would be shared out equally and the country would be run so that everyone was equal, too. There would be no need for money, or even laws, because everyone would live a simple life, sharing all they had with each other.

Not surprisingly, many poor ordinary workers liked Marx's ideas – a **communist** life sounded a lot better than the one they had! In fact, in the 1800s people in several countries rebelled against their leaders and tried to set up a communist country – but they all failed. And then the Russians tried in 1917…

Communists, like Karl Marx, believed societies were evolving and that workers would soon seize power. This, they believed, would lead to a better and fairer society.

SOURCE A: *Marx died in London in 1883. An inscription on his grave reads: 'Workers of all lands unite'. In the years following his death, Marx's ideas became more and more popular around the world – especially with poor people!*

SOURCE B: *The flag of the USSR. In 1922 Russia, together with the smaller countries it controlled, was renamed the Union of Soviet Socialist Republics (USSR). 'Soviet' is the Russian word for council and 'Socialist' is another word for communist.*

Wise Up Words

communism fascism

Case study 1: The USSR

The first country in the world to adopt the communist system was Russia. During the Great War, nearly two million Russian soldiers were killed and there were massive food shortages in the cities. In 1917, ordinary Russians who believed in the communist way of life rebelled against their king, Tsar Nicholas II. After a bitter civil war, the entire Russian royal family was killed and Russia officially became a communist country.

However, although Marx had written a great deal about how a communist society would work, he didn't explain exactly how one would be set up. Not everyone in Russia was keen on the changes that were taking place so the communists forced people to be equal and to share. They ran the country as a dictatorship.

- No other political parties were allowed to exist, only the Communist Party.
- Newspapers, books, films, and radio broadcasts were all controlled by the communists. Any person who spoke out against this was an 'enemy of the state' and sent to prison (or executed). Millions of people 'disappeared' in communist Russia.
- Nobody was allowed to have any open religious beliefs. Only the communist way of life was to be worshipped.
- All work, housing, healthcare, and education was controlled by the communists. Jobs, houses, hospitals, and schools were provided for all Russians. The state owned everything… and provided for everyone.

For many Russians, this was a much better way of life than what they were used to. Everything was provided for them as long as they were prepared to work and didn't complain! However, communism terrified people in other countries – especially the rich and members of royal families. Their worst nightmare was that communism would spread to their country. As a result, the USSR had few friends around the world and became more and more isolated.

FACT!

The flag of the USSR tells a story: the red background represents the revolution and the golden star represents power. This power is now controlled by the factory workers (who are represented by the hammer) and the farm workers (who are represented by the sickle). In reality, the power was controlled by one man – the leader of the Communist Party.

Work

1 Sum up communism in no more than 50 words. You could work with a partner if you like.

2 a Draw the flag of the USSR in your book.
  b Underneath the flag, write a sentence or two about its symbolism.

4.2B Two types of dictatorship

As you know, there are two different ways to run a country – democracy (where the people get to vote for leaders) and dictatorship (where there is one strong leader or group). So far (on pages 68 and 69) we have looked at one type of dictatorship – communism – so now it's time to look at another, known as **fascism**.

SOURCE A: *Italy's fascist flag used during the Second World War. The eagle is a traditional symbol of power and alertness, while the bundle the eagle is clutching is called a 'fasces'. The bundle of sticks represents strength in numbers, unity and law – the axe symbolizes power.*

A fascist dictatorship

Case study 2: Italy

Italy had fought on the winning side in the Great War. Over 600,000 Italians had been killed and the government hoped that this sacrifice would be rewarded with land from the losing countries. They were wrong – Italy gained hardly any new land at all.

By 1919 Italy seemed to have lost its way and the people were suffering from high unemployment and rising food prices. Bands of armed ex-soldiers roamed the countryside stealing and murdering. Those Italians that weren't suffering were terrified that communists might take over and take their money and belongings from them.

A new leader

Increasingly, Italians began to turn to a young politician called Benito Mussolini – a former soldier and schoolteacher. He promised to bring discipline, glory and pride back to Italy, but at a price. He had a theory called fascism (see **Source C**) and formed the Fascist Party in 1919. The idea behind fascism was that the country would be much stronger if everybody worked together rather than for themselves or the class they belonged to.

SOURCE B: *Mussolini, Italy's fascist leader, held enormous rallies like this one to make fascism and Italy appear strong.*

SOURCE C: *Mussolini mounted huge displays, with uniforms and special salutes. Mussolini once said, 'A minute on the battlefield is worth a lifetime of peace… better to live one day like a lion than a hundred years like a sheep'.*

Controlling the people

In reality, a fascist government controlled every aspect of someone's life (that's right; another type of dictatorship!). Education, newspapers, films, radio, and even sport all carried the same message: the needs of one person are not important; it's what Italy needs that counts. People were still free to run their own businesses and make money, but there were tight controls on the workers and strikes were banned. In return, the Fascist Party would 'look after' Italy and build roads and railways, which gave people jobs. Those still unemployed could join the army, which would be greatly increased in size. Unlike communists, fascists didn't believe in equality. They believed that men were superior to women and that some races and nations were superior to others. Mussolini argued that Italians were superior and used the Ancient Romans as evidence to support this. People seemed to like being told they were the best and the Fascist Party became more and more popular.

A takeover

In 1922 Mussolini (who wanted to be called 'il Duce' – the Leader) announced he was marching to Rome to take over the country. His supporters – known as 'blackshirts' because of their uniforms – marched with him and made a strong impression on the king. The king gave in and made Mussolini Italy's new Prime Minister. Soon, all opposition was banned and communists were beaten up or murdered.

Mussolini's tactics didn't go unnoticed by a 34-year-old up-and-coming politician living in Germany. His name was Adolf Hitler. Perhaps fascism could make Germany great too?

Work

1 a Draw Italy's fascist flag in your book.
  b Underneath the flag write a sentence or two about its symbolism.

2 Match up the names on the left with the correct description on the right.

Fascism	The fascist leader of Italy who took control in 1922
Communism	A German who first thought up the theory of communism
Mussolini	From 1922, this was the new name for Russia and the areas it controlled
USSR	One of the symbols of Italy's Fascist Party
Karl Marx	A political system where all people are equal and all property and business is owned by the state and run for the benefit of all
Fasces	A political system where the government controls all aspects of people's lives in an attempt to make the nation stronger than others

3 a Find two similarities and two differences between the dictatorships of the USSR and Italy.
  b Why were richer people across Europe worried about the spread of communism?
  c Why did Mussolini become popular in Italy after the end of the Great War?

4.3A Adolf Hitler: choirboy, artist, tramp, soldier, politician

Mission Objectives

- Recall at least five facts and dates about Adolf Hitler's life up to 1933.
- Outline Hitler's journey into politics.

Adolf Hitler is one of the most infamous men ever to have lived. He is known mainly for his association with the Second World War and his hatred of the Jews. But his time as leader of Germany only covers the last 12 years of his life! What about his early life? What was he like as a young man? How and why did he get involved in politics? And why was this Austrian (yes, he wasn't German at all) chosen to be Germany's leader in 1933?

Choirboy

Adolf Hitler was born in 1889 in Braunau, a small town in Austria. His dad was a hard-drinking bully who worked as a customs official. He died when Hitler was 13. Adolf's mum spoiled him and insisted he went to a respectable school in order to get good results and a well-paid job. But he failed his examinations and left school at 16. For the next two years he read books, listened to music and painted pictures. His mum died when he was 17. After her death, he left his home town and travelled to Vienna, the capital city of Austria, looking for work.

SOURCE A: *Hitler (circled) at school in 1899, aged ten. He was in the local church choir for five years.*

'He always wanted his own way. He was boastful, bad-tempered and lazy… He ignored advice and got angry if he was told off.'

▲ **SOURCE B:** *One of Hitler's teachers said this about him after he left school (from* The Twentieth Century *by J. D. Clare (1993)).*

SOURCE C: *A photograph of Hitler's mother, Klara. Her death due to breast cancer affected Hitler deeply. It is claimed he carried a photograph of her wherever he went and held it in his hand when he committed suicide in 1945. Klara had five children in total, but only Adolf and his younger sister, Paula, lived beyond childhood. When Hitler became leader of Germany, Paula changed her surname to Wolf (Adolf's nickname) to avoid any unwanted attention. She had no children and died in 1960.*

Artist and tramp

In 1907 Hitler arrived in Vienna hoping to 'make it big' as an artist. He tried to get into Vienna's Academy of Fine Arts, one of Europe's best art colleges, but failed to pass the entrance exam. Without any qualifications, he ended up living in a hostel for homeless people.

For the next five years, Hitler earned money any way he could – cleaning windows, painting houses, drawing and selling postcards in the street. He grew to hate people of foreign races, particularly rich Jewish people. He felt that foreigners were ruining Austria by taking over all the jobs and introducing their way of life.

Wise Up Words

swastika

'On the very first day there sat next to the bed that had been given to me a man who had nothing on except an old torn pair of trousers – Hitler. His clothes were being cleaned of lice, since for days he had been wandering about without a roof over his head.'

▲ **SOURCE D:** *Another homeless person in the hostel remembers Hitler's arrival (from* Weimar Germany *by Josh Brooman (1985)).*

SOURCE E: *One of Hitler's early paintings. He could draw buildings well but didn't draw people very well at all.*

Work

1 Answer the following questions in full sentences.

a Why did Hitler fail to get a place in Vienna's Academy of Fine Arts?

b While living in Vienna, why did Hitler begin to hate foreigners, especially Jews?

2 Read **Source D**. Why was Hitler in such a poor state?

4.3B Adolf Hitler: choirboy, artist, tramp, soldier, politician

SOURCE A: *Hitler (circled) as a soldier in the Great War. Hitler said that war was the greatest of all experiences.*

Soldier

Hitler left Austria in 1913 to avoid being called into the army. He went to live in Munich, Germany. When the Great War started in 1914, he decided to be a soldier after all, and volunteered to join the German army.

Hitler worked all through the war as a messenger in the trenches. It was a dangerous job and he was wounded several times, once when a piece of metal sliced through his cheek. He nearly died. He won six medals for bravery in total, including the Iron Cross, First Class.

Hitler was in hospital when the war ended, having been temporarily blinded in a gas attack. He wrote that he buried his head in his pillow and cried when he heard the news. He blamed Germany's surrender on weak politicians… and, of course, the Jews.

Report on Lance Corporal Hitler, Third Company (volunteers)

Hitler has been with the regiment since 1914 and has fought splendidly in all the battles in which he has taken part.

As a messenger, he was always ready to carry messages in the most difficult positions at great risk to his own life.

He received the Iron Cross (Second Class) on 2 December 1914 and I now feel he is worthy of receiving the Iron Cross (First Class).

◀ **SOURCE B:** *A report on Hitler by his commanding officer during the Great War. The Iron Cross was the highest medal awarded in the German army.*

From politician to prisoner

Hitler stayed in the army after the war, working as a 'V-man', spying on new political groups to see if they were dangerous. One group he investigated wasn't dangerous at all – they had few members and funds of only 7.5 marks – about £4. They were called the German Workers' Party.

After a few months, Hitler decided to join this new political party. He liked many of its ideas and became member number 555. Before long, he was making speeches and writing articles for local newspapers about the party's beliefs and ideas for a better Germany. Hitler spoke passionately about the need for Germany to gain a stronger leader who would get revenge for the defeat in the Great War. He also claimed that the Jews were 'germs' that must be 'destroyed'. In 1920 Hitler suggested the party change its name to the National Socialist German Workers' Party – or Nazi Party for short. By 1921 Hitler was running the Nazi Party himself!

Soon Hitler made the **swastika** the symbol of the Nazis and used brown-shirted 'storm troopers' to beat up the people who disagreed with him when he made speeches (see **Sources C** and **D**).

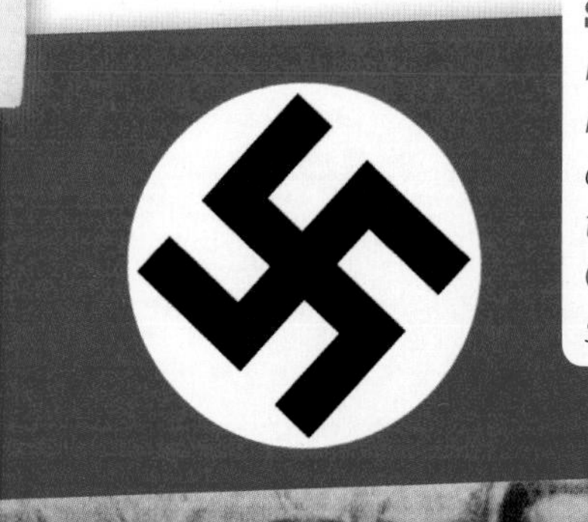

SOURCE C: *The Nazi flag. The symbol in the centre is known as the 'crooked cross' or the swastika. It became Germany's official symbol in 1935.*

SOURCE D: *Hitler pictured with his storm troopers. The 'brownshirts', as they were nicknamed, were Hitler's own private army of thugs that beat up people who criticized him.*

From prisoner to politician

Hitler's views made him popular and in 1923 he felt confident enough to try to take over Germany. He tried to start a revolution in Munich – one of Germany's largest cities – hoping it would spread to other places. It failed and Hitler was put in prison for treason. While in prison, he wrote a book about his life and his ideas called *Mein Kampf* (German for 'my struggle'). When Hitler was released in 1924 (for good behaviour), his book started to get him a reputation as a man whose ideas might be able to put Germany 'on the right track' again. And, while many ordinary Germans didn't quite understand (or agree) with all his views, many certainly liked his ideas for making Germany great again.

SOURCE E: *The front cover of an English translation of* Mein Kampf, *written while Hitler was in prison, which was published in 18 weekly parts.*

From politician to leader

When Hitler was let out of prison he went back to running the Nazi Party. By 1928, Hitler and the Nazis were very well known but they were still only the eighth largest political party in Germany. Then, in 1929, world trade began to slow down and a 'Great Depression' started. This means that countries stopped buying and selling to each other. German factories closed and millions lost their jobs. Lots of people lost their homes and in big cities the streets were full of starving people looking for work. Soon people, including Hitler, started to promise solutions to all Germany's problems. 'Vote for me,' was Hitler's message, 'and I'll provide you with work and bread.' As more and more people lost their jobs, the Nazis got more and more votes. By 1932, the Nazis were the largest political party and Hitler became Germany's Chancellor (or Prime Minister) in January 1933.

SOURCE F: *A Nazi election poster of 1932. The words mean 'Our last hope: HITLER.' Who do you think this poster was aimed at?*

'He is... one of the greatest speakers of the century. Adolf Hitler enters a hall. He sniffs the air. For a minute he gropes, feels his way, senses the atmosphere. Suddenly he bursts forward. His words go like an arrow to his target, he touches each private wound on the raw... telling it what it most wants to hear.'

◀ **SOURCE G:** *Otto Strasser, a German, wrote this after hearing Hitler speak. Strasser hated Hitler but recognized his excellent speaking skills.*

Work

1. a. Make a timeline of 12 important events in Hitler's life up to 1933. The first event in his life has been started for you:
   1889: Born in Braunau, a small town in Austria. His father…
   b. Choose two events in Hitler's life that you would regard as important turning points. Explain why each event you have chosen was so important.
2. Answer the following questions in full sentences.
   a. In your opinion, was Hitler a good soldier? Give reasons for your answer.
   b. What was a 'V-man'?
   c. Hitler always said he was the seventh member of the German Workers' Party, even though he wasn't. Even his membership card showed he wasn't one of the earliest members! So why do you think Hitler always claimed he was such an early member?
   d. What was the swastika?
   e. Who were the 'brownshirts' and how did they help Hitler?
   f. Write down three facts about *Mein Kampf*.
   g. In your own words, explain how Hitler's Nazi Party went from the eighth most popular political party in Germany in 1928 to Germany's most popular political party in 1932.

4.4A What was life like in Hitler's Germany?

Adolf Hitler was asked to become Chancellor by the President of Germany, Paul von Hindenburg. At this time, the President was the most powerful man in Germany and the Chancellor was his chief minister or 'second in command'. When President Hindenburg died one year later, Hitler made himself both Chancellor AND President. He started to call himself **Führer** (supreme leader) and immediately got all members of the army to swear an oath (promise) of loyalty to him (see **Source A**).

Mission Objectives

- Assess how life under the Nazi dictatorship differed from the democratic system we live in today.

'I swear by God that by this sacred oath I will give complete obedience to the Führer Adolf Hitler… and am ready as a brave soldier to risk my life at any time for him.'

▲ **SOURCE A:** *The Oath of Loyalty, 1934. Note that the promise is made to Hitler, not Germany. Why do you think making sure people took this oath was one of the first things Hitler did once he was in power?*

All change

Hitler quickly started to change things. Having worked so hard to get into power, he was determined to stay there. His secret police force, the dreaded **Gestapo**, hunted down anyone who might be against Hitler. They had the power to arrest and imprison people without trial and set up a web of informers who would report any 'moaners' to them. Children were encouraged to report their parents or teachers if they spoke out against the Führer and, by 1935, every block of flats or housing estate had a 'local ruler' who listened for negative comments. By 1939, there were well over 100,000 people in prison for 'anti-Hitler crimes'… they were known as Enemies of the State.

'The Nazi government must have total control over every aspect of life. Government will be in the hands of one person, a genius, a hero, with total responsibility for culling on behalf of a pure race in the national interest.'

▲ **SOURCE B:** *Part of a Nazi press release from 1934. 'Culling' means to kill or remove any unwanted people.*

Who was on Hitler's hate list?

Hitler was determined to crush anyone who didn't fully support him. He once declared that any opponents would 'have their skulls bashed in'. However, most of Hitler's hatred was based on race. He believed that humans were divided into races and some races were better or superior to others. Hitler said the best races were the 'pure' ones that hadn't interbred and 'mixed' with others. He added that the master race of pure Germans – or Aryans – were the rightful rulers of Europe. He felt that superior races (like the Germans) had the right to dominate 'inferior' races, such as Jews, Gypsies, Slavs (such as Russians), and black people.

'The prisons were full. Tramps, prostitutes and beggars were a common sight, but there were other prisoners too. Anyone who refused to join the army was sent to prison and so were people who'd been a member of any other political party except the Nazis. Trade union leaders were also inside and I once met a woman who had been reported for telling a joke at the Führer's expense. Another favourite tactic of the Gestapo was to accuse a man or woman of being homosexual – there were many in prison accused of this "crime".'

▲ **SOURCE C:** *Based on an interview with a former inmate of one of Hitler's prisons. They were known as* **concentration camps**.

Wise Up Words

concentration camp eugenics Führer Gestapo hereditary indoctrinate sterilize

People who were disabled in any way or had learning difficulties were also targets for Hitler because they damaged the purity of the German race. Hitler thought these people should be eliminated so their illnesses and disabilities could not be passed on to their children. 300,000 men and women were compulsorily **sterilized** in families with **hereditary** illnesses; 275,000 people with learning difficulties were gassed and 5000 babies killed.

Hitler reserved his greatest hatred for the Jews. He saw them as an inferior race that cared more about themselves than the greatness of Germany. He thought they were involved in a great conspiracy to take over the world and blamed them for Germany's loss in the Great War. Jews, Hitler said, must therefore be destroyed. **Sources D**, **E** and **F** show how Jews were persecuted in Nazi Germany in the 1930s.

LAWS AGAINST JEWS, 1933–1939

April 1933 All Jews banned from any sports clubs; all Jewish teachers sacked; all Jewish lawyers and judges sacked

September 1933 'Race studies' introduced in German schools

January 1934 All Jewish shops marked with a yellow Star of David – a symbol of the Jewish religion – or the word *Juden* (German for 'Jew'); soldiers stand outside shops turning people away

September 1935 Jews not allowed to vote. Marriages between Jews and non-Jews banned

January 1936 No Jew allowed to own any electrical equipment (including cameras), bicycles, typewriters or music records; Jews banned from using swimming pools

July 1938 Jewish doctors sacked

August 1938 Male Jews must add the name 'Israel' and female Jews must add the name 'Sara' to their first names

November 1938 Jewish children banned from German schools

December 1938 Jewish and non-Jewish children forbidden to play together

April 1939 Jews can be evicted from their homes for no reason

September 1939 Jews no longer allowed out of their homes between 8:00pm and 6:00am

SOURCE E: *Examples of laws that were designed to make life more and more uncomfortable for German Jews. There were approximately 500,000 Jews in Germany in 1934 (about 1 per cent of the population). By the time Hitler stopped Jews from leaving the country (1941), nearly 80 per cent had already left for new lives in other places.*

SOURCE D: *A photograph of a park bench in Berlin. The sign on the bench reads: 'Not for Jews.' Sometimes whole villages and towns displayed signs which read: 'Jews enter this place at their own risk.'*

Work

1. Write a sentence or two to explain the following words:
   - Führer • Gestapo • concentration camp • sterilization
2. Look at **Source E**.
   - **a** Write down five laws or policies that made life uncomfortable or difficult for German Jews.
   - **b** Next to each of your choices, explain why you think it was introduced by the Nazis. One has been done for you:

January 1934: Soldiers stood outside Jewish shops and told people not to shop there. I think this was introduced to ruin Jewish businesses – if they had to close their shops, they might leave Germany altogether.

SOURCE F: *This humiliating photograph of a married couple was taken in 1933. It shows an Aryan woman and a Jewish man being bullied by the Nazis. The woman's sign reads: 'I live with a pig and only go with Jews.' Her husband's sign reads: 'Instead of Jews, I only take young German girls to my room.'*

4.4B What was life like in Hitler's Germany?

Why were the young so important to Hitler?

Hitler took great trouble to make sure that young people were loyal to him and the Nazi Party. He realized that in future he may have to call on these people to put up with hardships, to fight and perhaps die for him. It was important therefore that young people thought that Hitler and the Nazis were the best thing that had ever happened to Germany. He needed young men who were 'as fast as a greyhound, as tough as leather and as hard as steel'. He wanted tough, strong, practical girls too… but for an entirely different reason – they were to be the wives and mothers of a future generation of soldiers. **Sources A**, **B** and **C** show how the Nazis changed Germany's school system.

SOURCE A: *A typical timetable for a day's education at a mixed school in Berlin, 1936.* ***Eugenics*** *is the scientific study of how to improve races. What major differences do you notice about the education process for the different sexes?*

	Lesson 1	Lesson 2	Lesson 3	Lunch	Lesson 4	Lesson 5	Lesson 6
BOYS	German	History/ Geography	Eugenics/ Nazi theory	Sport and music clubs	Physics and Chemistry	PE: boxing, football and marching	Maths
GIRLS	German	History/ Geography	Eugenics/ Nazi theory		Biology/ health and sex education	Cookery	Maths

Question 46:
The Jews are aliens in Germany. In 1933 there were 66,060,000 people living in Germany. Of this total, 499,862 were Jews. What is the percentage of aliens in Germany?

Question 52:
A bomber aircraft on take-off carries 144 bombs, each weighing ten kilos. The aircraft bombs a town full of Jews. On take-off with all bombs on board and a fuel tank containing 1000 kilos of fuel, the aircraft weighs about eight tons. When it returns from its victorious mission, there are still 230 kilos of fuel left. What is the weight of the aircraft when empty?

Question 67:
It costs, on average, four RM (reichmarks) a day to keep a cripple or a mentally ill person in hospital. There are currently 300,000 mentally ill, lunatics and so on in Germany's hospitals. How much would the German government save if they got rid of all these people?

◀ **SOURCE B:** *Youngsters were* ***indoctrinated*** *(brainwashed) to think like Nazis. Textbooks were rewritten to get across the Nazi message. Even teachers had to belong to the German Nazi Teachers' League and were made to put across Nazi ideas in their lessons – or face the sack. These questions are adapted and translated from a German textbook during the Nazi period.*

SOURCE C: *A picture from a German school textbook in 1936. Children were taught to recognize Jews at a glance. Look for: i) the way the Jewish children and adult (on the left) are drawn. Why have they been drawn this way?; ii) the reaction of the other children to the Jews' departure; iii) the Jewish boy on the right pulling another child's hair – why has this been included?*

Outside school, young people had to belong to a Nazi youth organization from the age of ten, though they sometimes participated from the age of six. Boys and girls were in separate groups and spent a few evenings a week and several weekends a year learning new skills and being taught how to show their loyalty to Hitler. Boys tended to learn military skills (model making, shooting practice and hiking) while girls learned mainly about cookery, housework and motherhood (see **Sources D** and **E**). As teenagers, boys were required to join the Hitler Youth, and girls joined the League of German Maidens.

SOURCE D: *A photograph of a smiling Hitler and a six-year-old member of the Hitler Youth Organization.*

1) Complete the following lessons:
- i) Life of Hitler
- ii) Germans abroad
- iii) Germany's rightful place in the world
- iv) National holidays of the German people
- v) Five flag oaths
- vi) Six Hitler Youth songs

2) Complete the following athletic tests:
- i) Run 60 metres in 10 seconds
- ii) Long jump 3.25 metres
- iii) Throw a small leather ball 35 metres
- iv) Pull up on a bar twice
- v) Somersault backwards twice
- vi) Swim 100 metres

3) Hiking and camping tests:
- i) A day's hike of 15 kilometres
- ii) Camp in a tent for three days
- iii) Put up a two-man tent and take part in putting up a twelve-man tent
- iv) Make a cooking pit and find water for cooking
- v) Know the names of the most important trees
- vi) Use the stars to find your place on a map

4) Target practice:
Hit a bull's eye on a target at a distance of eight metres with an air gun

▲ **SOURCE E:** *An extract from the guidebook of the boys' Nazi youth organization. It describes what ten- to fourteen-year-old boys had to do to get an 'Achievement Award'. Would you be tough enough?*

Work

1 Why do you think Hitler and the Nazis put so much effort into organizing the lives of young people?

2 Look at **Source A**.
- a In what ways is this timetable different to school timetables today?
- b Why do you think boys and girls were taught different things?
- c What is 'eugenics' and why do you think the Nazis put this on every school's timetable?

3 Look at **Source B**.
- a In what ways are these questions different from ones that appear in your Maths books today?
- b Why do you think questions like these appeared in German textbooks?

4 a Draw a poster showing how the Nazis were trying to organize the lives of young people. Choose to aim the poster at either the young people OR at their parents.
- b In what ways might the two posters differ?

4.4C What was life like in Hitler's Germany?

Was it a sexist society?

In Hitler's eyes, a woman's most important job was to have children – lots of them, and especially boys. Women were encouraged to stay at home and be good wives and mothers. Going out and getting qualifications and a professional job was frowned upon as it might get in the way of producing lots of babies. Loans were given to newly married couples – the equivalent of a year's wages – to encourage them to have children. On the birth of a first child, they could keep a quarter of the money. On the birth of another they could keep the second quarter. They could keep the third quarter on the birth of a third child and keep the lot on the birth of a fourth. Every year, on 12 August, the birthday of Hitler's mother, the Motherhood Medal was awarded to women who had the most children.

▼ **SOURCE A:** *A Nazi law written in 1943. It never came into effect.*

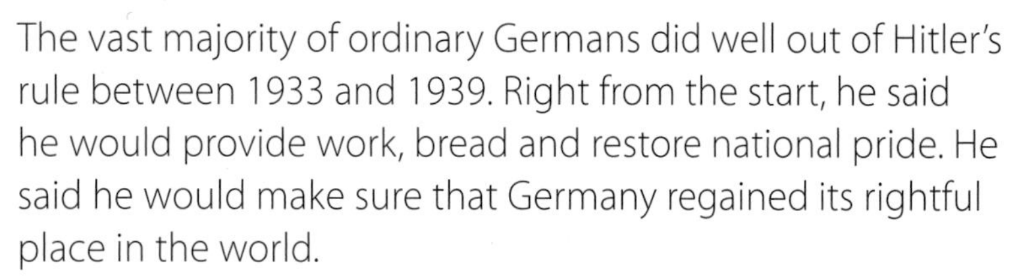

'All single and married women up to the age of 35 who do not already have four children should produce four children by racially pure German men. Whether or not these men are married is not important. Every family that already has four children must set the husband free for this action.'

SOURCE B: *A Nazi poster of 1937 showing what Nazis thought a woman's role in life should be. Look for: i) the plain, simple woman breastfeeding her baby. Wearing make-up and trousers was frowned upon by the Nazis. Permed or dyed hair was banned and slimming was discouraged because it was not thought to be good for childbearing; ii) her husband working on the land, providing for Germany while his wife takes care of things at home; iii) the church in the background. Hitler thought the ideal woman should stick to the 'three Ks' – Kinder, Kirche and Küche (children, church and cooking).*

How did Hitler please ordinary Germans?

The vast majority of ordinary Germans did well out of Hitler's rule between 1933 and 1939. Right from the start, he said he would provide work, bread and restore national pride. He said he would make sure that Germany regained its rightful place in the world.

In 1933 there were six million people out of work, but this figure had reduced to 200,000 by 1938. The Nazis provided work by building roads, schools, hospitals, railways… and by making the army bigger and building tanks, fighter planes and battleships. Hitler started to get back land Germany had lost after its defeat in the Great War and many Germans felt a sense of pride in this. If the German people were prepared to ignore some of the crueller things happening to a minority of people, and not complain too loudly, it seemed that life was better under Hitler's leadership.

▶ **SOURCE C:** *Adapted from* Hitler's Germany *by Josh Brooman (1991).*

'The Nazis drew up massive leisure programmes for working people. The biggest programme provided workers with cheap holidays. A cruise to the Canary Islands, for example, cost 62 marks, the equivalent of two weeks' wages. However, it was only loyal and hardworking members of the Nazi Party who were given places on the cruise liners. There were also walking holidays, skiing holidays, two weeks in Switzerland... or a tour of Italy. The Nazis arranged sports matches, outings to the theatre and the opera. It had its own symphony orchestra, which toured the country playing music in areas not usually visited by orchestras. It laid on evening classes for adults.'

SOURCE D: *Hitler introduced a savings scheme to help millions of ordinary Germans save up for an affordable car. The 'people's car' or 'Volkswagen' was launched in 1938. Built by Ferdinand Porsche (who went on to design sports cars), it was based on a sketch by Hitler himself. It was purposefully designed to look like a beetle because Hitler was a big admirer of the insect's fighting nature. In this photograph, Hitler is inspecting the first ever model. But the whole savings scheme was a big swindle. Not one ordinary German got their car; the money was used to buy weapons!*

How did Hitler get his message across?

Hitler was determined to control the way people thought. The Nazis controlled all newspapers, films, radio, plays, cinema, and books – and made sure they put across Nazi ideas. One of Hitler's most trusted friends, Joseph Goebbels, was put in charge of propaganda and censorship. He became a master of mind control. He had loud speakers placed on all city streets so that people could hear Hitler's speeches when they were doing their shopping and ordered all books written by Jews or communists to be destroyed. He banned jazz music because it was played mainly by black American musicians and even had a war film destroyed because it showed a drunk German sailor. He even introduced the death penalty for telling an anti-Hitler joke!

'I don't know how to describe the emotions that swept over me as I heard Adolf Hitler... when he spoke of the disgrace of Germany I was ready to spring on any enemy... I forgot everything but Hitler. Then, glancing around, I saw that the thousands around me were drawn to him like a magnet as well.'

▲ **SOURCE E:** *The feelings of a man who attended a Nazi rally in 1937.*

Hungry for More?

Why do you think Hitler wanted so many boys to be born in Germany?

Work

1 Read **Source A**. In your own words, explain how this law tried to encourage Germans to have more children.

2 a How did Hitler create jobs?
  b What effect do you think the creation of lots of jobs had on his popularity?

3 a In 1937 a leading Nazi said, 'The only people who have a private life in Germany today are those who are asleep.' Use the information and sources on pages 76 to 81 to give examples of how people's private lives were affected by the Nazis.
  b Why do you think Hitler put someone in charge of propaganda and censorship?
  c Why do you think he gave the job to one of his most trusted friends?

4.5A Why was there another world war?

Adolf Hitler, who became leader of Germany in 1933, was determined to make Germany great again. He had fought for the defeated German army in the Great War of 1914–1918 and, like millions of Germans, was humiliated by the punishment Germany received at the end of the fighting (see **Source A**).

Mission Objectives

- Outline Hitler's aims.
- Examine why war broke out in 1939.

Hitler's aims

Hitler had three main aims in his dealings with other countries:

- Firstly, he wanted to do everything in his power to get back all the land that Germany had lost after the Great War. He felt he would have to build up his army, navy and air force to do this, despite the fact that this would mean breaking the rules laid down at the end of the Great War. Hitler was determined to ignore the Treaty of Versailles and carry on regardless.
- Secondly, he wanted to join together anyone who spoke German into one big country.
- Finally, he wanted to make Germany bigger by taking land from other, weaker countries. He believed that true Germans were such a great and powerful race that they needed the extra living space (he called it '*Lebensraum*') to reach their full potential.

Be a Top Historian

Top historians know that big events, like wars, usually have many **causes** – and it's often possible to **link** some of these causes together. Identify a variety of causes for the outbreak of the Second World War – and try to link some of these causes together.

THE

TREATY OF VERSAILLES

- *The Great War was Germany's fault.*
- *The Germans must pay for the war... until 1988. The money will go to the British and French.*
- *Germany should only have a small army (100,000 men), a small navy (six battleships) and no submarines, air force or tanks.*
- *Germany must hand over huge areas of its land to the winning nations. Some of the land will be used to make new countries like Poland and Czechoslovakia.*
- *Germany must never unite with Austria again.*
- *No German soldiers can go into an area known as the Rhineland, a German region close to France.*

Signed Britain, France, Italy, the USA, and all other victorious nations.

SOURCE A: *This is a summary of the punishments Germany received at the end of the Great War.*

Making Germany stronger

Three days after becoming leader of Germany, Hitler told his military chiefs to start building up the army, navy and air force in secret. This was known as **rearmament**. By 1935 Hitler had aeroplanes, dozens more battleships than he was allowed, and thousands more soldiers! In late 1935, Hitler even told the world about his increased armed forces, but no one did anything. Some countries didn't want to stand up to Hitler for fear of starting another war, while others felt that the Germans should be allowed to build up their armed forces if they wanted to. After all, they were only protecting themselves, weren't they?

Wise Up Words

appeasement rearmament

More rule-breaking

In 1936 Hitler broke the rules again by sending his soldiers into the Rhineland area of Germany. Remember – his soldiers were not allowed anywhere near France (see **Source A**)! Once again, no country stopped him – after all, he wasn't invading another country, just moving his soldiers around *within* his own, they thought!

Yet Hitler's aggressive moves worried some politicians. British politician Winston Churchill, for example, made many speeches in Parliament about the need to stand up to Hitler. But Churchill was not Prime Minister at this time; he was just an ordinary MP… and many people ignored him! But Hitler's actions were starting to make world news. What would be his next daring move?

SOURCE B: *This is a German poster published after Germany had been forced to accept the Treaty of Versailles. The man on the left (in boxing gloves) represents France, while the man on the right represents Great Britain. Germany is tied up.*

Work

1 a Why did Hitler (and millions of other Germans) hate the Treaty of Versailles?
  b Explain how Hitler broke the Treaty of Versailles between 1933 and 1936.
  c Why did the leaders of some countries refuse to stand up to Hitler at this time?

2 Look at **Source B**.
  a Which countries do each of the three people in the cartoon represent?
  b What point do you think the cartoonist was trying to make about the way Germany was treated in the Treaty of Versailles?
  c Do you think the cartoon helps explain why many Germans, including Hitler, were unhappy with the Treaty of Versailles?

4.5B Why was there another world war?

What Happened When?

1938

In 1938 Otto Hahn and his assistant Fritz Strassmann discovered nuclear fission, the process by which nuclear power is generated.

SOURCE A: *A photograph of the German invasion of Austria, March 1938.*

Invasion of Austria

In 1938 German troops marched into Austria, the country of Hitler's birth. Once again, Hitler had broken the rules laid down at the end of the Great War in the Treaty of Versailles. Once again, no country stopped him. After all, many Austrians *wanted* to be part of Germany… and Hitler himself was Austrian (see **Source A**)!

Unstoppable?

By 1938, it seemed as if Hitler was unstoppable. His armed forces were getting stronger and he was demanding more land. He next turned his attention to the Sudetenland, a small area of Czechoslovakia that contained many people who spoke German as their first language (see **Source B**). Hitler told the world that he wanted this region. In September 1938 Neville Chamberlain, the British Prime Minister, visited Hitler in Germany to discuss Hitler's demands. On 30 September the British and the French agreed to let Germany have the Sudetenland. The Czechoslovakian leaders were not even at the meeting, but went along with the more powerful countries' decision! Hitler said he was happy and the world breathed a sigh of relief. In Britain, Chamberlain was a hero. He had even got Hitler to sign a piece of paper saying that he was satisfied with everything and didn't want anything else!

SOURCE B: *A map of Europe in the 1930s.*

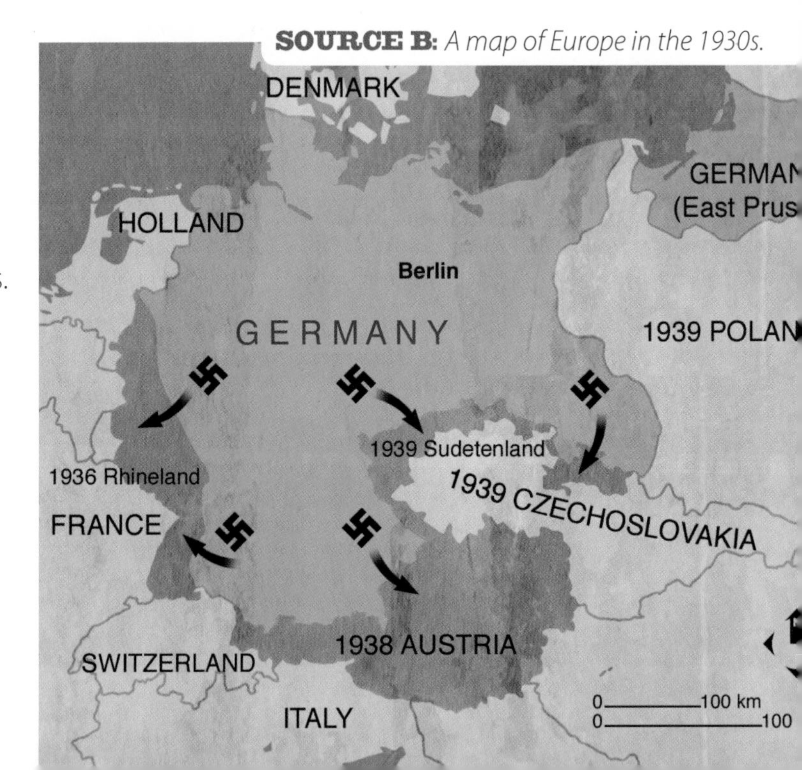

Hitler the liar!

But all Hitler's promises were exposed as lies in March 1939 when his soldiers took over the rest of Czechoslovakia. It seemed that he wasn't satisfied with just the Sudetenland at all… he wanted more and more. Suddenly, the countries of Europe realized that Hitler could never be trusted, and prepared for war. They wondered if they would be next. Britain and France had had enough of letting Hitler get away with things (giving Hitler what he wanted was known as **appeasement**) and agreed to help Poland if Hitler invaded.

War approaches

Sure enough, Poland was next on Hitler's hit list. He threatened to invade in August 1939, but only after he made a clever alliance with the USSR. Hitler thought that the Russians might feel threatened if he continued to push his soldiers in their direction, and so he made a deal with Stalin, the Russian leader. A secret part of the deal agreed that the Russians could have part of Poland if they let the Germans invade.

War breaks out

On 1 September 1939 German troops invaded Poland. Chamberlain decided that enough was enough. Two days later, on 3 September 1939, Britain declared war on Germany. Later that day, Chamberlain went on the radio to tell the British public the news (see **Source D**). France declared war, too.

SOURCE C: *A British cartoon published in a satirical magazine in the 1930s featuring Neville Chamberlain. The cartoon is called 'Still Hope'.*

Hungry for More?

Poland was defeated quickly. Hitler's troops then went on to invade Norway, the Netherlands, Belgium, and even France. On 10 May 1940 Winston Churchill, the man who had warned the world about Hitler, took over as British Prime Minister. Hitler eventually invaded the USSR in June 1941 (so much for his alliance!) but was forced back in the winter after getting to within 95 kilometres of Russia's capital, Moscow. If you're hungry for more information on what happened, get researching!

'This country is at war with Germany… May God bless you all. It is evil things we are fighting against – brute force, bad faith, injustice, oppression and persecution; and against that, I am certain that right will prevail [win].'

▲ **SOURCE D:** *Part of Chamberlain's speech on 3 September 1939.*

Work

1 Look at **Source A**. What does this photograph tell us about the feelings of ordinary Austrians when Hitler invaded in 1938? Give reasons for your answer.

2 Look at **Source C**.

a Who is the man pictured in the cartoon?

b Where is he going?

c Why do you think the cartoon is called 'Still Hope'?

5.1A The Second World War: an overview

The Second World War lasted from 1939 to 1945 and is the largest global conflict the world has ever known. It was fought over six continents, and during six long years more than 50 million men, women and children were killed. So when, exactly, did war break out? Which countries fought? What were the war's key events and turning points? And how did it end?

Mission Objectives

- Recall key terms such as 'Blitzkrieg', 'Blitz' and 'D-Day'.
- Identify key turning points of the war.

Blitzkrieg

Germany invaded Poland on 1 September 1939 using a new method of fighting called **Blitzkrieg** ('lightning war' – see **Source A**). The Polish army was beaten in about a week. Blitzkrieg involved fast-moving columns of tanks supported by infantry soldiers and dive-bomber attacks. Parachutists were dropped behind enemy lines the night before to destroy enemy strongholds and cut their telephone wires.

Britain and France had promised to protect Poland, but were too far away to stop the invasion. As a result, there was very little fighting for about six months after Poland was defeated. Instead, the British army crossed over to help its allies, France and Belgium, to set up defensive positions along their borders.

SOURCE A: *The Blitzkrieg method of warfare.*

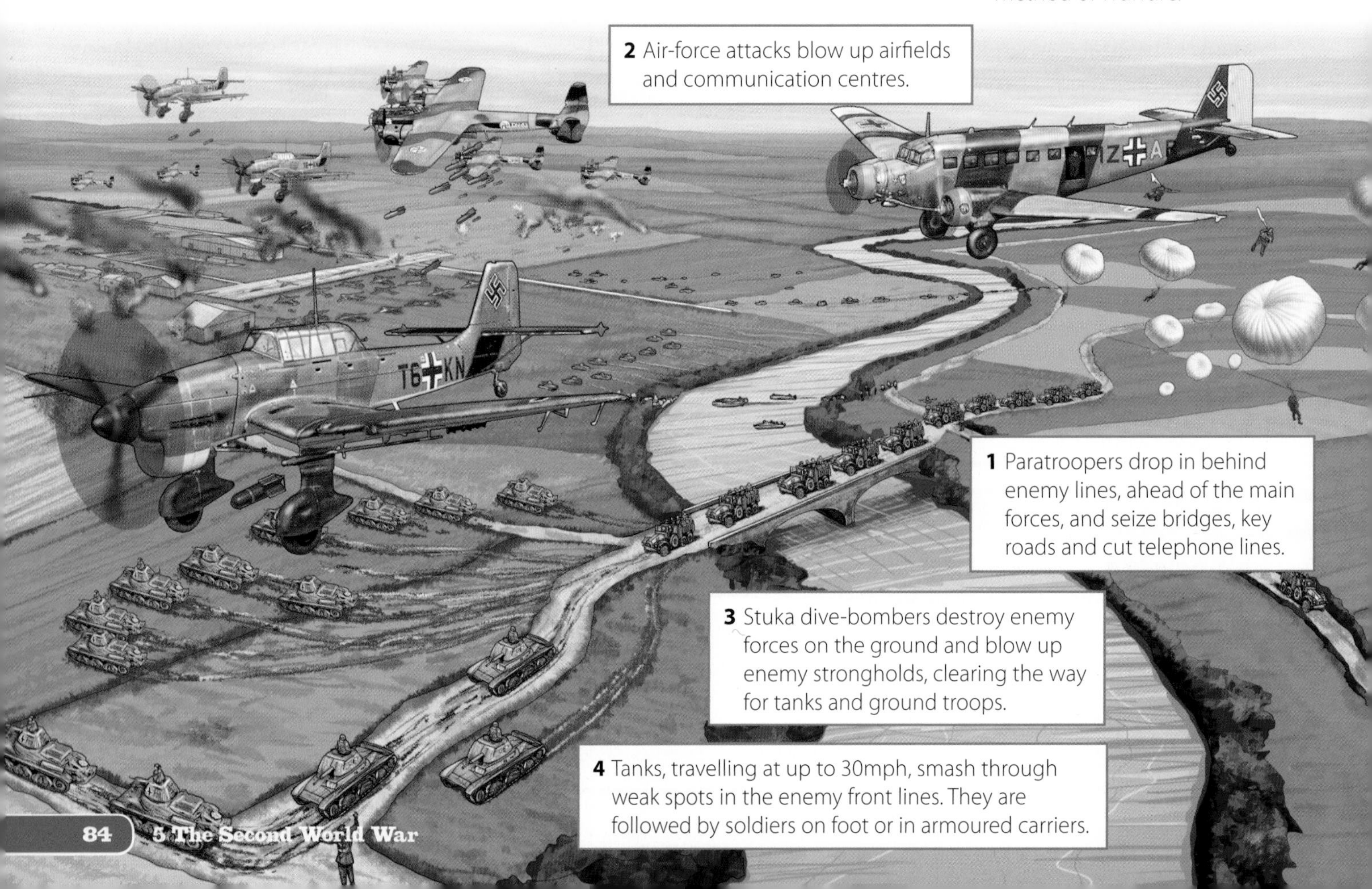

SOURCE B: *An artist's impression of the evacuation of Dunkirk.*

Wise Up Words

Blitz Blitzkrieg

Evacuate!

Then, in the spring of 1940, the German Blitzkrieg tactics were used to attack France, Denmark, Norway, the Netherlands, and Belgium. In just a few months, Hitler's armies occupied much of the centre of Europe and there was little the defending armies could do. Thousands of British, French and Belgian troops escaped from Dunkirk to England in a fleet of yachts, paddle steamers, warships, and even rowing boats (see **Source B**).

The Battle of Britain and the Blitz

As a result of Blitzkrieg, in 1940 Britain stood alone without any powerful countries as allies except for those in its Empire (such as India) and those that used to be (such as Australia, which had recently gained its independence). However, Hitler wanted to complete his domination of Europe by invading Britain. But before he could transport his troops across the English Channel, he had to destroy Britain's air force. He began by carrying out a series of air raids on military air bases in southern England in the summer of 1940. The British air force fought back and, in August and September, the skies over Kent, Surrey, Sussex, and Essex were a smoking mass of aeroplanes as British Spitfires and Hurricane fighters fought against German Messerschmitts and Heinkels (see **Source C**).

Hitler lost the Battle of Britain and abandoned his plans for invasion for the time being. Instead, he launched massive night bombing raids on major British cities, hoping to force Britain to surrender (see **Source D**).

SOURCE C: *British aircraft defeated a larger German force in the Battle of Britain.*

SOURCE D: *A photograph of the results of German bombing in London. On 14 October 1940, a bomb killed 64 people who were sheltering in an underground station in London. This period was known as the* ***Blitz****.*

FACT!

During the **Blitz**, German bombers dropped 18,800 tons of bombs on London and 11,700 tons on other British cities such as Bristol, Plymouth, Coventry, Glasgow, and Hull. They killed 61,000 civilians. Of every 26 houses in Britain in 1939, 17 were untouched, 8 were damaged and 1 was destroyed by air raids.

5.1B The Second World War: an overvie

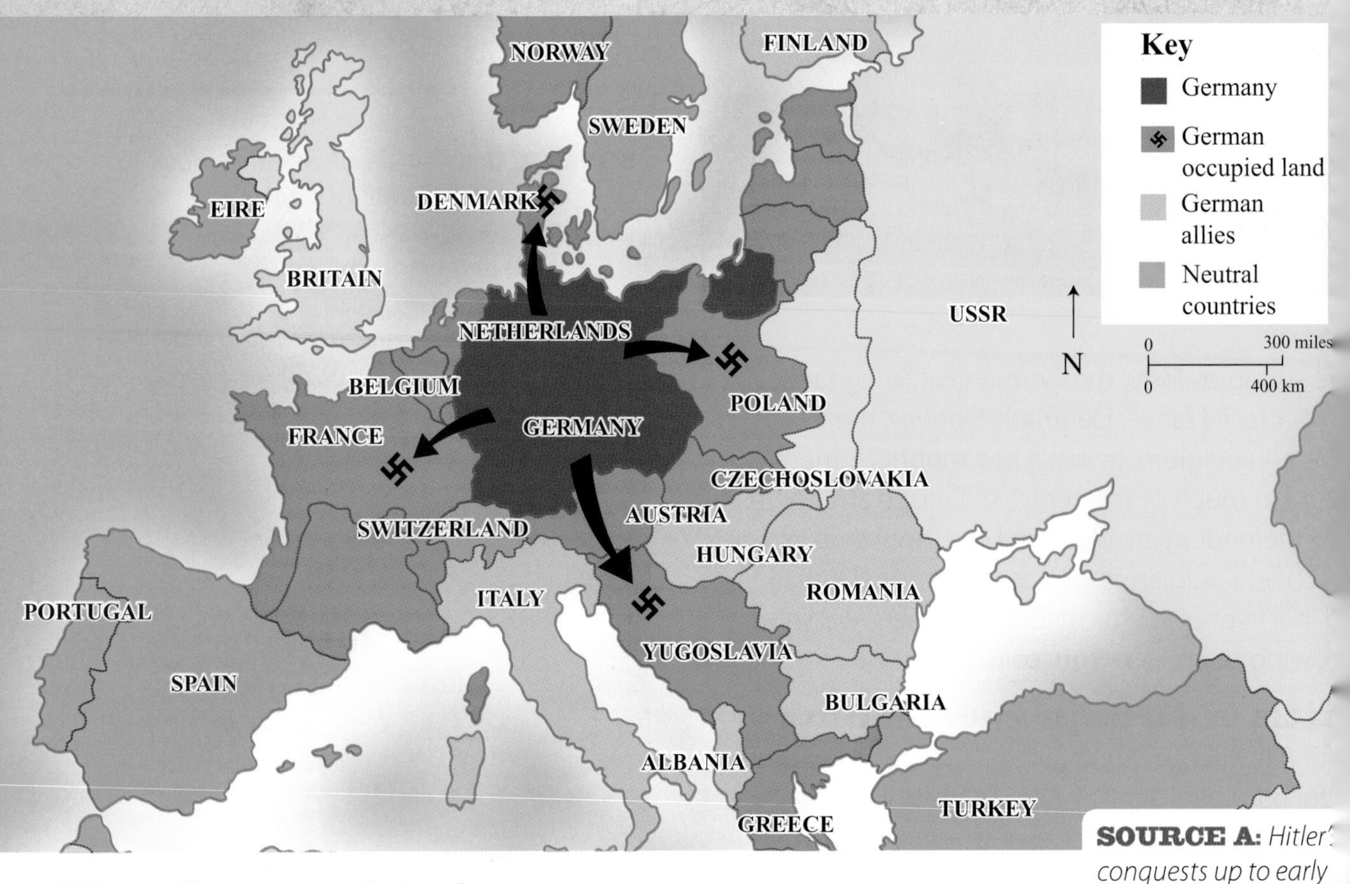

SOURCE A: *Hitler'*
conquests up to early

More German victories

Despite the nightly onslaught by German bombers, the British held on. And, by 1941, Hitler had turned his attention towards his old hated enemy – Russia.

In April 1941, the Germans helped their Italian allies invade Greece and Yugoslavia. They had invaded some parts of Africa where the British were based, too.

When Germany attacked Russia in June 1941, the Russians were pushed back and back until, in October, Hitler was only 95 kilometres from the capital city, Moscow. As winter started to set in, it seemed that the German army was unstoppable.

Japan enters the war

Then, at the end of 1941, the Japanese entered the war. In an attempt to knock out America's navy in one go (and give them control of the rich lands in the Far East), they launched a surprise attack on the great American naval base of Pearl Harbor in Hawaii. Thousands of American soldiers were killed and dozens of US fighter planes and warships were destroyed, so the USA declared war on Japan and its allies (Italy and Germany). Japan won victory after victory against America. Japanese troops seized the British colonies of Hong Kong, Malaya and Burma, too, as well as the French colony of Indo-China. By early 1942, the war seemed lost for Britain, Russia and America.

The Germans were almost in Moscow and had nearly pushed the British out of Africa. In the east, Japan was pushing back American forces and was close to invading India and Australia. Then, in the space of a few months, three major battles changed the course of the whole war!

SOURCE B: *The attack on Pearl Harbor.*

Key turning points

- **The Battle of Midway (June 1942):** In the Pacific Ocean, the Japanese were beaten by American forces in the great air and sea battle of Midway Island. The Japanese advance was stopped and gradually the Americans began to drive them back, island by island.
- **The Battle of Stalingrad (July 1942–February 1943):** In Russia, after four months of very fierce hand-to-hand, house-to-house fighting in the city of Stalingrad, a significant proportion of the German army surrendered. Gradually, Soviet forces began to push the German army out of Russia and back towards Germany. This was the first time the Germans had retreated. At the same time, British and American bombers began night and day air raids on Germany itself.
- **El Alamein (October–November 1942):** In Africa, at El Alamein, British troops defeated the Germans. With help from the Americans, the British drove the Germans out of North Africa and invaded Italy. British war leader, Winston Churchill, called El Alamein 'the turning point of the war'!

SOURCE C: *Through the windowless side of a ruined building, a photographer records the horrific street fighting that proceeded, literally, from one building to the next in Stalingrad.*

Work

1. **a** What was 'Blitzkrieg'?
   b Why do you think Blitzkrieg was so effective?
2. In your opinion, by the end of 1940, how well was the war going for:
   • Germany • Britain?
3. When and why did the USA enter the war?
4. **a** What do you think is meant by the term 'turning point'?
   b Why do you think the battles of Midway, Stalingrad and El Alamein are known as 'turning points'?

5.1C The Second World War: an overview

Italy surrenders

By the end of 1943, the invasion of Italy was in full swing. As Italian forces surrendered, their leader, Mussolini, was captured and shot.

In Britain, an invasion of France that aimed to push German forces back towards Germany was planned. The invasion date was set for June 1944.

D-Day

On 6 June 1944, British, American and other Allied troops landed on beaches in Normandy, France, and forced the Germans back, despite brutal fighting. On top of this, in July, Hitler's opponents in Germany tried to assassinate him and a German attempt to retake some of the land they had lost in December failed.

Germany surrenders

By April 1945, British and American forces were moving quickly towards Berlin (Germany's capital city). Along the way, they were freeing villages, towns and even countries from the German occupation. In the east, the Russian armies were advancing too. The German army was being beaten in battle after battle and food supplies in major German towns were running short.

Hitler and his closest followers retreated to a special underground bunker under Berlin's streets and, on 30 April, Hitler killed himself. Within days, Germany surrendered and the war was over… in Europe!

Nuclear bombs

Victory in Europe meant that more Allied troops could be sent to fight the Japanese. However, before the invasion could take place, the American President made the decision to drop two nuclear bombs on the Japanese cities of Hiroshima and Nagasaki. The Japanese, rather than face the complete destruction of their islands, surrendered on 14 August. The Second World War was over.

FACT!

The Second World War was fought between two main groups of countries. On one side were the Axis Powers, including Germany, Italy and Japan. On the other side were the Allies, including Britain, France, Canada, Australia, New Zealand, India, the Soviet Union, China, and the USA.

SOURCE A: *American troops arriving at Normandy beaches (north-west France) as reinforcements during the historic D-Day landings.*

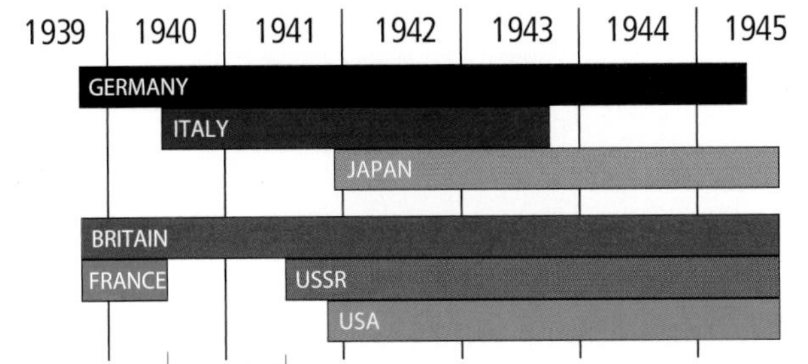

SOURCE C: *When countries joined (and left) the war.*

SOURCE B: *This is a photograph of a test explosion of a nuclear bomb on 25 July 1946 (you can see some of the old warships they used to test the blast). The man who developed the bomb, Robert Oppenheimer, was so overwhelmed by its power that he said, 'Now I am become Death, the destroyer of worlds.' The bomb dropped on Hiroshima was the equivalent of 20,000 tons of dynamite. When US President Harry S. Truman heard of the bombing, he said, 'This is the greatest thing in history.'*

SOURCE D: *Second World War deaths.*

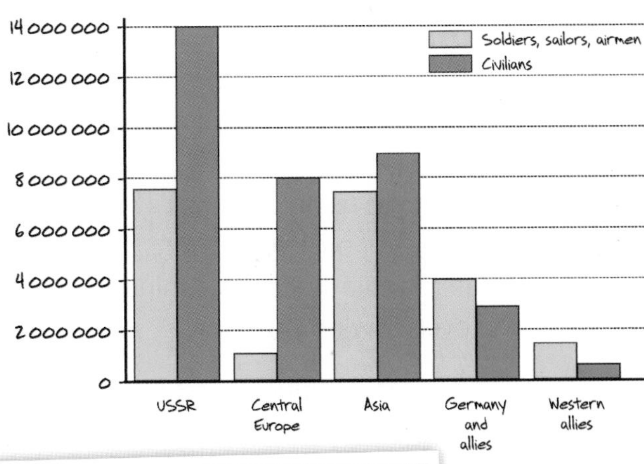

Work

1. Draw a timeline from 1939 to 1945. Add at least ten key battles, events or interesting facts.
2. Look at these three headings:
   - 'Bad times for the Brits'
   - 'The tide turns'
   - 'Victory'.

   a Add the headings to your timeline in the places you think they fit best. It is OK for the headings to cover a number of months or even years.

   b Explain why you have put each heading in the place you have chosen.
3. Look at **Source E**. With a partner or in a small group, discuss what the source means. Do you think the money should have been spent on defeating Nazi Germany and its allies, or building houses, roads and schools?
4. You have been given the job of choosing an image for the front of a new school textbook about the Second World War. You can choose either one or two images, but you can only choose from ones that appear on pages 84 to 89 of this book. What image(s) will you choose? Explain your decision.

SOURCE E: *The cost of the war.*

5.2A Dunkirk: victory or disaster?

When war officially began in September 1939, British troops crossed the English Channel into France to help the French to prepare for a German attack. When German troops finally invaded France in May 1940, they quickly pushed the British and French back towards the English Channel. By the end of May, nearly half a million British and French soldiers had been pushed back so far that they were trapped between the sea and the advancing Germans (see **Source A**). At that moment, it looked as if all was lost for Britain and France. Hitler was close to wiping out the entire British army (and thousands of French troops) before the war had really got under way!

Mission Objectives

- Identify reasons why Dunkirk could be considered a success.
- Identify reasons why Dunkirk could be considered a failure.
- Assess why interpretations of Dunkirk have changed over time.

Operation Dynamo

At the last moment, the British government organized a huge rescue operation known as 'Operation Dynamo'. The plan was to evacuate the troops to Britain using warships. They were helped by dozens of ordinary citizens in hundreds of small boats, paddle steamers, fishing boats, yachts, and even rowing boats.

Between 26 May and 4 June over 800 boats rescued 215,587 British soldiers and 127,031 French soldiers from the beaches of Dunkirk.

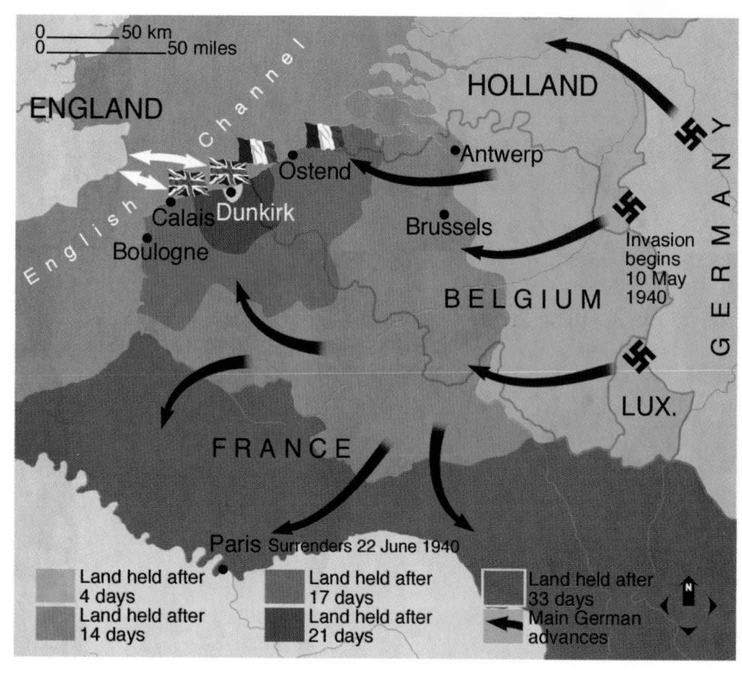

SOURCE A: *The German advance of 1940.*

Reporting Dunkirk

The events at Dunkirk are viewed in different ways. What happened there is sometimes viewed as a triumph or victory… but sometimes it's seen as a disaster. As top historians, you are going to investigate how Dunkirk has been reported and why it's been reported differently. Firstly, study **Sources B** to **F** carefully. The sources show how the evacuation was reported at the time.

'More cheering evidence of the success of this amazing military exploit is the presence in Britain of large numbers of French soldiers. They are showered with hospitality and find the tea of old England almost as refreshing as their coffee… Enjoying an unexpected seaside holiday, they lie in the sun, awaiting orders to return to France.

The story of that epic withdrawal will live in history as a glorious example of discipline [among the troops]… Every kind of small craft – destroyers, paddle steamers, yachts, motor boats, rowing boats – has sped here to the burning ruins of Dunkirk to bring off the gallant British and French troops.'

▲ **SOURCE B:** *From cinema newsreels, May 1940.*

SOURCE C: *A photograph taken on the beaches of Dunkirk in May 1940.*

'Bloody Marvellous.'

SOURCE D: *A headline from the Daily Mirror.*

▼ **SOURCE E:** *From BBC Radio's Six O'Clock News, 31 May 1940.*

'All night and all day men of the undefeated British Army have been coming home. From interviews with the men, it is clear they have come back in glory; that their morale is as high as ever, and that they are anxious to be back again "to have a real crack at Jerry [the Germans]".'

'Dunkirk has been a miracle escape. But we must be very careful not to call it a victory. Wars are not won by evacuations.'

▲ **SOURCE F:** *Winston Churchill, British Prime Minister, 4 June 1940.*

Work

1. a. How did ordinary civilians help out during the evacuation of Dunkirk?
   b. Can you suggest reasons why the news articles were so keen to report how ordinary civilians had helped out?
2. Look at **Sources B** to **E**. After studying these sources, which word best describes the events at Dunkirk – 'victory' or 'disaster'? Give reasons for your answer.
3. Look at **Source F**. In what way is Churchill's opinion of Dunkirk different from some of the other sources you've read on these pages?

5.2B Dunkirk: victory or disaster?

A game of two halves

Now look at **Sources A** to **F** on these pages. They were published some time after 1940 and give a different version of the events at Dunkirk.

SOURCE A: *This French poster was published by French people who believed that the British had deliberately left 40,000 French soldiers behind at Dunkirk. In fact, the British did take out some of their own troops before they told the French army about the evacuation, so the French held back the Germans while the British were loaded onto ships. The poster says: '1940 – Dunkirk. The English stop the last of the French who came to protect their retreat from getting on the boats.'*

2500 guns, **20,500** motorbikes, **64,000** other vehicles, **77,000** tons of ammunition, **416,000** tons of supplies and **165,000** tons of petrol. **68,000** soldiers were killed or taken prisoner.

▲ **SOURCE B:** *The numbers of weapons, vehicles and other supplies that the British Army left behind at Dunkirk.*

'Dunkirk was a military disaster – and took the British public by surprise... but almost at once, victory was being plucked from defeat and the newspapers began to manufacture the Dunkirk myth... The government encouraged it to flourish – and allowed nothing to be published which might damage morale... Dunkirk was a military defeat but a propaganda victory.'

▲ **SOURCE C:** *A BBC reporter commenting in 2000.*

'The troops had to leave all their tanks and heavy guns behind, so although Operation Dynamo became known as "The Miracle of Dunkirk", really the allies had been soundly beaten.'

▲ **SOURCE E:** *From* The Second World War *by Sean Lang (1993).*

Be a Top Historian

GCSE

Top historians should understand that events from the past (like the Dunkirk evacuation) can be presented – or **interpreted** – in different ways. Students working at a higher level (or at GCSE level) should try to understand not just how, but **why** past events have been interpreted in different ways.

What Happened When?

1940

In the same year as the Dunkirk evacuation, German bomber planes attacked London in what is known as the 'Blitz'.

'The British government hoped that at least 50,000 men could be rescued. In fact, around 340,000 men were rescued. The escape was referred to as a miracle but huge amounts had to be abandoned, including 475 tanks, 1000 heavy guns and 400 anti-tank guns. The BEF [British Expeditionary Force] had been forced to retreat, leaving the French to fight on alone. Churchill turned the evacuation into a national triumph playing up the role of the small boats and trying to build up morale and create "The Dunkirk Spirit".'

▲ **SOURCE D:** *From Steven Waugh's* Essential Modern World History *(2001).*

- British and French troops getting drunk during the retreat
- A soldier shooting another to stop him capsizing an overcrowded boat
- Soldiers arriving back in Britain and throwing away their rifles.

▲ **SOURCE F:** *These are summaries of accounts from a book called* The Sands of Dunkirk, *written in 1961 by Richard Collier. For his book he interviewed over 1000 eyewitnesses and looked at government papers on Dunkirk that no member of the public had seen before.*

Work

1.  Look at **Source A**. Why do you think this poster wasn't shown in Britain?
2. Look at all the sources on these two pages.
   - **a** What are the main differences between these sources and the sources you studied on pages 92 and 93?
   - **b** Why do you think that these differences exist?
3. **a** Why do you think that, at the time, Dunkirk was mainly reported as a victory?
   - **b** Do you think that the British government was right to report Dunkirk as a victory?
4. Is it possible for an event (such as Dunkirk) to be both a victory *and* a disaster? Explain your answer carefully.

5.3A Who were 'the Few'?

Towards the end of 1940, posters like **Source A** began to appear all over Britain. This poster featured five smiling fighter pilots and a famous quotation from Britain's Prime Minister, Winston Churchill. So why was the poster published? Why were the pilots smiling? And why did 'so many' people have to be thankful to 'so few'?

Mission Objectives

- *Explain what 'Operation Sealion' was.*
- *Decide why Hitler wasn't able to invade Britain in September 1940.*

By July 1940, Hitler was close to becoming the 'Master of Europe'. He was friendly with, or his armies had successfully invaded, most European countries (see **Source B**). Britain and the USSR were two of the more powerful nations that could stop him... but Britain was firmly in Hitler's sights and he was hoping to invade in September 1940!

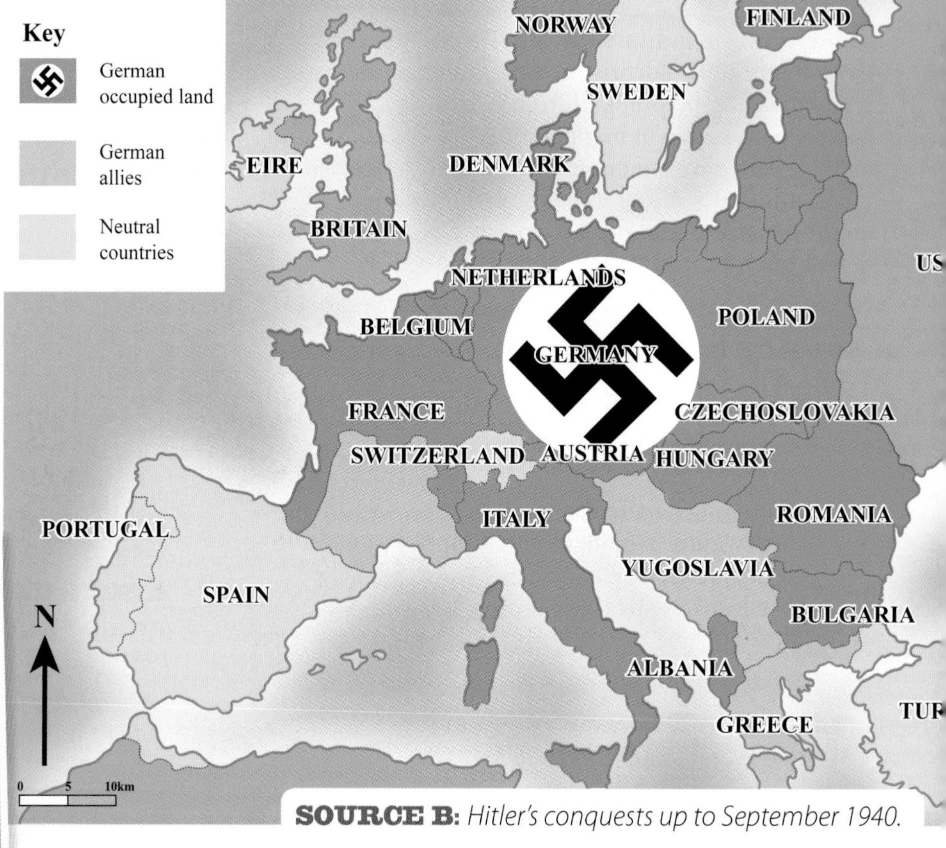

SOURCE B: *Hitler's conquests up to September 1940.*

SOURCE A: *A poster which first appeared in 1940.*

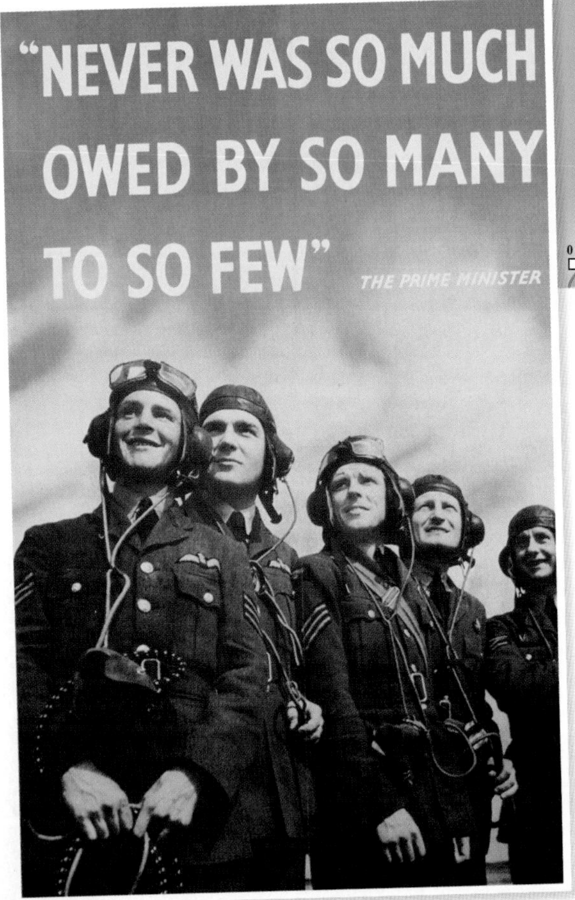

Hitler on top

On 1 August 1940, Hitler signed top secret plans to begin the invasion of Britain. Code-named 'Operation Sealion', the aim was to get German soldiers onto British soil by 15 September (see **Source C**). After that, German troops would move towards London and other major British cities with the goal of controlling the whole country by Christmas.

FACT!

In total, over 3000 pilots fought against the Germans in the Battle of Britain. Over 2000 were from Britain but they were joined by New Zealanders (102), Poles (141), Canadians (90), Czechs (86), South Africans (21), Americans (7), and many more.

TOP SECRET

GERMAN GOVERNMENT
TOP SECRET DIRECTIVE NO. 17,
1 AUGUST 1940

FROM: ADOLF HITLER

In order to establish the conditions necessary for the final conquest of Britain, I intend to step up the air and naval war more intensively.

i) From 5 August German bombers should attack British airfields and destroy all the RAF's aircraft. These bombers should be protected by fighter aircraft.

ii) If Britain does not surrender after all her aircraft are destroyed, the German army, escorted by the German navy, will land on beaches between Folkestone and Brighton on 15 September.

SOURCE C: *A summary of the order to launch air strikes in the build-up to Hitler's planned invasion. The* ***RAF*** *was the Royal Air Force, the official title of Britain's air force.*

SOURCE D: *A photograph of RAF pilots 'scrambling' to get to their planes to intercept approaching enemy aircraft.*

For Operation Sealion to have any chance of success, Hitler knew he had to destroy Britain's air force. He believed that if the **Luftwaffe** (German air force) could win control of the skies, it would be far easier for German ships to transport soldiers over the English Channel to begin the land invasion of Britain. If the RAF was destroyed, British planes could not attack the ships bringing across Hitler's troops.

Throughout the summer of 1940, German and British pilots fought each other in the Battle of Britain high above southern England. From the start, the odds were stacked against the British:

- The Germans had 824 fighter planes and 1017 bombers in service. Britain only had about 600 fighter planes.
- It took five minutes for German planes to cross the Channel from France. However, it took 15 minutes for British planes to take off and reach the invading planes after they were spotted.
- Many of the British pilots were part-timers and had not received the same level of training or experience as the Germans. Germany trained 800 new pilots a month, while the British trained just 200.

Work

1 Why were some people calling Hitler the 'Master of Europe' by July 1940?

2 a What was 'Operation Sealion'? Try to give a really detailed answer.

b Do you think Hitler had good reason to believe that an invasion of Britain was possible by 15 September? Give reasons for your answer.

5.3B Who were 'the Few'?

War in the air

Throughout the summer of 1940, the fate of the entire British nation rested on the shoulders of a handful of young men. The outcome of the Battle of Britain not only depended on the bravery and skill of the pilots, but on the performance of the machines they flew. Look at the British and German planes below that fought to the death in the skies above England.

The planes of the RAF

THE HAWKER HURRICANE

Max Speed: 328mph
Weapons: Eight machine guns mounted in wings
Crew: Pilot only
Recognition: A short, sturdy plane with a wooden body (fuselage) that could turn sharply and take a lot of damage before the pilot had to 'bail out'. The **Hurricane** was the most common RAF **fighter** and shot down more German aircraft than the **Spitfire**.

THE SUPERMARINE SPITFIRE

Max Speed: 362mph
Weapons: Eight machine guns mounted in wings
Crew: Pilot only
Recognition: Sleek and beautiful, the Spitfire is one of the most famous planes in the world. It was fast, handled extremely well, and was more than a match for the German fighters.

The planes of the Luftwaffe

MESSERSCHMITT BF 109

Max Speed: 357mph
Weapons: Two machine guns mounted on the engine and two cannons in the wings
Crew: Pilot only
Recognition: This fast, shark-like plane had square-tipped wings and a bright yellow nose. It was the most deadly and feared of all the German aircraft.

MESSERSCHMITT BF 110

Max Speed: 349mph
Weapons: Four machine guns and two cannons in the nose, one rear-firing machine gun in cockpit
Crew: Pilot and gunner
Recognition: Heavily armed and able to fly long distances, this twin-engined plane was slow and clumsy to turn and was easy meat for the RAF fighters.

HEINKEL HE 111

Max Speed: 247mph
Weapons: Three machine guns in the nose, top and belly and 2000kg of bombs
Crew: Pilot, gunner and bomb-aimer
Recognition: The most common German **bomber**, the Heinkel was slow, lightly armed and had large sections of glass over the cockpit. This allowed the pilot to see clearly – but offered no protection from a hail of bullets. When they did get past the RAF, they inflicted heavy damage on British airfields, towns and cities.

Battle of Britain

By the end of August, the RAF was only days away from defeat. Its airfields were badly damaged and it didn't have enough pilots. However, the Germans were encountering big problems too. Brand-new radar technology meant that the British could detect enemy planes before they reached Britain. A system of 51 radar stations directed British fighters to the Germans in a matter of minutes, leaving them enough fuel to attack the German planes time and time again. In fact, it soon became clear that the Germans were losing more planes than the British. More importantly, the Germans were only making about 150 new planes a month while the British were producing over 550!

Victory or defeat?

At 2:00pm on 15 September, Prime Minister Winston Churchill asked his air force commander what British fighter planes were available other than the ones in the air. 'There are none,' came the reply. However, 15 September saw the final major engagement of the Battle of Britain. On that very day, Germany lost 60 aircraft to Britain's 25! Two days later Hitler postponed Operation Sealion 'until further notice'. He had failed to defeat the RAF by his 15 September deadline and was forced to cancel his invasion plans. Instead, he started to target London in huge night-time bombing raids in an attempt to force the British into surrender. This was known as 'the Blitz'.

The RAF pilots who fought in the Battle of Britain became known as the 'Few', after Winston Churchill honoured their victory with a speech in which he said, 'Never in the field of human conflict was so much owed by so many to so few.'

Wise Up Words

bomber fighter Hurricane Luftwaffe RAF Spitfire

Work

1 a Draw a simple bar chart displaying the top speeds of the planes involved in the Battle of Britain. For an example of a bar chart, see page 89.

b Which plane would you choose to fly into combat? Give reasons for your answer.

c Why do you think the Spitfire is better known than the Hurricane? Remember, the Hurricane shot down more German planes.

2 Look at this list of reasons why Germany lost the Battle of Britain. Explain, in your own words, how each reason made a difference to the outcome of the battle:

- The British had radar.
- Hitler lost patience and started bombing London.

Can you add any reasons of your own to explain why Germany lost the Battle of Britain?

3 a In your own words, explain what Churchill meant when he said, 'Never in the field of human conflict was so much owed by so many to so few.'

b Write a brief for a design company to produce a poster to thank the 'Few'. Briefly describe what the poster should look like and why. Your explanation to the designer should include who the 'Few' were, what they did, and why it is important that we thank them for it. Look at **Source A** on page 94 for inspiration.

Date	Official British figures	Official German figures	Figures agreed after the war
8–23 August	755	213	403
24 August–6 September	643	243	378
7–30 September	846	243	435
TOTAL	**2244**	**699**	**1216**

SOURCE A: *Fighters and bombers lost by the Luftwaffe in the Battle of Britain. Which set of figures do you think is most accurate and why?*

Hungry for More?

Other aircraft were used by both sides during the Battle of Britain. See if you can find out more and work out why they are not as well known as the ones on this page.

5.4A 'Mr and Mrs Jones would like a nice little boy'

During the First World War, some of Britain's cities had been bombed by the German air force and over 1000 people had been killed. During the years between the First and Second World Wars, great advances had been made in aircraft technology. As a result, many believed that Britain's towns were once more going to be targeted from the air – and this time on a much bigger scale. The government was determined to be ready and, in addition to digging lots of air raid shelters, they decided to move over one million people away from the danger areas. This was known as **evacuation** and it changed the lives of many people forever. So where were people evacuated from? Where were they moved to? And what did this mean for the people of Britain?

Mission Objectives

- Define the word 'evacuation' and explain why it took place.
- Assess the typical experiences of an evacuee and their hosts.
- Explore a number of sources relating to 'evacuation'.

City slickers and country bumpkins

For four days in September 1939 the government took over Britain's entire transport system. All of the buses and trains were used to move the more vulnerable people away from the places most likely to be bombed (large towns and cities full of factories) and into the countryside where they would be safer.

Armed with suitcases full of clothes, a gas mask packed into a cardboard box, and a name tag tied to their coats, thousands of children left the familiar surroundings of city life for a completely new experience in the countryside (see **Source B**). Some would love their new life… but many others would hate every second of it!

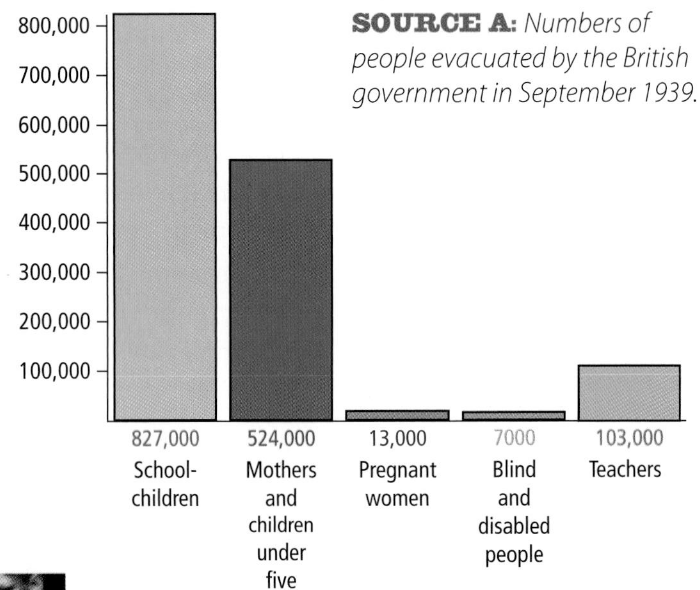

SOURCE A: *Numbers of people evacuated by the British government in September 1939.*

What Happened When? 1939

In 1939 in Bombay, India, Mohandas Gandhi (see page 135) began a fast in protest against British rule in India. Later that year he wrote to Adolf Hitler, addressing him as 'my friend', urging him not to go to war.

SOURCE B: *An evacuated child, photographed in September 1939.*

None of the children knew where they were going and nothing prepared them for the ordeal they would go through when they reached their countryside reception areas.

There were two main methods of finding a new home or 'foster family'.

METHOD NO. 1

GRAB A CHILD – the children were lined up and local people would choose the ones they wanted. Obviously, the smarter, cleaner girls would go first… and the dirtier, scruffy little boys would be left until last.

METHOD NO. 2

HUNT THE HOME – evacuated children, or evacuees as they were called, were led around the town or village and taken door-to-door. Homeowners were asked if they would foster a child for a while.

'Villagers stood around watching us as we got out of the bus and went into the school. What followed was like an auction. Villagers came in to choose children. "Mr and Mrs Jones would like a nice little boy." Nobody wanted the awkward combination of a girl of 11 and such a small boy, from whom I had promised my mother never to be separated. We were left until the very last. The room was almost empty. I sat on my rucksack and cried.'

▲ **SOURCE C:** *The thoughts of one young girl remembering what happened to her and her brother when they were evacuated. From* Peace & War *by Shepard, Reid and Shepherd (1993).*

'They unloaded us on the corner of the street; we thought it was all arranged, but it wasn't. The billeting officer [the man in charge of housing the children] walked along knocking on doors and asking if they'd take a family. We were the last to be picked. You couldn't blame them; they didn't have any coloured people there in those days.'

▲ **SOURCE D:** *An example of a family who had to hunt for a home. From an oral interview with evacuee Anita Bowers in 1983, printed in* Keep Smiling Through *by Caroline Lang (1989).*

Wise Up Words

evacuation

Work

1 Look at **Source A**.
  - a What is meant by the word 'evacuation'?
  - b Look at the different groups of people evacuated in September 1939. Do you think the government got it right? Which groups of people would you have moved first? Give reasons for each of your choices.

2 Look at **Source B**. By looking at the photograph, write down all you can find out about this boy and what is happening to him. Consider the following questions:
  - Why do you think he has a label tied to his coat?
  - What is his suitcase for? What do you think it contains?
  - Who do you think the woman is?
  - Why is there a line of children behind him? And why is the boy out of line?
  - How do you think the boy feels? Describe his emotions.

  Compare your answers to the rest of the class.

3 Read **Sources C** and **D**.
  - a Describe the two different methods used to find these two young families a new home.
  - b Write down the reasons why each person had problems finding a new home.
  - c Do either of the reasons surprise you? Give reasons for your answer.

FACT!

Britain wasn't the only country that evacuated people. The French moved thousands away from their border with Germany. And the Germans did the same.

Hungry for More?

Suppose you were evacuated now. You can take just ten of your things with you. Write a list of what you would take, giving reasons for each.

5.4B 'Mr and Mrs Jones would like a nice little boy'

A better life?

Evacuation wasn't easy for anyone – evacuees or hosts. Some children settled down happily and loved their new lives in their new homes and schools – others hated country life and were homesick. The country people had to put up with a lot, too. Some of the children arrived badly clothed, very thin and covered in lice and nits. Some of the 'rougher' evacuees shocked their foster families by swearing and being naughty. One young evacuee in Northallerton, Yorkshire, spent a whole day blocking up the local stream – later that night it was found that he'd flooded six houses and the local church! Study **Sources A** to **F**, which outline some of these experiences.

'Rosie whispered. She whispered for days. Everything was so clean. We were given face cloths and toothbrushes. We'd never cleaned our teeth up till then. And hot water came from the tap and there was an indoor toilet. And carpets. And clean sheets. This was all very odd and rather scary.'

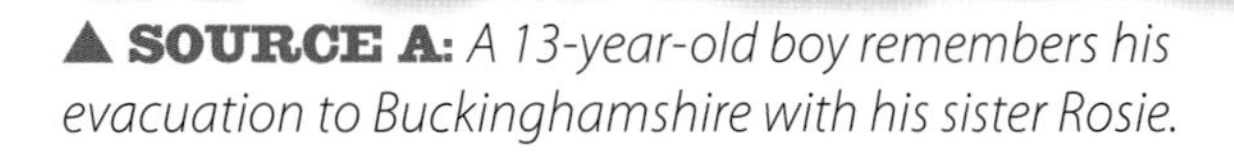

▲ **SOURCE A:** *A 13-year-old boy remembers his evacuation to Buckinghamshire with his sister Rosie.*

'My foster mum thought she was onto a good thing with me and the other 11-year-old girl I was put with. We did her shopping for her, cleaned her house, cooked, washed up and even looked after her whining three-year-old when she went out.'

▲ **SOURCE B:** *Unhappy times for an 11-year-old girl evacuated to Cambridgeshire.*

'One evacuated child from the South of England… on arrival at the billet [his new home], was asked by the hostess, "Would you like some biscuits, dear?" "Biscuits?" the boy replied. "I want some beer and some bloody chips. That's what I get at home!"'

▲ **SOURCE C:** *An extract from the* Newcastle Evening Chronicle *in 1940. Some boys found country life hard to get used to!*

'I love my six lads from London as if they were my own. They've made this dreary, lonely war quite enjoyable for me.'

▲ **SOURCE D:** *One rich woman from Devon, commenting on the evacuees in her house.*

SOURCE E: *Children had to carry gas masks everywhere in case poison gas was dropped.*

SOURCE F: *The countryside was a whole new world to many inner-city kids. Here they are nervously looking at a tame fox.*

FACT!

When some of the evacuated children finally returned home after the war, they found their homes had been bombed and their parents were missing. Some parents had even abandoned their children on purpose. About 40,000 children remained 'unclaimed' after the war!

FACT!

Many city children had never seen a farm animal before. They were shocked to see what cows, chickens and sheep looked like. In October 1939 BBC News broadcast this description of a farm animal written by a young evacuee. Can you guess what animal he's describing?

'It has six sides… at the back it has a tail on which hangs a brush. With this it sends flies away so they don't fall into the milk. The head is for growing horns and so that the mouth can be somewhere… the mouth is to moo with. Under the animal hangs the milk… when people milk, the milk comes and there is never an end to the supply. How the animal does it I have not realized… one can smell it far away. This is the reason for fresh air in the country…'

In case you weren't sure, the boy is describing a cow!

A safe return?

After a few months of life in the British countryside, many children returned to their lives in the city. The enemy bombers hadn't arrived as expected, and by March 1940 nearly one million children had gone home. However, later that year the mass bombing of British cities – 'the Blitz' as it was known – began and many children, but not all, returned to the country.

SOURCE G: *A British government poster issued in 1940.*

Work

1 Look at **Source A**. It tells you a lot about the kind of life Rosie led before she was evacuated.
   a Write down at least five things it tells you.
   b How had her life changed?

2 a Who do you think enjoyed evacuation more – the evacuated children or their new families? Try to give reasons for your answer.
   b Did everyone enjoy evacuation? What evidence is there on these pages that some children and their hosts did not like evacuation at all?

3 Look at **Source G**.
   a Who is standing next to the tree?
   b What is he doing – and why?
   c Why was this poster produced?
   d What is the message of the poster?

4 Imagine you are a child in one of the sources you have been reading. Write a short letter home about your new life. Use your imagination to build up a picture of your new surroundings for your family back home. Compare your letter with other people's letters in your class. Can they guess which source you based your letter on?

5.5 Total war

The Second World War did not just involve soldiers, sailors and airmen. The armed forces may have been the ones who went off to fight the enemy on foreign soil, but the people left at home had their part to play, too, and were greatly affected by the conflict. So what impact did the war have on people back in Britain?

Mission Objectives

- Recall key terms and concepts such as rationing, Home Guard and total war.
- Identify ways in which the Second World War affected ordinary citizens.

The Germans tried to cut off supplies of food and other goods by sinking the ships that brought the supplies to Britain. So, in 1940, the government introduced rationing. This meant that every person was entitled to a fixed weekly amount of fuel, clothing and certain types of food. The government also encouraged people to grow their own food in their back gardens or allotments. The slogan for the campaign was 'Dig for Victory'.

When the war began, everyone expected to be bombed from the air – so civilians prepared for it. Millions of people built their own bomb shelters in their back gardens.

In May 1940 the government urged all men aged between 17 and 65 who weren't in the army to join what became known as the 'Home Guard'. These men worked part-time in their local area to prepare it for attack. Many of the men in the Home Guard were not permitted to join the regular army because their jobs were necessary to the war effort – farm workers, teachers, grocers, bank workers, and railwaymen, for example. Others were too old to join up or had health problems. They weren't paid and to begin with they didn't have any weapons… so some made their own!

In late 1940 German bombers began to bomb Britain's major cities. This was known as 'the Blitz'. Swansea, Cardiff, Bristol, Southampton, Plymouth, Birmingham, Coventry, Liverpool, Glasgow, Manchester, Sunderland, Aberdeen, Sheffield, and many other cities were targeted. London suffered the heaviest bombing – for one 11-week period, London was bombed every night except one! By the end of May 1941, over 30,000 civilians had been killed in the bombing raids and 87,000 were seriously injured. In London alone, over one million homes were destroyed or damaged.

Air Raid Precaution (ARP) wardens had the job of patrolling the streets at night to make sure that no light was visible and helping out if there was an air raid. There were 1.4 million ARP wardens altogether, many of them part-time volunteers who also worked full-time during the day.

People put up thick curtains that they could shut at night to prevent any glimmer of light from escaping and helping enemy bombers to locate their target. Street lights were switched off or dimmed, too, and cars were fitted with masked headlights. Windows were taped to stop glass from shattering all over the place if a bomb exploded nearby.

FACT!

When a country uses all its resources to try and win, and the war involves all its people in some way, the conflict is often called a 'total war'. This term is often used to describe the Second World War.

Britain was organized like never before during the Second World War. The government had the power to move people to any job they felt necessary to help win the war. Millions of women worked in weapons factories, on farms, and in army, navy and air force bases. Single women were forced to work but married women weren't. However, many decided to work anyway, as well as looking after their families.

When war broke out, the government was worried that large British cities would be targets for aircraft bombing and raids. So schoolchildren (and their teachers) were evacuated from the cities that were considered to be in danger. Pregnant women, blind and disabled people, and women with children under five were also sent by road and train to safer countryside areas.

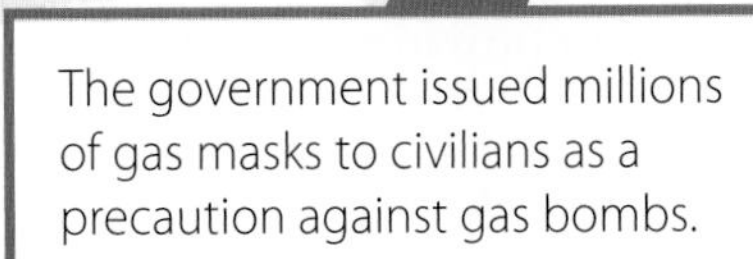

The government issued millions of gas masks to civilians as a precaution against gas bombs.

Work

1 In your own words, define 'total war'.

2 Imagine you've been asked to either a) give a short talk or b) design a poster aimed at primary school students that explains what life was like in Britain during the Second World War. You may wish to include details about:

- the Blitz
- air raid precautions
- evacuation
- changing roles of women
- the Home Guard
- rationing
- the Dig for Victory campaign
- your own family's contribution to the war.

NOTE: You might want to emphasize what you think have been the biggest changes.

5.6A Sir Arthur Harris: war hero or war criminal?

At about 9:00pm on 13 February 1945, 805 British bomber planes dropped 2690 tons of bombs on the German city of Dresden. Before long, an area of 28 square kilometres was burning so ferociously that temperatures reached 1000 degrees Celsius – that's ten times hotter than a boiling kettle! The city blazed for seven days, during which time an estimated 150,000 people were burned to death.

Mission Objectives

- Explain the difference between precision and area bombing.
- Formulate an opinion on why you think Dresden was bombed.

'Bomber' Harris

In 1992 a bronze statue of a man in RAF uniform was unveiled in London. The statue was of Sir Arthur 'Bomber' Harris, the Head of Bomber Command and the man whose idea it was to bomb Dresden (see **Source D**). Immediately, protesters threw paint at the statue and demanded its removal.

So do you agree with the protesters – should the statue be removed? Was it wrong to bomb Dresden? Or, as Sir Arthur Harris thought, was the attack necessary to shorten the war and save British lives?

Your task over the next four pages is to formulate an opinion. You must establish:

- why the attack happened in the first place
- why the raid caused so many deaths
- what the bombing of Dresden achieved.

You will then use your ideas and opinions to complete an extended piece of work.

Why bomb Dresden?

Bomber planes changed the face of war between 1939 and 1945. American and British planes dropped nearly three million tons of bombs on 131 German cities. This killed nearly one million men, women and children, and made eight million people homeless. German planes dropped bombs on British cities, too – 40,000 people died in air raids on London, Coventry, Glasgow, Hull, and other cities.

When the war began, both sides had tried to use **precision bombing** to hit key targets, such as factories, ports, bridges, major roads, and railway stations. The idea was to destroy the enemy's ability to fight by making it impossible to manufacture weapons, build ships, or move soldiers around. However, precision bombing didn't work – bombs didn't always hit their targets and damage was often easily repaired – so **area bombing** was introduced instead. This devastating new type of attack meant that whole towns and cities were bombed in order to make sure that *everything* was destroyed… including the enemy's will to fight!

'Investigations seem to show that having your house destroyed is most damaging to morale… there seems little doubt that this will break the spirit of the [German] people.'

▲ **SOURCE A:** *Advice given to the British government in 1942 by a senior scientific advisor.*

'Destroy a factory and they rebuild it. If I kill all their workers it takes 21 years to provide new ones.'

▲ **SOURCE B:** *Sir Arthur Harris, Head of RAF Bomber Command, 1942.*

In October 1944, a detailed report by the British on Dresden concluded that the city was an 'unattractive target'. In other words, there was no point in bombing the place. However, in January 1945 British spies reported that thousands of German soldiers were collecting in Dresden before being sent off to fight. All of a sudden, Dresden had turned into a key bombing target – and this very likely influenced the decision to attack.

Wise Up Words

area bombing firestorm incendiary precision bombing

> 'Dresden had become the main centre of [the] defence of Germany. It had never been bombed before. And, as a large centre of war industry, it was very important.'

▲ **SOURCE C:** *Sir Arthur Harris, speaking about the bombing of Dresden*

SOURCE D: *The statue of Sir Arthur Harris that was put up in London in 1992. Interestingly, he was the only war commander to not have a statue made immediately after the war!*

SOURCE E: *A British poster showing Lancaster bombers attacking a target in Germany. What was the purpose of this poster?*

THE ATTACK
BEGINS IN THE FACTORY

Work

1 What is the difference between precision and area bombing?

2 What evidence is there so far that Dresden was targeted for *military* reasons?

3 What evidence is there so far that Dresden was *not* targeted for military reasons?

5.6B Sir Arthur Harris: war hero or war criminal?

Why did so many die?

The planes dropped a mixture of **incendiary** and high explosive bombs. Incendiary bombs are specifically designed to start fires. Dresden, being a very old city with many wooden-framed buildings, started to burn very quickly. The fact that the city was packed with people running away from the Soviet army meant that any large fire was sure to kill thousands of people.

The bombs soon created a **firestorm**. In a firestorm, the hot air that rises from burning buildings is replaced by cooler air rushing in from outside. Soon, hurricane-force winds of up to 120mph were 'superheating' the fire.

'I saw people clinging to the railings, burnt to cinders. I kicked what I thought was a big tree stump – but it was a person, burnt to death. There was a big heap of arms, legs, bodies, everything – I tried to piece together a leg, arm, fingers, body – to recognize one of my family – but I passed out.'

▲ **SOURCE A:** *One survivor remembers the firestorm. She was interviewed in 1985.*

'Many German towns were severely devastated by bombing, but the effect on the amount of weapons, tanks and fighter planes the Germans produced was small... the bombings didn't make the German people lose the will to fight either. The German people proved calmer and more determined than anticipated.'

▲ **SOURCE B:** *Adapted from the report of the British Bombing Survey Unit, set up at the end of the war to study the effects of area bombing on Germany.*

'Every day that the war went on cost the lives of countless more... so the numbers killed at Dresden, dreadful as they were, were nothing like so dreadful as the numbers of people Hitler was killing... A decisive blow was needed to end the war quickly.'

▲ **SOURCE C:** *From an article written by a historian, Dr Noble Frankland, in 1985.*

'Attacks on cities... tend to shorten the war and so preserve the lives of allied soldiers... I do not personally regard the whole of the remaining cities of Germany as worth the bones of one British soldier.'

▲ **SOURCE D:** *From a letter written by Sir Arthur Harris in response to a letter written by Winston Churchill. Churchill had begun to doubt whether the raid on Dresden was justified.*

What did the attack achieve?

Historians have argued for years about the bombing of Dresden – did the attack help Britain win the war? Some are sure it helped while others questioned whether it was necessary at all. Perhaps the following sources will help you form your opinion.

SOURCE E: *Victims of the bombing of Dresden, February 1945. The bodies have been piled up to be burned.*

SOURCE F: *A photograph of Dresden after the bombing. The main railway station and the headquarters of the air force escaped total destruction.*

What other research might a researcher need to collect before forming a fuller opinion of Harris?

	1940	1942	1944
Fighter/bomber planes	10,200	14,200	39,500
Tanks	1600	6300	19,000
Heavy guns/cannons	4400	5100	19,000

SOURCE H: *German war production, 1940–1944.*

'It struck me at the time, the thought of women and children down there. We seemed to fly for hours over a sheet of fire – a terrific red glow. You can't justify it.'

▲ **SOURCE G:** *The view of an RAF pilot who took part in the attack.*

Work

 You might wish to work in pairs, threes or fours for this task.

A television company has decided to stage a debate on whether the statue of Sir Arthur Harris should be removed or not. Use the information from pages 106 to 109 (and anything else you can find) to produce an opening speech for the televized debate. Your speech must be either in support of or against the actions Harris decided on. Whether your team is for or against, you should try to consider:

- whether Dresden was an acceptable target or not; does the use of incendiary rather than explosive bombs tell us anything about the attack?
- whether Harris was acting in Britain's best interests by trying to win the war – or was he a war criminal guilty of killing innocent people?
- what you think people felt about the bombing of German cities at the time; was Harris doing something that most British people supported?
- whether, in a war, everyone who helps build weapons – including workers and their families – is a fair target; can Harris be criticized for killing Germans – after all, weren't they all part of Hitler's evil empire?
- whether the bombings actually achieved anything; did they help Britain win the war?

Hungry for More?

Look at all the sources written by Sir Arthur Harris (**Sources B** and **C** on pages 104 and 105 and **Source D** on page 106). What is your opinion of Harris based on these sources? Try to use quotations from the sources to back up your statements about him.

5.7A Why is Winston Churchill on a £5 note?

In 2013 Britain's Prime Minister during the Second World War was chosen to feature on a new-look £5 note for 2016. The Bank of England, which decides on the historical figures who appear on the notes, said that Sir Winston Churchill was 'a truly great British leader' and a 'hero' whose 'energy, courage, eloquence, wit and public service' should be an 'inspiration to us all'. But do you agree? Was he a great British leader? Do you think he should appear on a £5 note?

Mission Objectives

- Outline why Winston Churchill appears on a £5 note.
- Determine whether you think he was a 'truly great leader' or not.

What makes a good leader?

Before looking through these sources relating to Churchill, take a moment or two to think about the sort of qualities that make a good leader.

- List some words that would describe a good leader. Can you give examples of good leaders you know of?
- What are the most important qualities of good leaders? List your top three.
- Do you think leaders during wartime need any different qualities to the ones who lead when there's peace?

Who was Winston Churchill?

In the years before the Second World War broke out, the British government followed a policy called 'appeasement'. This meant that Britain (and France) allowed Hitler to get away with things (like building up his army or taking over other countries) in order to keep on friendly terms with him. It was hoped that Hitler would soon have all the land he wanted and eventually stop! Winston Churchill, who wasn't part of the government at this time, felt appeasement was wrong. He said that Britain must stand up to Hitler! So, when the idea of appeasement failed, and war finally broke out, it was clear that Britain needed a new leader. In May 1940, Winston Churchill became Britain's Prime Minister.

Winston Churchill

Born: Blenheim Palace, Oxfordshire, England
30 November 1874

Education: Harrow School and Royal Military Academy Sandhurst

Early career: Joined the army, fought in battles in India and Africa during 1897–1898.
Worked as a war reporter during Boer War

Politics: 1900 – Elected as an MP
1910 – Became Home Secretary (in charge of law and order and policing)
1911 – Put in charge of Royal Navy
1915 – During First World War he planned an attack on Turkey that went badly wrong; many soldiers died and Churchill resigned
1924–1929 – Back in politics, became Chancellor of the Exchequer (in charge of the country's money and taxes), but was not a success
1929–1940 – Remained an MP and said Britain should watch Hitler carefully, stand up to him, and get ready for a war; people took little notice of his warnings
1940 – Became Prime Minister

SOURCE A: *Winston Churchill will appear on the first plastic British banknote in 2016.*

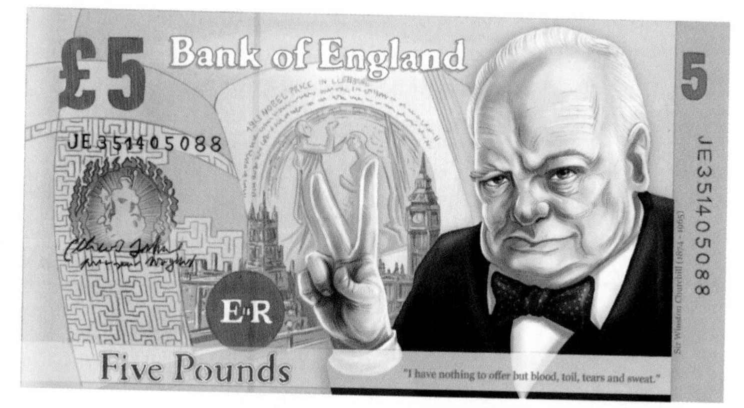

Winston during wartime

The British government wanted the new Prime Minister to be seen in a particular way during wartime. Look through **Sources B** to **F** carefully.

SOURCE B: *A poster produced during the Second World War that shows Churchill as a British bulldog.*

'Never give in – never, never, never, never, in nothing great or small, large or petty... Never yield to force; never yield to the apparently overwhelming might of the enemy.'

'I have nothing to offer but blood, toil, tears and sweat. We have before us an ordeal of the most grievous kind. We have before us many, many long months of struggle and of suffering. You ask, what is our aim? I can answer in one word: victory. Victory at all costs – victory in spite of all terror – for without victory there is no survival.'

'We shall go on to the end... We shall defend our island whatever the cost may be. We shall fight on the beaches, we shall fight on the landing grounds, we shall fight in the fields and in the streets, we shall fight in the hills; we shall never surrender.'

▲ **SOURCE C:** *Extracts from some of Winston Churchill's most famous wartime speeches.*

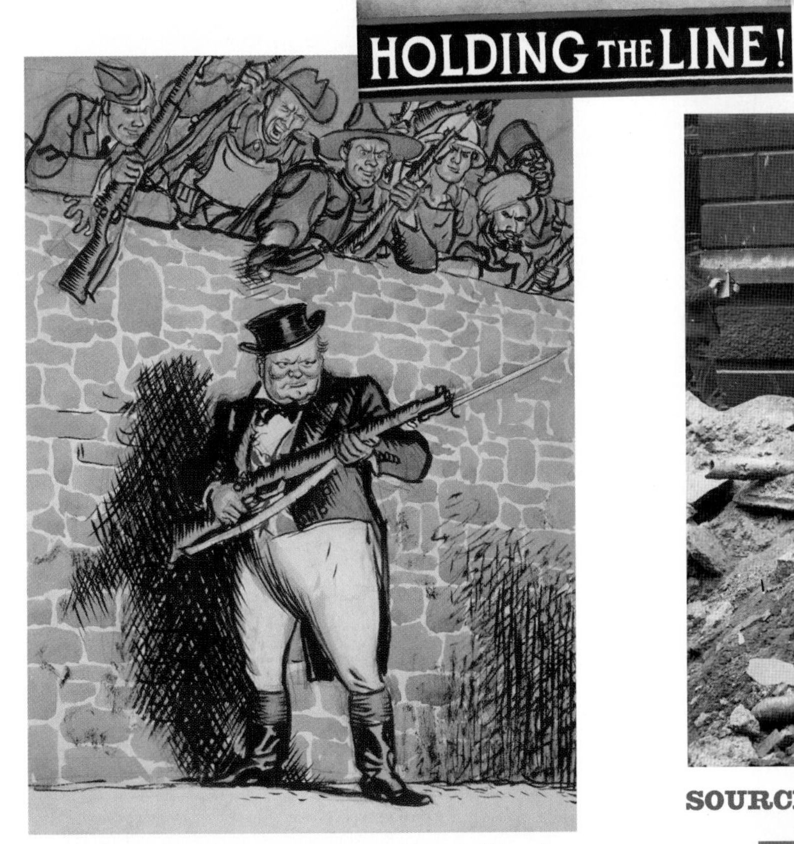

SOURCE D: *This poster shows Churchill leading troops from many allied countries into battle.*

SOURCE E: *Winston Churchill inspecting a bomb crater.*

'The ideas, the persistence in flogging proposals, the goading of commanders to attack – these were all expressions of that blazing, explosive energy which helped steadily steer civilians and soldiers through so many setbacks and difficulties.'

▲ **SOURCE F:** *Adapted from an account by an assistant to Churchill.*

Work

1. Look at **Source B**. Why do you think Churchill is drawn in this way?
2. Look at **Sources C** and **D**. If you were an ordinary citizen who lived during the war, how would speeches and cartoons like these make you feel?
3. Look at **Source E**. Why do you think Churchill was keen to be photographed visiting lots of bomb sites?

5.7B Why is Winston Churchill on a £5 note?

Churchill: after the war

However, Churchill wasn't always viewed in such a positive way as in the sources you've studied on pages 108 and 109. Some cartoons at the time were critical of him (see **Source A**), and in the years after the war, some people questioned Churchill's leadership. Study all the sources carefully.

What Happened When?

1945

In the spring of 1945 Princess Elizabeth (who was to become Queen Elizabeth II) joined the Auxiliary Territorial Service – the women's branch of the British Army during the war – as a driver and mechanic.

SOURCE A: *A cartoon of Churchill published after the war. The caption says, 'Man goeth forth unto his work and to his labour until the evening.' Churchill hated the picture and was upset by it. He even said, 'There's malice in it. Look at my hands, I have beautiful hands… I shall have to retire if this sort of thing goes on.'*

FACT!

Churchill was defeated in the 1945 General Election, held shortly after the end of the war. He was seen as a great war leader, but the public didn't think he could run the country in times of peace. He won the 1951 election, though, and became Prime Minister again for another four years.

Be a Top Historian

GCSE

Individuals (like Winston Churchill) are viewed by many people as **significant**. But it's very important to understand why a person might be viewed as significant. People use different categories to decide how significant a person is. Most often, though, for a person to be significant they must have done important things that had far-reaching consequences **at the time** AND they must still be viewed as important **today**. So do you think Winston Churchill 'qualifies' as a significant person?

'Churchill's ideas about the army annoyed some of the chiefs and generals. They said that if his ideas were adopted then the war might go badly. They may have been right, but I wonder if Churchill just said these things to get them thinking harder.'

▲ **SOURCE B:** *Adapted from the autobiography of an MP who knew Churchill, written in 1960.*

'There was criticism of Churchill. Some said he was the cause of much of our setbacks because he took too much on all by himself.'

▲ **SOURCE C:** *From* Of This Our Time *by Tom Hopkinson (1982).*

'The spring of 1940 saw Churchill back the disastrous invasion of Norway, hoping to stop the Nazis invading. The operation was a failure.'

▲ **SOURCE D:** *Adapted from a BBC online article from 2009.*

- 'The PM is not a good listener and rarely listens to expert opinion.
- He gets through a lot of work, more than we do. He speaks simply and effectively.
- No one disagrees with Winston, he is surrounded by people saying "yes" to him all the time. His colleagues fear him – the people have set him up as a God, and he is terrifically powerful.
- He loves war and spends hours with charts and maps. There isn't a proper policy for growing food.'

▲ **SOURCE E:** *Adapted from the diary of Robert Menzies, the Australian Prime Minister, who visited Britain in 1941.*

'When you are up against the threat of defeat, as we were, and when we were standing alone, then you have to have somebody like Churchill who isn't rational, who isn't weighing up chances soberly, but who is describing his fantasy life in his speeches and who rallies everyone round, so that people become heroes and work thrice as hard.'

▲ **SOURCE F:** *Written by Dr Anthony Storr, a psychiatrist. It is said that Storr is referring to Churchill's heavy drinking in this extract.*

FACT!

Churchill came from a rich, important family. He was born in a palace near Oxford. He was sent away to school aged seven, but hated it. He was beaten by his teacher and never got enough to eat. And he didn't do particularly well in some exams – during one he wrote his name and nothing else!

Hungry for More?

Find out about the person who Winston Churchill will replace on the £5 note. Then, find out what other changes are planned for England's banknotes and £2 coins.

FACT!

Churchill died on Sunday 24 January 1965 at the age of 90. 350 million people watched his funeral on television and 112 nations sent representatives to attend the service in St Paul's Cathedral, London.

Work

1. Look at **Source A**. What is the cartoonist trying to say about Churchill?
2. a. Make a list of Churchill's strengths and weaknesses as a war leader. You should look back at the sources on pages 108 to 111 to help you. For each strength or weakness, write a short sentence about the source that you got your information from.
   b. Think carefully. Can a strength also be a weakness? You might want to discuss your ideas with a partner.
3. As you know, Churchill is to appear on a £5 note and has been described as a 'great British leader'. So, do you think he was a great leader? Does he deserve his place on a new note? Explain your views.

5.8A What was a death camp like?

Between 1942 and 1945, millions of people were sent by force to one of six specially built camps in Eastern Europe. The camps were surrounded by electrified razor wire fences and tall watchtowers packed with machine gun-carrying guards. Once inside the 'prisoners' were either shot or gassed to death. Not surprisingly, the camps soon picked up a terrifying nickname – 'death camps'. But who committed these appalling crimes? And why? What sort of people were sent to these death camps? And what exactly happened once inside them?

Mission Objectives

- *Investigate how and why the Nazis organized the mass murder of millions of Jews.*

Why were they built?

The six death camps were built by the Nazis during the Second World War when they controlled most of Europe. Hitler saw this as an opportunity to get rid of all the people he hated – tramps, those with learning difficulties, the chronically sick, disabled people, Gypsies, homosexuals, political opponents… and especially Jews. In total, approximately six million Jews were killed, three million of whom were killed in Hitler's death camps.

The persecution begins

Jews had been treated badly in Germany for many years. As soon as Hitler became leader of Germany in 1933 he introduced laws and rules that made their lives more and more difficult. Jews were sacked from their jobs and banned from voting, for example. Soldiers stood outside Jewish businesses and turned shoppers away and Jews were openly attacked in the street (see **Source A**). Lots of Jews left Germany to live in nearby countries, but found themselves back under Nazi rule when Germany invaded during the Second World War. And as the war went on, more Jews became trapped under Hitler's rule all over Europe – three million Jews in Poland, 2.7 million in western Russia and over one million in France, the Netherlands, Belgium, Denmark, Norway, and the Balkans.

FACT!

Anti-Semitism, as hatred of Jewish people is known, has been common in Europe for many centuries. Among other things, Jews have been blamed for the death of Jesus Christ and the outbreak of Black Death in the fourteenth century. At one time or another, they were driven out of almost every country in Europe and there are few European nations without some record of anti-Semitic violence in their history.

SOURCE A: *A Nazi storm trooper standing outside a shop owned by a Jew, preventing shoppers from going inside. The sign reads: 'Germans, defend yourselves. Do not buy from the Jews.'*

Ghettos and the execution squads

Hitler's method of dealing with the Jews under his control was brutal. In some countries they were bricked into separate areas outside the cities (called **ghettos**) or sent to work in labour camps. Execution squads (called '*Einsatzgruppen*') even went out into the countryside in mobile vans and shot, or gassed, as many Jews as they could find. But to many fanatical Nazis, the destruction of Europe's Jews was not happening quickly enough – and by the end of 1941 leading Nazis had begun working on plans for what they called 'a final solution to the Jewish question'.

The 'final solution'

On 20 January 1942, Nazi leaders met to finalize their plans for the mass murder of every Jew in Europe, either by working them to death or killing them in poison gas chambers. This amounted to an estimated eleven million people – and six death or extermination camps were to be specially built for this purpose.

Wise Up Words

anti-Semitism genocide ghetto Holocaust

SOURCE B: *A photograph of local workers under Nazi order in Warsaw, Poland, building a brick wall round the Warsaw Ghetto in 1940. At this time, the population of the ghetto was estimated at 440,000 people – nearly 40 per cent of the whole Warsaw population. However, the ghetto itself was only about 5 per cent of the size of Warsaw!*

SOURCE C: *The main entrance to Auschwitz, one of the largest and probably the most infamous of the death camps. The photograph shows the railway lines upon which the cattle trucks would arrive with their 'cargo' of Jews.*

FACT!

The Nazis' attempt to wipe out the Jewish race is often known as the **Holocaust**. However, many Jews object to this term as it means 'sacrifice'. Some prefer to use the word 'churban', which means 'destruction'.

Work

1. a What was the 'final solution'?
   b In what way was the 'final solution' different from the way the Nazis treated Jews in the first few years of the war?
2. Write a sentence or two about the following terms:
   - ghetto
   - *Einsatzgruppen*
3. a Explain what the word 'holocaust' means.
   b Why do you think some people don't approve of the word 'holocaust' when describing what happened to Jews during the war?

5.8B What was a death camp like?

Inside a death camp

The death camps – Auschwitz, Belzec, Chelmno, Majdanek, Sobibor, and Treblinka – were filled with Jews from the countries that the Nazis had taken over… and the killing was on a vast scale (see **Source A**).

When they arrived at a death camp, the prisoners were immediately sorted into two groups: those who looked over 15 years old and were strong and healthy were sent to the left; the old, the sick, pregnant women, and women with young children were sent to the right. Those on the left (usually about 10 per cent) were put to work helping to murder the ones on the right. Any refusals would result in an immediate death sentence.

Those selected to die weren't informed of their fate. To prevent panic, they were told they were going to have a shower and were given soap and towels as they were marched into big chambers disguised as shower rooms. With as many as 2000 prisoners packed inside at any one time, the doors were sealed and poisonous gas was poured through the vents. In about 30 minutes, everyone was dead. The bodies were later burned.

FACT!

There were occasional rebellions in death camps. The most famous of all was in Treblinka in 1943. After setting the camp on fire, 150 prisoners managed to escape and 15 guards were killed. However, the Nazis soon regained control and all of the escapees were killed. 550 other prison workers were also killed in revenge.

	Number of Jews killed	%
Poland	3,000,000	90
Germany	210,000	90
Czech	155,000	86
Holland	105,000	75
Hungary	450,000	70
Ukraine	900,000	60
Romania	300,000	50
Russia	107,000	11

Key
- Extermination camps
- Concentration camps
- Transport routes (rail)

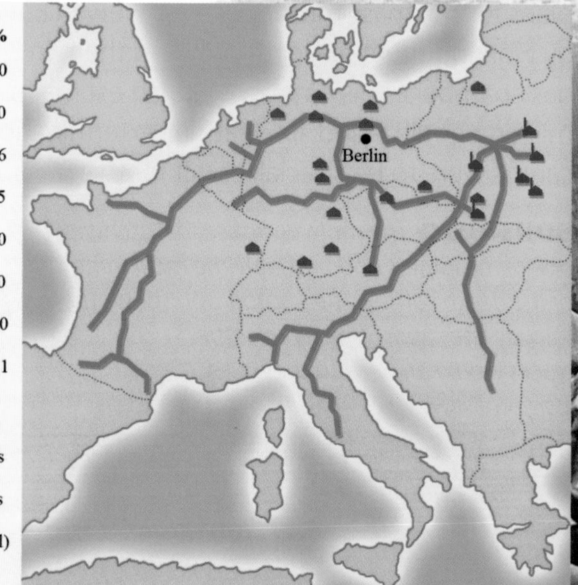

SOURCE A: *A map of Europe showing the main concentration and extermination camps. Concentration camps tended to be more like prisons where inmates were put to work in terrible conditions. They were often worked to death. The extermination camps' only purpose was to kill.*

'At last, after 32 minutes, they are all dead... The dead stand like pillars pressed together in the chambers. There is no room to fall or even to lean over. Even in death one can tell which are the families. They are holding hands in death and it is difficult to tear them apart in order to empty the chambers for the next batch.'

▲ **SOURCE B:** *An eyewitness account of a gassing by a Nazi death camp guard, August 1942 (by SS Officer Kurt Gerstein, Belzec, from* Investigating History *by Neil DeMarco (2003)).*

'The children were taken to an enormous ditch; they were shot and thrown into the fire… If mothers managed to keep their babies with them, a guard took the baby by its legs and smashed it against a wall until only a bloody mess remained in his hands. The mother then had to take this "mess" with her to the "bath" [gas chamber].'

▲ **SOURCE C:** *Another eyewitness account.*

'Among ourselves we can talk openly about it, though we will never speak a word in public... I am speaking about... the extermination of the Jewish people… That is a page of glory in our history that... will never be written.'

▲ **SOURCE D:** *Heinrich Himmler, the man in overall charge of the 'final solution', speaking at a meeting in 1943.*

Who knew?

Around three million people, mainly Jews, were killed in death camps like Auschwitz as part of the 'final solution'. Thousands of people, not only loyal Nazis, helped with this – ordinary people like railway workers, office clerks and policemen. 150 German companies used Auschwitz prisoners as slaves – other firms even competed for the contract to design and build the gas chambers and the ovens in which people were murdered and burned. As reports and photographs of this mass murder started to make their way around the world in newspapers and on news programmes, a new word – **genocide** – entered the vocabulary of a shocked world. It was hoped that genocide – the deliberate extermination of a race of people – would never happen again!

What Happened When? 1943

In 1943 three pigeons named White Vision, Winkie and Tyke became the first recipients of the Dickin Medal, which honours the work of animals in war. They all carried important messages to conflict locations during the Second World War.

Work

1. a What is the difference between a concentration camp and an extermination camp?
   b In your own words, explain what happened to Jewish prisoners as soon as they arrived at Auschwitz.
2. a Why did the Nazis tell the Jews they were going for a shower?
   b In your own words, describe what really happened in the 'shower rooms'.
3. Look at **Source D**.
   a Who was Heinrich Himmler?
   b Why do you think Himmler wanted people to be secretive about the 'final solution'?
   c Do you think Himmler was proud of his work on the 'final solution'? Give a reason for your answer.
4. Today, Auschwitz extermination camp is a museum. Many people were against turning it into a museum and wanted it to be pulled down.
   a Why do you think some people wanted Auschwitz destroyed?
   b Do you think we should forget a place like Auschwitz or not? Give reasons for your opinions.
5. a What does the word 'genocide' mean?
   b Find out if genocide has ever happened again.

SOURCE E: *Piles of dead bodies waiting to be buried at a Nazi death camp. It has been estimated that, on average, 4000 people were murdered every day for four years in these camps.*

5.9 The war goes nuclear

At 7:55am on Sunday 7 December 1941 two waves of around 180 Japanese bomber planes each launched a surprise attack on Pearl Harbor, a huge American navy base in Hawaii. In less than two hours, 21 US warships were sunk or damaged and over 2000 Americans were killed. The next day, the USA (and its ally, Britain) declared war on Japan. Three days later, Germany and Italy showed their support for Japan by declaring war on the USA. The Second World War had gone truly global with the major powers of the USA and Japan entering the conflict. The fighting in the Pacific was brutal and was only brought to an end when the most terrible weapon in the history of the world was used. But why did Japan attack an American base? In what ways was the fighting different from that in Europe? And how did the dropping of nuclear bombs finally end the war?

Mission Objectives

- Explain how and why the USA joined the Second World War.
- Assess the immediate impact of the nuclear attack in 1945.

Japan's eastern empire

The USA and Japan had been rivals for many years. Both countries wanted influence and control over the rich lands of the Far East, which contain coal, oil, rubber, and copper. Japan itself has very few of these natural resources so had been invading other countries throughout the 1930s to get them. By attacking Pearl Harbor, the Japanese were hoping to destroy the massive American Pacific fleet – the only thing that could stop them taking all the land they wanted. The plan seemed to work – for a while at least. Japanese forces swept through the Far East, conquering Hong Kong, Malaya, Singapore, the Dutch East Indies, and parts of New Guinea by May 1942.

The Empire falls back

But the Japanese advances did not last long. By the end of 1942, the USA – with the help of thousands of British Empire troops – was winning battles and taking back land in the Far East. By 1944, American troops were getting nearer and nearer to Japan, capturing one small island after another. The Japanese fought fanatically, believing it was a great honour to die for their country and a disgrace on their families if they were taken prisoner. Thousands of suicide bombers called kamikaze flew planes packed with explosives into American ships. Despite the desperate defence, by July 1945 the Japanese were fighting a losing battle. The war in Europe was over and the USA, Britain and Russia could now concentrate all their efforts on defeating Japan.

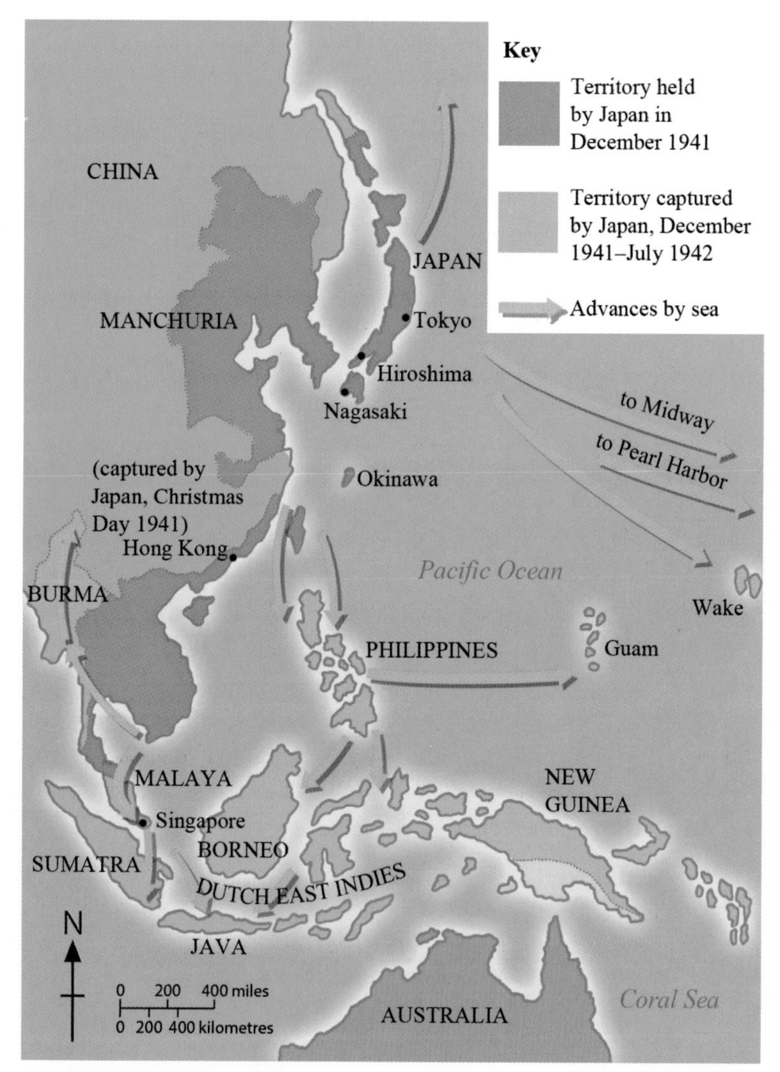

SOURCE A: *The Japanese advance seemed unstoppable. Their committed army, navy and air force quickly defeated British forces – taking 80,000 British soldiers prisoner in Singapore.*

Final victory

The American President, Harry S. Truman, had to decide how to end the war. The choice he made changed the world for ever. On 6 August 1945 a B-29 bomber dropped a single bomb on the Japanese city of Hiroshima. The bomb exploded 570 metres above the ground in an enormous blast many times brighter than the sun. Those closest to the explosion were evaporated in the 300,000 degree Celsius heat, leaving nothing but burnt shadows on the ground. Anyone within half a mile of the bomb when it went off was turned into smoking black ash within seconds. The Americans estimated that 79,000 people were killed. The Japanese claimed 240,000 lost their lives. On 9 August a second bomb was dropped on the port of Nagasaki. The Americans claimed 20,000 died in this blast – the Japanese claimed it was 50,000. Japan surrendered and the Second World War was over.

'Their faces were burned, their eye sockets hollow, the fluid from their melted eyes had run down their cheeks. Their mouths were mere swollen, pus-covered wounds, which they couldn't open wide enough to take a drink from a teapot.'

▲ **SOURCE B:** *A description of some men found hiding in bushes after the bombings (from J Hershey's account of the effects of the bomb, 1946, in* Peace & War *by Shepard, Reid and Shepherd (1993)).*

'In Hiroshima, 30 days later, people who were not injured in the bombing are still dying mysteriously and horribly from an unknown something which I can only describe as the atomic plague.'

▲ **SOURCE C:** *The account of one of the first British journalists to visit Hiroshima. He is describing the effects of radiation sickness, which caused death and illness decades after the bomb was dropped.*

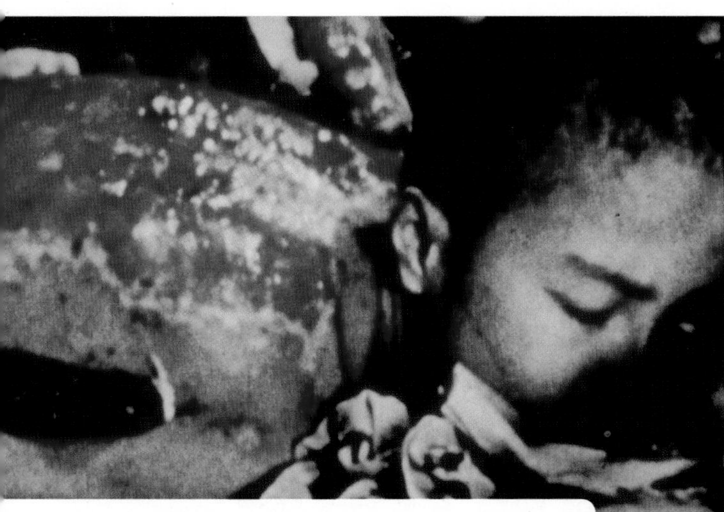

SOURCE D: *One of the thousands of civilians who suffered terrible burns from the bomb blast.*

SOURCE E: *An aerial photograph of the bomb that destroyed Hiroshima.*

Work

1. In no more than 50 words, explain why Japan launched a massive attack on Pearl Harbor.
2. **a** Define the word 'kamikaze'.
   b Why do you think so many people were willing to become kamikaze pilots?
3. Why do you think Japan finally surrendered?
4. Look at **Sources B** and **C**.
   a What is the difference between a short-term and a long-term effect?
   b Which of the sources shows short-term effects and which shows long-term effects? Explain your choices.

Hungry for More?

Research the effects of the bombs dropped on Hiroshima and Nagasaki. Think about the short-term, immediate effects as well as the long-term, lasting ones.

5.10 A United Nations

Towards the end of the Second World War, Britain, the USSR and the USA realized that they had to do something to prevent such a war happening again. They believed that if there was more cooperation between countries, they could work together to stop someone like Hitler before they got too powerful and started a war. They formed the United Nations (UN), which is still an important organization today. So just how do countries get together and cooperate? How do they decide what action to take? And what decisions have they made to improve the lives of people around the world?

Mission Objectives

- Explain what the United Nations is, what it does, and how it's organized.
- Outline some of the successes of the UN.

The UN Charter

When the UN was set up, a number of aims and rules were agreed. The 'Charter of the United Nations' says:

- the UN can't interfere in the way countries run themselves (elections, policing etc.)
- the UN should encourage cooperation at all times and promote **human rights** (see **Source A**)
- the UN should promote peace and can send 'peace keeping forces' to settle disputes in war-torn countries.

UN DECLARATION OF HUMAN RIGHTS

- *All human beings are born free and equal.*
- *Everyone has the right to life, liberty and freedom from fear and violence.*
- *Everyone has the right to protection of the law without discrimination.*
- *Everyone has the right to a fair trial and will not be arrested without good reason.*
- *No one shall be a slave.*
- *No one shall be tortured or punished in a cruel, inhumane or degrading way.*
- *Everyone has the right to seek asylum from persecution in other countries.*
- *Adult men and women have the right to marry, regardless of their race or religion.*

SOURCE A: *All countries must sign the Universal Declaration of Human Rights before being allowed to join the UN.*

Security Council

The five most powerful countries at the end of the Second World War (Britain, France, the USA, the USSR and China) formed the permanent **Security Council** and were joined by ten other countries (temporary members). The Security Council meets when it looks like a dispute could turn into a war. They can stop countries attacking each other by:

- asking all UN members to stop trading with them until a shortage of supplies forces them to back away from war
- sending in soldiers – or peacekeepers – to prevent or contain the fighting.

Any decisions need a 'yes' from all five permanent members and peacekeepers are sent from armies of several countries.

World Health Organization (WHO)

Mounts health campaigns, does research, runs clinics and vaccinates against infectious diseases. One of the WHO's greatest successes was the elimination of smallpox, one of history's biggest killers, through a massive vaccination programme.

The General Assembly

A sort of world Parliament, with each country having one vote. There were 51 member countries in 1945. By 2011 there were 193.

Secretary-General

A key person who manages the UN and speaks on its behalf.

Children's Fund (UNICEF)

Helps underfed, poorly treated or neglected children throughout the world.

Work

1 Imagine you are representing your country at one of the first meetings of the UN. You are holding a press conference. What would be your answers to these questions?
- Why is this new organization necessary?
- What is the Security Council and how can it stop one country attacking another?
- Are all nations of the world in the UN?
- How do all countries get a say in UN decisions?
- Why do all countries have to sign the Universal Declaration of Human Rights before being allowed to join the UN?
- People throughout the world are weak and vulnerable after the war – how will the UN help them?

2 Look at **Source A**. Do you think that some of the rights are more important than others? Explain your answer carefully.

3 **a** Draw the logo of the UN.
b Explain what you think the logo means.

SOURCE C: *The logo of the UN. What do you think it means? By 1960 99 countries were members of the UN. This increased to 127 members by 1970, 154 by 1980 and 193 by 2011.*

International Labour Organization (ILO)

Tries to protect workers all over the world by improving their conditions, pay, rights, and insurance.

International Court of Justice

Based in the Netherlands. Fifteen judges, each from a different nation, settle legal disputes between countries before they lead to war.

Educational, Scientific and Cultural Organization (UNESCO)

Tries to get countries to share each other's films, books, music, sport, and scientific discoveries so that they understand each other more and are less likely to fight.

Wise Up Words

human rights Security Council

Assessing Your Learning 2

Why did the USA drop nuclear bombs?

This assessment exercise aims to get you working with sources to help you construct an extended answer to a question. Good historians can select the sources, or parts of sources, which are most useful in investigating an enquiry, answering a question or telling a particular story.

In the summer of 1945 fierce fighting was still taking place in the Far East between Japanese and American forces. The number of casualties was enormous.

Eventually, US President Harry S. Truman decided to use a new weapon on the Japanese – nuclear bombs. On 6 August a nuclear bomb was dropped on the city of Hiroshima, killing around 80,000 people instantly. Three days later a second nuclear bomb was dropped on Nagasaki, killing around 40,000. A few days later Japan finally surrendered and the Second World War was over.

Over the years it has been claimed that there were a number of reasons (some not as obvious as you'd think) why President Truman ordered the bombs to be dropped. Broadly speaking, there are three reasons that have been suggested:

Reason No. 1
The bomb cost a lot of money to develop (over $2 billion) so the Americans wanted to test it properly.

Reason No. 2
The USA wanted to show the world, in particular the USSR, how powerful and advanced it was.

Reason No. 3
The Japanese had been very cruel to any soldiers they had captured. Some Americans felt they needed to be taught a lesson.

What do I do next?

Now you've looked at some of the possible reasons why President Truman dropped the bombs, it's time to gather evidence to support some of these views. Study the sources carefully, and try to match them to one (or more) of the reasons above.

'There is no doubt in my mind that these bombs saved many more lives than the tens of thousands they killed. They saved prisoners of war… allied servicemen and millions of Japanese – for, let there be no mistake, if the [Japanese] Emperor and his cabinet had decided to fight on, the Japanese would, literally, have fought to the last man.'

▲ **SOURCE A:** *A British prisoner of war (adapted from* The Emperor's Guest 1942–45 *by John Fletcher-Cooke (1971)).*

'Even killing one American soldier will do. Use your awls [woodwork tools] for self defence. Aim for the enemy's belly. Understand? The belly? If you don't kill at least one, you don't deserve to live.'

▲ **SOURCE B:** *This is what Kasai Yukiko, a secondary school pupil, was told to do by her teacher if the Americans invaded in 1945.*

SOURCE C: *A British cartoon from 1960.*

'This barbarous weapon was of no real use in our war against Japan. They were already defeated and were ready to surrender.'

▲ **SOURCE D:** *Admiral William Leahy, one of President Truman's chief advisors in 1945. He wrote this in 1950.*

'The bombs had been developed at a cost of $2000 million. It would have been difficult to justify not using it after such a vast financial investment. Two types of bomb had been developed – Nagasaki was simply an experiment to try out the second type.'

▲ **SOURCE E:** *From a booklet against nuclear weapons, published in 1985.*

Task 1

a Copy out the list of three different reasons that have been suggested to explain why the USA dropped nuclear bombs on Japan in 1945.

b Look through **Sources A** to **F**. All the sources can be matched to at least one of the reasons. Try to match up each of the six sources to at least one reason from your list.

Task 2

Now it's time to put all you've learned on this controversial topic into practice by writing an extended answer (or essay) to the following question: 'Do you think the USA was right to use nuclear bombs?'

This is a very difficult question to answer so think carefully about it and weigh up all the evidence. Remember, there are good arguments on both sides!

'To damage Japan and demonstrate the power of the allied countries.'

'Because Hiroshima was a big city which was worth destroying. There was a military base there.'

'Because they had them.'

'This is not a simple issue; there are many reasons. They were: to stop the war, to save American soldiers and to show their power.'

'To experiment with their new technology, but couldn't they have dropped it on an uninhabited island nearby?'

▲ **SOURCE F:** *Some comments made in interviews by people who lived in Hiroshima in 1995. They are in answer to the question: 'Why do you think the bombs were dropped?'*

Assessing your work

Good	In a **good** extended answer, you would…	• describe some of the reasons why the USA might have dropped nuclear bombs • identify and use some of the information from the sources to support some of the reasons • use historical words • produce work which shows some structure.
Better	In a **better** extended answer, you would…	• **explain** in your own words each of the reasons why the USA might have dropped nuclear bombs • select and use relevant information from a **variety of sources** to support **different views** • produce **well-structured work** with a conclusion.
Best	In the **best** extended answer, you would…	• **analyse** the reasons why the USA might have dropped nuclear bombs. You might suggest other reasons too • select and use relevant information (including quotations) from **all sources** to support a variety of different views • produce work that is **carefully and clearly structured** and has a **supported** conclusion.

6.1 Why don't we pay to see a doctor?

There is almost no one in Britain who isn't helped at some time or another by what is known as the **welfare state**. This is the name of the system by which the government aims to help those in need – mainly the old, the sick and the unemployed. It is sometimes called **social security**. It aims to make sure that nobody goes without food, shelter, clothing, medical care, education, or any other basic need as a result of not being able to afford it.

Mission Objectives

- Define the 'welfare state' and explain its origins.
- Outline how a report, written in the 1940s, still affects everyone in Britain today.

Study **Source A** carefully. It gives a basic outline of the welfare state. You and your family will almost certainly have been helped out by this system at one time or another.

A caring country

Although we take the things outlined in **Source A** for granted today, it is not a system that has been in place for many years. From 1906, the government had introduced *some* help for the most vulnerable sections of society – free school meals for poorer children, free school medical check-ups and treatment, small old-age pensions for the over 70s, and basic sick and 'dole' pay – but nothing on the same scale as what was introduced after the Second World War.

Rebuilding Britain

In 1942 a man named Sir William Beveridge wrote a report about the state of Britain. It outlined some of the problems that Britain would have to face once the war was over and suggested ways to improve things. In a Britain where people hoped that life would be better once the war was over, it became a surprise bestseller.

As the war ended, an election was held to decide who would run the country after the war. The Labour Party promised to follow Beveridge's advice but the Conservative Party, led by Winston Churchill, refused to make such a promise. The Labour Party won the election easily – and Winston Churchill, the man who had led Britain during the war, was out of power!

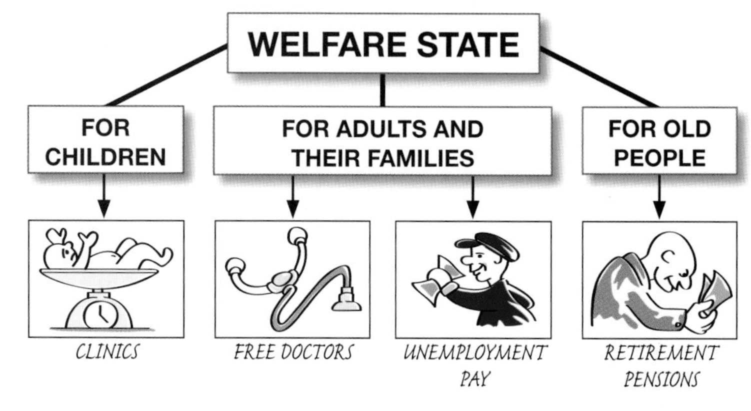

CHEAP/FREE MILK AND FOOD

FREE HOSPITALS

TRAINING

SPECIAL HOMES

CHEAP/FREE SCHOOL MEALS

CHEAP MEDICINE

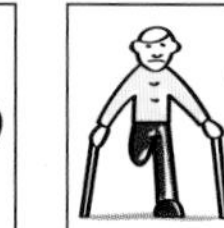

PENSIONS FOR THOSE UNABLE TO WORK

HOME HELP

EDUCATION

FAMILY ALLOWANCES

MONEY FOR LOW INCOME FAMILIES

MEALS AT HOME

FREE GLASSES AND DENTAL CARE

SICK PAY

MATERNITY GRANTS

HELP WITH FUNERAL COSTS

SOURCE A: *When this system was first designed, it was hoped that it would provide 'security from the cradle to the grave'. What do you think this means?*

Helping the most vulnerable

Almost immediately, the new government began to put Beveridge's plan into practice. It was a huge success:

- A National Health Service (NHS) was set up to provide healthcare for everyone. This made all medical treatment – including that offered by doctors, hospitals, ambulances, dentists, and opticians – free to all who wanted it.
- A weekly family allowance payment was introduced to help with childcare costs.
- The very poor received financial help or 'benefits'.
- Pensions for the elderly and disabled were increased.
- The school leaving age was raised to 15 to give children a greater chance of a decent education and more free university places were created.
- Twelve new towns were created. By 1948, councils were building 280,000 homes each year that local people could rent (known as council houses).

Is it really free?

Of course, all this costs money. All workers would have to pay for the service through taxes and **National Insurance** contributions. This is how the welfare state is paid for today… and everyone must pay National Insurance when they get a job (including you!).

Despite the huge cost of the welfare state, it still remains a remarkable achievement. It didn't stay totally free for long – working people today have to pay for prescriptions, dental treatment and other things – but, on the whole, the welfare state ensures that no one is deprived of food, shelter, clothing, medical care, education, or any other essentials as a result of not being able to afford them.

Wise Up Words

nationalize National Insurance social security welfare state

'We were sorry to see Churchill voted out, he was our war leader, but he never promised to give the new ideas a go. The Labour Party did, you see, and they publicized this in all the papers… servicemen [men in the army, navy and air force] like me expected so much after the war, perhaps Utopia [a perfect world], and the welfare state seemed to be a good start. I didn't mind the idea of paying a bit more of my salary to know that a doctor or dentist was there if I needed them... I think there was a bit of a rush when the NHS first started. There were stories of people going and getting whole new sets of teeth, new glasses, even wigs.'

▲ **SOURCE B:** *Nottingham resident Frederick Rebman, remembering the introduction of the welfare state.*

SOURCE C: *A Labour Party election poster from 1945. As well as introducing the welfare state, the Labour Party also* **nationalized** *large industries including electricity, coal and the railways. This meant they came under the control of the government, not private companies.*

Work

1 Copy and complete this paragraph.

Sir William ________ wrote his report about the state of ________ shortly before the end of the ________. He suggested that the government provide a national ________ service and provide social ________ 'from the ________ to the ________'. In the general election of ________, the ________ Party was elected and decided to try out his ideas.

2 a In your own words, explain what the term 'welfare state' means.

b Draw your own version of **Source A**, showing the different benefits a person may receive at different stages in their life. Call your diagram, 'From the cradle to the grave'.

3 Look at **Source B**.

a According to the source, why did the Labour Party win the election in 1945?

b Why do you think people rushed out to get 'whole new sets of teeth, new glasses, even wigs' when the NHS first started?

6.2A Why was there a Cold War?

During the Second World War the USA and the USSR (and Britain of course) fought together to defeat Nazi Germany and its allies. As the war came to a close, it became clear that the enormous differences between these countries would be a lot harder to ignore once the fighting had stopped. So just what were these differences? Why had allies turned into enemies so quickly? And why did the two sides' armies never actually go into battle with each other?

Mission Objectives

- Explain the reasons why the allies of the Second World War became enemies.
- Define what was meant by 'Cold War'.
- Outline why the Cold War eventually ended.

Different ways to run a country

By the end of the Second World War, the USA and the USSR had emerged as the two **superpowers** of the world. This meant that they were the two most powerful countries in the world… by far! However, they may have been on the same side during the war against Hitler, but there were many differences between them. To begin with, the two countries organized themselves in entirely different ways – the USSR was communist, the USA was capitalist. Both believed their way was best… and it would set them on a deadly collision course! (See **Source B**.)

SOURCE A: *American and Soviet soldiers meet at the end of the Second World War. Soviet troops had arrived from the east while the Americans arrived from the west and met up around Berlin, Germany's capital.*

SOURCE B: *Communist and capitalist countries are organized very differently. What sort of country do you think you live in today?*

Differences over the past

The USA and the USSR disagreed on other things, too!

- There was a history of bad feeling between some countries that went back to the First World War. When the USSR had a revolution in 1917, Britain and the USA sent troops and supplies to help destroy the new communist government. The Soviet leader, Joseph Stalin, had not forgotten this.
- Stalin had been very unpopular in Britain and the USA during the 1930s because of his brutality and because he had signed a peace deal with Hitler just before the war started. It was this deal that effectively brought Britain and France into the war. The 'West' had not forgotten this.
- Nine out of ten German soldiers killed in the Second World War died fighting the **Soviets**. The combined deaths of Britain, France and the USA were less than a million. The USSR lost 11 million soldiers and 12 million civilians. Stalin was convinced that the USA and Britain had waited for the Soviet armies to do all the fighting and dying before invading in 1944.

Differences over the future

What to do with war-ravaged Europe quickly caused disagreement. Britain and the USA wanted the countries of Europe – including Germany – to recover quickly so they could trade goods with them. Stalin wanted to keep Germany weak and create a 'buffer' of countries that he controlled between the USSR and Germany. Despite several attempts to come to an agreement, Europe became divided in two by what Winston Churchill called an '**Iron Curtain**'. The countries to the west of the curtain became 'capitalist' and had close relationships with the USA. The countries to the east became 'communist' and were controlled by the USSR (see **Source C**). Relations between East and West grew worse and worse. Capitalism and communism were in a deadly struggle for control of the world. The Cold War had begun.

Work

1. In fewer than 50 words, try to explain the differences between capitalism and communism.
2. a. List different reasons why the wartime allies fell out.
   b. Which reason do you think was most important? Explain your answer.

Wise Up Words

Iron Curtain Soviet superpower

SOURCE C: *How Europe was divided after the Second World War.*

6.2B Why was there a Cold War?

A 'cold war'

Despite the bad feeling and threats exchanged between the two sides, no actual fighting took place – that is why it became known as the Cold War. If the two sides had sent their armies into battle, it would have become a 'hot war' – just like all the others in history. So why didn't the bullets start flying this time?

A MAD idea

The USA dropped the world's first nuclear bombs to be used in warfare on Japan in 1945 to end the Second World War. In 1949 the Soviet Union detonated its first nuclear bomb on a test site. Both sides were terrified that the other would soon have more of these horrific weapons than them, so they quickly began making nuclear bombs. They hoped that by having so many, they would put the other side off launching an attack as it would mean the certain destruction of both countries – and the world! This theory became known as Mutually Assured Destruction – or MAD for short.

A close call

Soldiers from the two major Cold War nations – the USA and the USSR – never actually fought directly against each other in over 40 years of tension... but they came very close. In October 1962, for example, the two sides went to the brink of war when an American spy plane saw that Russian ships were taking nuclear missiles to the small Caribbean island of Cuba, just 140 kilometres from the American coast. Thankfully, after 13 days of unbearable tension, the two countries worked out a deal and the weapons were withdrawn – and the world breathed a huge sigh of relief! However, hostility remained for many years after the Cuban Missile Crisis and the Cold War became a war of nerves, a war of threats and bluffs, and of spies and propaganda.

Be a Top Historian

GCSE

Top historians should be able to **relate topics** they're already studied to new ones. For example, whilst studying the world wars you learned about the idea of 'total war'. As you can see from **Source B**, the idea of total war applied during the Cold War... and still does to this day.

The Cold War thaws

Towards the end of the 1980s the USSR began to struggle to afford its huge army and massive stock of nuclear weapons. The Soviet people were very poor and started to demand an improved quality of life. The Soviet Union began to collapse. One by one, the countries of Eastern Europe won their freedom from Soviet control. In 1991 the 15 republics that made up the USSR split up and began to rule themselves. By 1993 the people of Russia had free speech and free elections. The Cold War had come to an end.

The USSR is sometimes known as Russia… or the Soviet Union.

What Happened When?

1949

In 1949 Britain officially recognized the independence of the Republic of Ireland, ending its membership of the British Commonwealth. Northern Ireland remained part of the United Kingdom.

Work

1. Explain why the Cold War got its name.
2. In no more than 50 words, explain the theory of Mutually Assured Destruction.
3. What are the dangers of MAD?
4. Do you think MAD was a good idea? Explain your answer carefully and try to think of reasons why World War Three was avoided and why the Cold War came to an end.

SOURCE A: *One hundred nuclear weapons would have guaranteed the total destruction of the world. By the end of the Cold War, the USA and USSR had 40,000 between them. For 40 years, every time the two superpowers fell out, every living thing on the planet faced annihilation.*

SOURCE B: *American children were taught to 'duck and cover' under their school desks in the event of a nuclear attack. It would have given no protection whatsoever.*

History Mystery

6.3A Did man really land on the moon?

During the 1950s and 1960s, the USA and the USSR were competing in a frantic '**space race**' to be the first to conquer space and put a man on the moon. Both sides were determined to prove that their country and way of life were superior.

Space race

American pride was dented in April 1961 by the news that Yuri Gagarin, a Russian astronaut, had become the first human to orbit the Earth. It seemed that Russia had won the space race… but not for long! The US President, John F. Kennedy, responded by setting what many thought was an impossible target: 'To land a man on the moon and return him safely to earth… by 1970!' Just eight years later, on 20 July 1969, America's *Apollo 11* moon mission triumphed and Neil Armstrong became the first man to walk on the surface of another world. Millions watched the event 'live' on their television sets. To many Americans, and other countries of the world, landing a man on the moon was more of an achievement than putting one in space – it showed the greatness of the American way of life and its superiority over the Russians.

Space sham?

But as news of the moon landing spread, another famous story was just beginning. As photographs and film were released, some people began to say the whole mission, including the moon landing itself, was faked. They said that, in 1969, Americans didn't have the technology to land men on the moon (and get them back safely) and started to pick apart each and every part of the mission. Even the photograph on this page came under scrutiny (**Source A**). Some wondered why the photograph was of such good quality. And where are the stars – aren't they meant to be in the background? **Sources B** and **C** also point to the theory that the mission was faked.

SOURCE A: *This picture is often used to back up the argument that the landing was faked. They say the photograph is too perfect – it looks like the astronaut posed for it. Some of the other key points made about this picture are listed below.*

- *The cameras were mounted on the front of each astronaut's space units (with no auto focus). So why is it such a good picture? Did a professional photographer take it in a special studio?*
- *Why is the flag fluttering? There's no atmosphere on the moon, no breeze at all. A flag wouldn't wave in a vacuum so there must have been a slight wind on the film set.*
- *Why do the footprints look like they've been set in wet sand? There is no water on the moon to make this happen, so surely the footprints should have disappeared like in the dry sand on a beach.*
- *And where are the stars? The sky should be full of them!*

Wise Up Words

space race

SOURCE B: *A photograph of a moon rock. Can you see the letter 'C' below? The people who think the landings were faked use this photograph to back up their theory that the whole thing was filmed in a television studio. They suggest that every rock on the 'faked' moon surface was individually labelled, starting at 'A'. This is a close-up photo of rock 'C' (which the people who built the set forgot to turn over!).*

Fake or fact?

Controversy still rages over this historic event today. Did the Americans fake the landings just to 'get one over' on the Russians? Was it faked in 1969 because the President had promised the American public to put a man on the moon before 1970? Were the moon landings filmed in a television studio rather than on the moon itself? These pages will ask you to form your opinions on this great debate – was man on the moon in July 1969… or not?

In 2001 a survey in the USA showed that 20 per cent of US citizens believed the 1969 moon landings were faked. It has clearly remained a very 'hot topic', not just in the USA, but all over the world. Study these photographs, facts and written sources very carefully. These cover the most controversial areas of the whole topic.

'NASA [the US government agency responsible for space travel] couldn't make it to the moon, and they knew it! In the late 1950s a study on astronauts landing on the moon found that the chance of success was 0.0017 per cent. In other words, it was hopeless. As late as 1967 three astronauts died in a horrendous fire on the launch pad without even taking off. It was well known that NASA was badly managed and had poor quality control. Yet by 1969 they suddenly put men on the moon. And got them back again with complete success! It's just against all common sense and statistical odds.'

▲ **SOURCE C:** *Based on an interview by Rogier van Bakel with Bill Kaysing published in 1994. Bill Kaysing is famous for co-writing the book* We Never Went to the Moon, *published in 1974.*

Work

1 Based on the evidence you have seen so far, what is your opinion? Were the moon landings faked or not? Start a table of evidence with a column 'for' and a column 'against' the argument that the landings were faked.

6.3B Did man really land on the moon?

What are the arguments that it *wasn't* faked?

Now study the following arguments carefully. The Work section will ask for your opinion as to whether the moon landings were faked or not.

ARGUMENT A

From a science website.

'Pictures from astronauts transmitted from the moon don't include stars in the dark lunar sky – an obvious production error! What happened? Did NASA film-makers forget to turn on the lights? Most photographers already know the answer: it's difficult to capture something very bright and something else very dim on the same piece of film... astronauts striding across the bright lunar soil in their sunlit spacesuits were dazzling. Setting a camera up properly for a glaring space suit could make the background stars too faint to see.'

ARGUMENT B

From a website that tries to prove that the moon landings were not faked. This source is referring to Source B on the previous page.

'[The mark on the rock] is not a "C". The photograph is a copy of the original photograph. If you look at the original, taken in 1969, the "C" disappears. This is simply because all it is, is a tiny hair that has got into one of the copies along the way.'

ARGUMENT C

Another argument that the moon landings were not faked.

'The astronauts received a great deal of training before they left earth; part of this was in the operation of cameras, which were specially designed to be used by the astronauts with their suits on. The Apollo astronauts took around 17,000 photographs... and there's plenty of not-so-great ones that NASA have never published... only the best ones were released to the world.'

ARGUMENT D

From a space website, www.badastronomy.com.

'The flag isn't waving. It looks like that because of the way it's been put up. The flag hangs from a horizontal rod, which pulls out from the vertical one. In *Apollo 11*, they couldn't get the rod to extend completely, so the flag didn't get stretched fully. It has a ripple in it like a curtain that is not fully closed... it appears to have fooled a lot of people into thinking it waved.'

Be a Top Historian

GCSE

Top historians, whether studying at KS3 or GCSE level, ask relevant questions about the past, investigate issues critically and use a range of sources to demonstrate their knowledge and understanding when reaching conclusions.

SOURCE A

The three astronauts of the Apollo 11 *moon mission: Neil Armstrong, Michael Collins and Buzz Aldrin.*

ARGUMENT E

An answer to the question: 'The first man on the moon: real or fake?' posted on the Internet in 2008.

'The Russians were watching the USA space programme like hawks and analysing everything the Americans did. If there was the slightest suggestion that a hoax was happening, the Russians would have been falling over themselves to tell the world about it.'

Work

Now you've had a chance to look through the arguments, it's time to decide whether YOU think the USA put man on the moon in 1969.

Step 1 Find reasons why the USA felt it was really important to put a man on the moon before the USSR. What was the 'space race'? How had the USSR dented American pride in 1961? What had President Kennedy promised and why? Why would the USA want to beat the Soviets and put a man on the moon before them?

Step 2 Find evidence that the moon landings were faked. Think about the photographs. What is 'wrong' with some of them? Make notes on the suspicions surrounding the moon landings.

Step 3 Find evidence that the moon landings were not faked. Can any of the 'errors' on the photographs be explained? Make notes that answer some of the suspicions about the landings from **Step 2**.

Step 4 Time to make up your mind! Were the moon landings faked? Write the script for a short report for a children's television programme about the moon landings. In your report, you should express your opinion about the moon landing debate. Remember, you must back up your theory with evidence.

ARGUMENT F

In 2002 a man from Beverly Hills, California, complained that the retired Buzz Aldrin had punched him in the face after he had asked Aldrin to swear on a Bible that he had been to the moon. The man explained that he did not believe Aldrin, or anyone else, had ever walked on the moon.

6.4 A united Europe

During the first half of the twentieth century, Western Europe was devastated by two of the most horrific wars that the world had ever seen. During the second half of the twentieth century, Europe witnessed peace, increased wealth and close cooperation. So why was Europe suddenly so peaceful? Just how closely do the countries of Europe cooperate? And which countries are members of the European Union?

Mission Objectives

- *Explain why the countries of Europe cooperated more and more in the second half of the twentieth century.*
- *Outline which countries belong to the European Union and investigate when they joined.*

Europe in ruins

Wars between European nations – particularly between Germany, France and Britain – had been raging on and off for centuries. At the end of the Second World War, the leaders of Europe saw that things had to change. They had an idea that if they put aside differences in language, culture and history, they could work together and wars between them would be unthinkable. Rather than compete as rivals, they could work together to increase wealth and ensure peace. This vision of a united Europe – that is as closely linked as the United States of America – has gradually evolved over the decades. Today, hundreds of millions of Europeans now share the same **currency**, vote in European elections and live under the same laws and regulations. So how did this happen?

The evolution of the European Union

1950s

In 1951, six countries joined their iron and coal industries together to form the European Coal and Steel Community (ECSC). That way, they could never build up their armies on their own. In 1957, the Treaty of Rome was signed, joining the group together as the European Economic Community (EEC) and paved the way for greater cooperation.

1960s

The Common Agricultural Policy was signed, which meant that all farmers in the EEC were paid the same for their produce. In 1968, the EEC began to trade with other countries as a single state – the biggest trading **bloc** in the world.

1970s

The success of the EEC attracted other countries and it expanded to include three more members. In 1979, the European Parliament was elected by EEC citizens. At first it could just advise, but now it can pass laws that apply in all member countries.

1980s

Three more members joined the EEC and a '**single market**' was created. This meant that goods, services, money, and people could move freely between all 12 EEC countries.

1990s

The Maastricht Treaty was signed, which renamed the community the European Union (EU). All countries agreed to extend cooperation even further – including **foreign affairs**. Another three countries became members and the EU agreed to accept more members in the future.

2000s

On 1 January 2002 12 member countries adopted new **Euro** notes and coins as their currency. Three hundred million Europeans now carried the same coins and notes in their pockets. In 2004, ten more countries joined the EU, joined by another two in 2007 and a further country in 2013. It is planned that more European countries will follow.

Hungry for More?

Several other nations in Europe are keen to join the EU. Find out which countries. Investigate and assess their chances of joining.

Hungry for More?

Cooperation between EU members is increasing more and more – to the point where there might one day be a European army or police force. Some people don't agree with this and there is a UK Independence Party that campaigns for Britain to leave the EU. Why do you think some people are against the EU increasing its power?

SOURCE A: *The EU flag.*

SOURCE B: *The European Union has grown steadily since it was formed in 1951.*

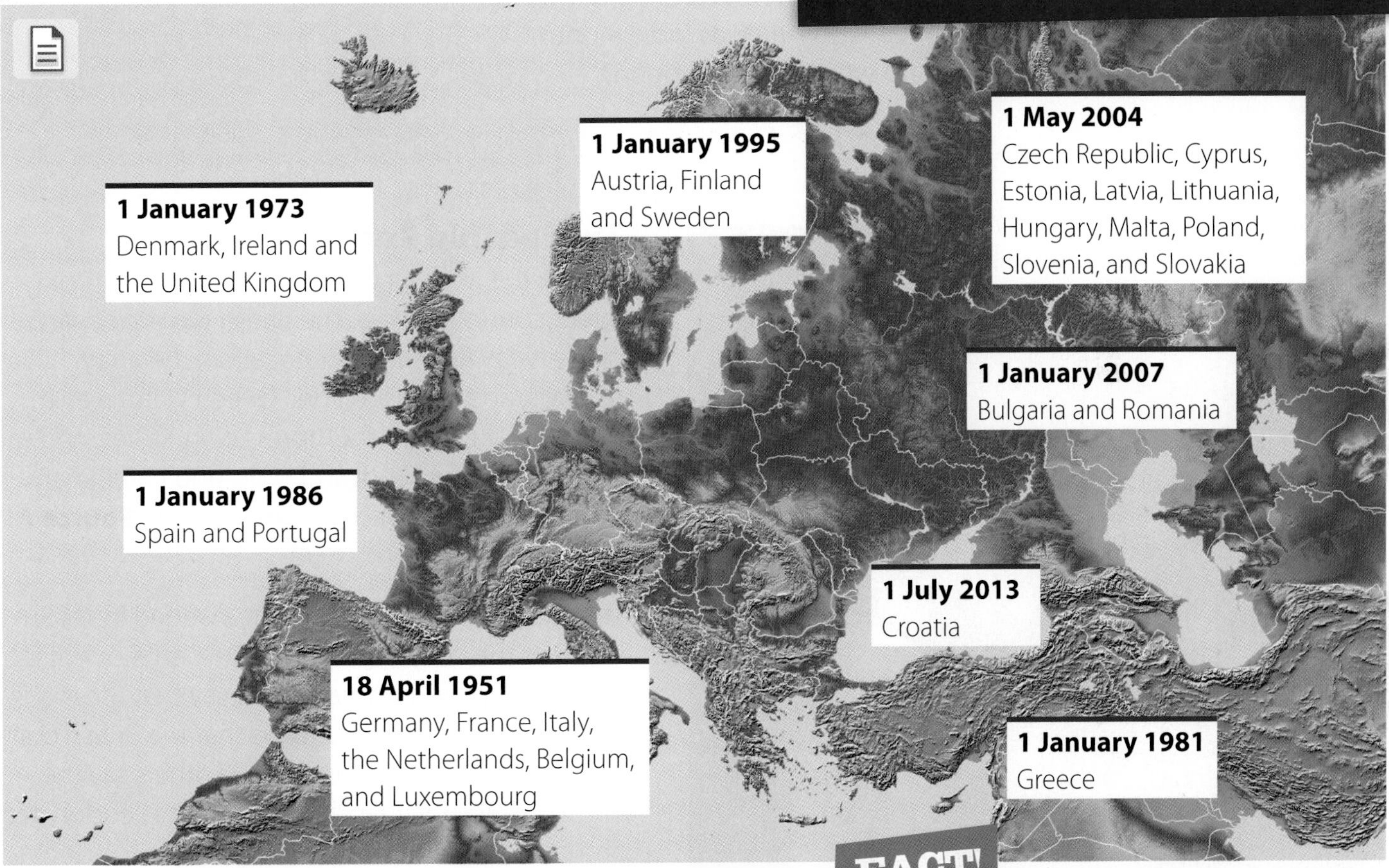

1 January 1973
Denmark, Ireland and the United Kingdom

1 January 1995
Austria, Finland and Sweden

1 May 2004
Czech Republic, Cyprus, Estonia, Latvia, Lithuania, Hungary, Malta, Poland, Slovenia, and Slovakia

1 January 2007
Bulgaria and Romania

1 January 1986
Spain and Portugal

1 July 2013
Croatia

18 April 1951
Germany, France, Italy, the Netherlands, Belgium, and Luxembourg

1 January 1981
Greece

Work

1 a Explain why many Europeans wanted to increase the cooperation between countries in the 1950s.
  b Has their plan for Europe worked? Explain your answer.

2 a List the original six member states that joined in 1951.
  b List the countries that joined in the 1970s.
  c List the countries that joined in the 1980s.
  d List the countries that joined in the 1990s.
  e List the countries that have joined since the year 2000.
  f How many members does the EU have in total?

3 What do you think have been the three most important developments in the evolution of the EU? Explain your choices.

FACT!

Many people from the poorer countries in the EU have moved to the wealthier ones to work. This has caused tension in some communities when large numbers of people (known as 'immigrants') who speak a different language and have a different culture have settled and opened businesses.

Wise Up Words

bloc currency Euro
foreign affairs single market

7.1A Independence for India

From the 1600s onwards, Britain conquered foreign lands all over the world and claimed them as part of the British Empire. During Queen Victoria's reign (1837–1901) Britain ruled over 450 million people living in 56 different places (or colonies) all over the world. Put simply, the British Empire was the biggest empire the world had ever known! But 50 years later, after two world wars, the British Empire was breaking apart. More and more countries wanted nothing to do with Britain and wanted to run themselves. And one of the first nations to break away from British rule was India – one of Britain's largest colonies. So how and why did this happen?

Mission Objectives

- Compare opinions on British rule in India.
- Assess factors that led to the Partition of India in 1947.

SOURCE A: *Queen Victoria pictured with her Indian secretary, Munshi Abdul Karim.*

Incredible India

During the reign of Queen Victoria, Britain took direct control of India. The British ran many parts of everyday life, such as education, the army, railways, and law and order. Queen Victoria even proudly called herself 'Empress of India', learned to speak and write Hindi and Urdu, and had Indian food on most of her dinner menus (see **Source A**).

British rule

There is little doubt that Britain changed India. But whether the changes were for the better or not is a matter of opinion. Some people say that the roads, hospitals, schools, and railways that the British built made India a better place – while others say the British just took valuable goods (such as cotton, tea and precious jewels) and forced people to adopt the British language, customs and lifestyle (see **Sources B** and **C**).

'British brains, British trade and British money changed India. Many bridges, 40,000 miles of railway, and 70,000 miles of roads show how hard the British worked. They brought water to vast areas of farmland. They built sewers, gave good wages, built canals and handed out food. As a result, famines almost ended.'

▲ **SOURCE B:** *Adapted from* The English in India *by British historian Sir John A.R. Marriott (1932).*

'Can these thieves really be our rulers? These thieves… import a huge number of goods made in their own country and sell them in our markets, stealing our wealth and taking life from our people. Can those who steal the harvest of our fields and doom us to hunger, fever and plague really be our rulers? Can foreigners really be our rulers?'

▲ **SOURCE C:** *From a leaflet written by Indians who wanted the British out. Who do you think the thieves were?*

Towards independence

By 1900, many educated Indians started to believe that India should be free from British control. A political group called the Indian National Congress had been formed to bring this about, but despite holding meetings and organizing demonstrations, the British ignored their demands.

In 1914 Indians fought alongside British soldiers in the Great War (see **Source D**). India itself gave Britain a huge amount of money, food and materials – and nearly 64,000 Indian soldiers died in the war.

In 1919 the British government made slight changes to the way India was governed. Law-making councils were set up in each province and over five million wealthy Indians were given the vote. However, the British government, based in London, still controlled taxation, the police, the law courts, the armed forces, education, and much more. While some Indians welcomed the changes as a step in the right direction, others were bitterly disappointed. A demonstration was organized in the town of Amritsar in the province of Punjab. The local British commander ordered his men to fire into the crowd, killing 379 men, women and children.

The Amritsar incident was a turning point for the Indian National Congress and the man who would soon become its leader, Mohandas Gandhi. He wrote, 'When a government takes up arms against its unarmed subjects, then it has lost its right to govern.' The Congress, more loudly than ever, demanded an independent India.

Wise Up Words

Partition viceroy

SOURCE D: *A picture of Naik Darwan Singh Negi, one of the first Indian winners of the Victoria Cross, Britain's top bravery medal, in 1914. He was part of an Indian battalion fighting as part of the British Army during the Great War.*

Gandhi

Gandhi, a holy man and a very clever politician, told Indians to do all they could to make life difficult for the British without using violence. Today, this is called passive resistance. By 1935, after many years of protests, a Government of India Act gave Indians the right to control nearly everything except the army. India, however, was still part of the British Empire and was still ruled by a **viceroy**. Many Indians, including Gandhi, continued to demand complete independence.

SOURCE E: *A photograph of Gandhi, taken in 1931. Every day he spun cotton on a small spinning wheel to encourage people to lead simple lives. He wanted Indians to be proud of their country and realize that they didn't need British rule.*

7.1B Independence for India

SOURCE A: *Indian soldiers with captured German artillery in the Libyan desert in 1943.*

India at war again!

In 1939, when the Second World War began, India was still part of the British Empire. As in the First World War, thousands of Indians joined up to fight as part of the British Empire force. In total, 2.5 million Indians fought in what was the largest volunteer army in history.

After the war, it was clear that Britain would have to give India its independence. Britain wasn't strong enough to hold on to a country that was so desperate to rule itself – and the people in Britain, tired of war, weren't keen to see their soldiers trying to control marches and demonstrations that could easily turn to violence.

But the whole matter of independence was complicated by the increasing violence between Hindus and Muslims. Relations had been bad for a long time, but after 1945 they started to break down completely. Muslims didn't want to be ruled by a mainly Hindu government if India gained its independence (there were a lot more Hindus than Muslims in India). Instead, Muslims wanted a country of their own, made up of areas where mainly Muslims lived. They wanted to name the new country after these areas – P for Punjab, A for Afghanis, K for Kashmir, S for Sind, and TAN for Baluchistan. The word 'Pakistan' also means 'land of the pure' in Urdu.

As violence between Muslims and Hindus continued, the British hurriedly made plans to split India into two countries – India for Hindus and Pakistan for Muslims. The million Sikhs, who felt they didn't belong in either, would have to choose one or the other.

'How can you even dream of Hindu-Muslim unity? Everything pulls us apart. We have no inter-marriages. We do not have the same calendar. The Muslims believe in a single God, the Hindus worship idols… The Hindus worship animals and consider cows sacred. We, the Muslims, think it is nonsense. We want to kill the cows and eat them. There are only two links between the Muslims and the Hindus: British rule – and the common desire to get rid of it.'

▲ **SOURCE B:** *From a 1943 interview with Mohammed Ali Jinnah, the leader of an Indian political party called the Muslim League. He eventually became Pakistan's first leader.*

Partition of 1947

On 15 August 1947, Britain stopped ruling India. The whole subcontinent was divided into Hindu India and Muslim Pakistan (itself divided into two parts – see **Source C**). Immediately, there were problems. As it was impossible to make sure that boundaries were drawn so that all Muslims were in Pakistan and all Hindus were in India, millions now found themselves in the wrong country. As they fled across the boundaries to be in the country of their religion, whole trainloads were massacred by the 'other side'. Nobody knows exactly how many were killed, but some have estimated as many as one million. Then, at the height of this violence, Gandhi himself, the man who had believed in peaceful protest, was assassinated by a Hindu extremist.

Sadly, the troubled start for the new, independent nations of India and Pakistan continued. Major differences still exist today.

Be a Top Historian

GCSE

Top historians, whether studying at KS3 or GCSE level, should always be looking to extend their knowledge and understanding of how different countries around the world influence and are influenced by each other. Your studies of Britain's relationship with India is a good example of how you can do this.

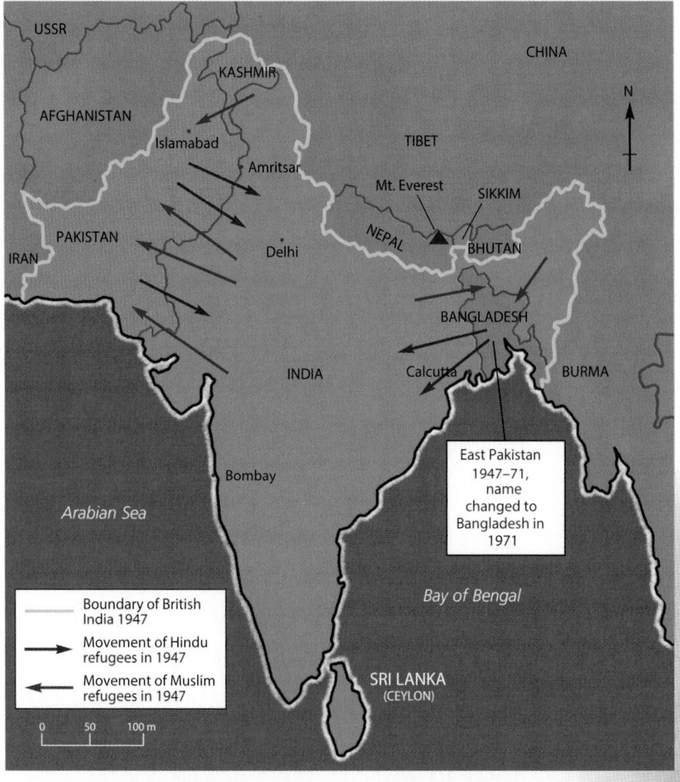

SOURCE C: *How India was divided in 1947. Areas where more than half the people were Muslim became Pakistan while areas where over half the people were Hindu became independent India. It has been estimated that over 14 million fled to the 'other side' in 1947. Thousands from both religions were slaughtered on the way.*

Hungry for More?

Find out which countries or colonies are still part of the British Empire. Then, make a timeline showing when different nations gained their independence from Britain. What is the British Commonwealth?

Work

1. How do we know that Queen Victoria was proud and pleased about Britain's connection to India?
2. **a** Read **Sources B** and **C** on page 134. Describe two opposing views of the impact of British rule in India.
   b Why do you think there is such a difference of opinion on this issue?
3. **a** How did India contribute to the Great War?
   b What changes were made to the way India was governed after the Great War?
   c Why were some Indians happy with these changes? Why were others disappointed?
   d What happened in Amritsar in 1919?
4. **a** Why was India split into two countries in 1947?
   b Why did violence continue even after the split?
   c Look at **Source B** on page 136. In your own words, explain why Jinnah thought unity between Hindus and Muslims was impossible.

SOURCE D: *Jawaharlal Nehru and Mohammed Ali Jinnah, the first leaders of the new, independent India and Pakistan.*

7.2A Independence for Africa

Look at **Source A** carefully. The map shows the huge continent of Africa – and the colours indicate which European nation owned that particular area in 1900. You will notice that almost all of Africa was ruled by seven European nations – Britain, France, Germany, Spain, Portugal, Belgium, and Italy.

Mission Objectives

- Recall why Africa became the focus of expansion for several European nations in the 1800s.
- Explain how African nations regained their independence during the twentieth century.

Dividing Africa

As you can see in **Source A**, in 1900 there were a few independent African countries, but most had been taken over or colonized by Europeans. In fact, between 1880 and 1900 over 80 per cent of Africa was divided up among European powers. They were attracted to Africa because of valuable raw materials such as diamonds and gold and cheap labour. Britain itself took control of 16 colonies in Africa, including Egypt, the Sudan, Nigeria, Kenya, Rhodesia (now Zimbabwe), and South Africa. This, combined with other colonies, such as India, Australia and Canada, made the British Empire the largest the world had ever known.

Now look at **Source D** on the opposite page. Again it shows Africa, but this time at the start of the twenty-first century, in the year 2000. You will notice that there is no key this time showing which European power owns which area. Instead you can see a whole continent of independent countries, not tied to or ruled by anyone other than themselves. So how was independence achieved?

SOURCE A: *Africa in 1900.*

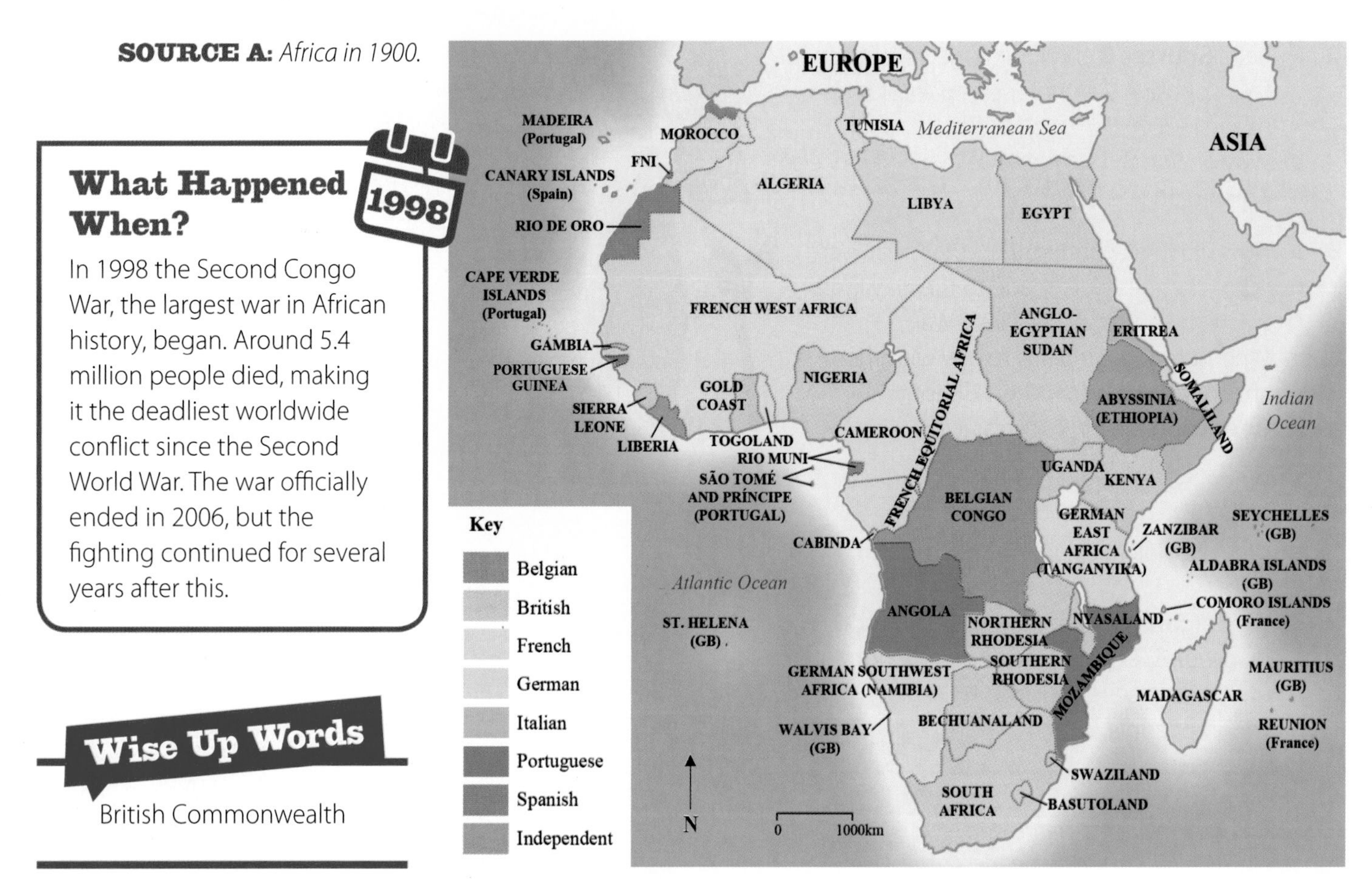

What Happened When? 1998

In 1998 the Second Congo War, the largest war in African history, began. Around 5.4 million people died, making it the deadliest worldwide conflict since the Second World War. The war officially ended in 2006, but the fighting continued for several years after this.

Wise Up Words

British Commonwealth

Controlling Africa

As you can see from **Source A**, there were four main European powers that controlled Africa in the early 1900s: Britain, France, Belgium, and Portugal… and each of these countries viewed their colonies differently. Britain thought of itself as a parent – the mother country – helping its colonies to develop. Queen Victoria herself said that Britain's role was to 'protect the poor natives and advance civilization'. France believed its role was to turn Africans into Frenchmen. Its colonies were run from Paris and treated as part of France. Belgium and Portugal ruled their colonies very harshly and were determined to hold on to them for as long as possible. In general, though, all European powers exploited their colonies in some way. They took their raw materials and used the natives as a cheap workforce. Africans had no say in how their countries were ruled and European settlers banished Africans from the best land and took it for themselves.

> When they first came they had the Bible and we had the land. Now we have the Bible and they have the land.

SOURCE B: *An African saying.*

SOURCE C: *An amazing photograph showing a white European settler using local men as servants at his colonial mansion in Africa.*

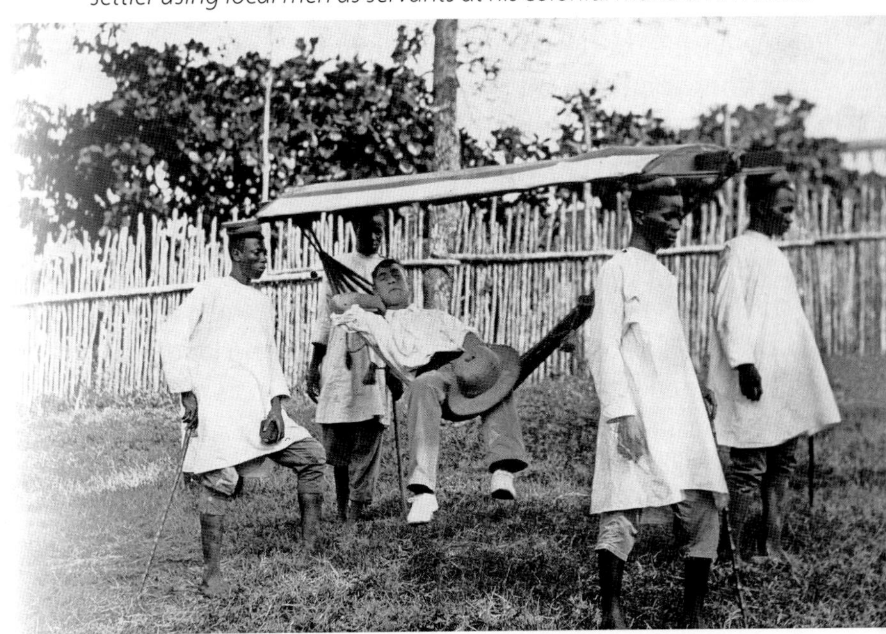

SOURCE D: *Africa in 2000.*

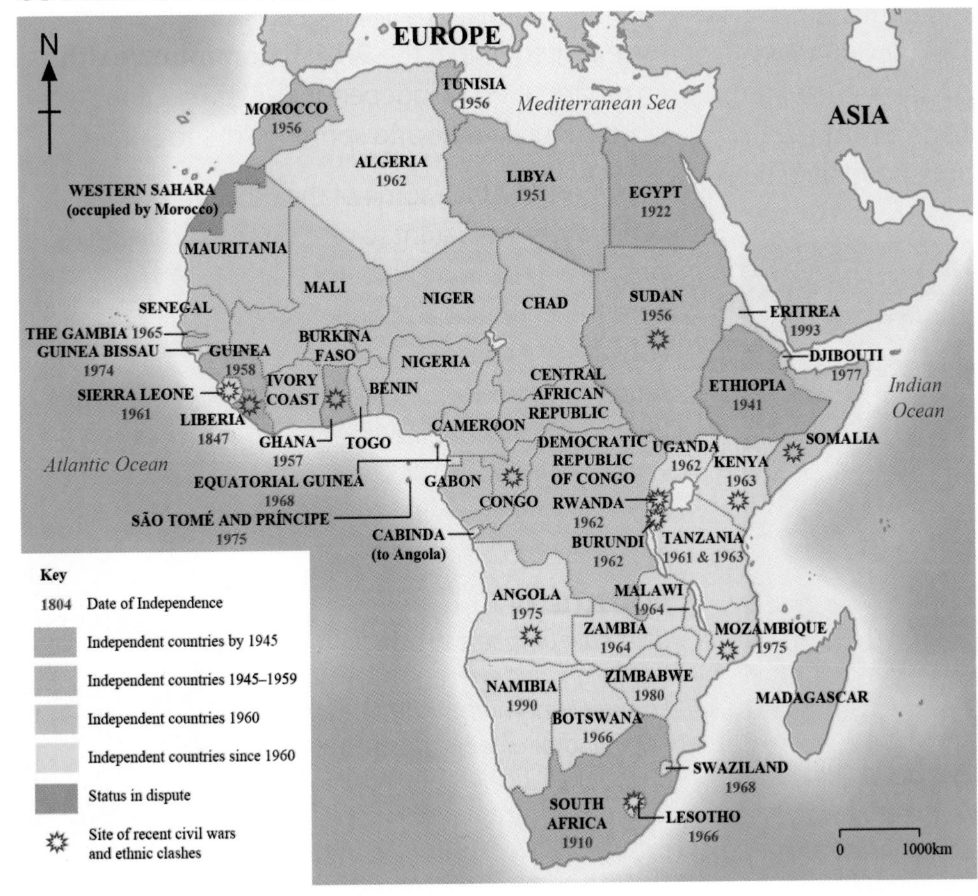

Work

1. a Describe how **either** the British, the French, the Belgians, **or** the Portuguese ruled their colonies.
   b Why were African colonies seen as such a rich prize?
2. Look at **Source B**. Write a short paragraph explaining what point this saying is trying to make.
3. Look at **Source C**.
   a What is happening in the photograph?
   b Do you think the source helps us understand how some Europeans viewed Africa and Africans? Explain your answer.

7.2B Independence for Africa

The impact of the Second World War

Some of Britain's colonies – such as Canada, Australia, New Zealand, and South Africa – had been running their own affairs for years. Australia, for example, had been part of the British Empire since 1770, but by 1901 it had its own Parliament that was making most of the key decisions about the country. New Zealand became a British colony in 1840, but had gained the freedom to run its own affairs by 1907. In Africa, South Africa had been self-governing since 1910 and Egypt since 1922.

By the end of the Second World War, more and more colonies were demanding the right to govern themselves. And by 1945 countries like Britain and France no longer had the strength or wealth to hold on to their colonies. Many Africans had fought for Britain and France against Nazi Germany too. They felt they were fighting to defend freedom but were frustrated that their own countries were not yet free.

Indian example

When India won its independence from Britain in 1947, it led to a whole host of other countries demanding their freedom. In 1957, the first British colony in Africa got its independence when the Gold Coast (as it was known under British rule) became Ghana. **Source D** on page 139 shows the speed at which independence then spread through Africa.

SOURCE B: *The Commonwealth Games, once known as the British Empire Games, is a sports competition held every four years in one of the former colonies of the British Empire. Athletes from former British colonies are invited to participate.*

SOURCE A: *A jubilant crowd carries Julius Nyerere, Premier of Tanganyika (Tanzania), after being granted internal self-government. The following year he was made president when the country was given independence.*

The transfer of power

In the British colonies, independence for African nations was achieved fairly peacefully. There were riots in some places like Kenya, but on the whole the transfer of power went smoothly. Newly independent nations like Nigeria, Gambia and Kenya were invited to join the **British Commonwealth**, an organization of independent, free countries with close cultural, trade and sporting links to Britain.

Elsewhere in Africa some of the other European nations were reluctant to give up their colonies. In Angola and Mozambique, for example, Portugal's determination to hang on to these colonies led to a long war between African and Portuguese soldiers. In Algeria, French forces fought to keep control from 1945, until independence was finally agreed in 1962.

SOURCE C: *In recent years there have been several high-profile campaigns and events (such as Make Poverty History and Live 8) aimed at helping some of the world's poorest countries, including many in Africa. Comic Relief, for example, raises millions of pounds with its Red Nose Day to fund aid projects all over Africa.*

A new Africa

For many newly independent nations, freedom produced its difficulties as well as its benefits. Some nations, like Morocco, Tunisia and Egypt, have developed thriving tourist industries, while others have made good use of raw materials such as rubber, gold and diamonds. However, some countries have seen rivalries between tribes flare up into bloody civil war. This happened in Nigeria in the 1960s, Uganda in the 1980s, and Sierra Leone, Rwanda and Somalia in the 1990s. Many new nations have struggled to create their own systems of government, build up their own industry and trade, and cope with internal divisions. **Source D** shows some of the problems faced by some of the newly independent African nations in the years after they gained freedom. Yet perhaps the greatest problem the newly independent nations have had to deal with is poverty. Of the 25 poorest countries in the world, 17 are in Africa… and despite offers of loans and aid from richer countries the problems of poverty and long-term debt still remain.

	Country	Ruler	Date of independence	The price of freedom?
	Algeria	France	1962	Independence was achieved only after unrest and an armed rebellion.
	Angola	Portugal	1975	There was a civil war in Angola between 1975 and 2002.
	Congo	France	1960	Congo had a civil war after independence and its first president was driven out.
	Ghana	Britain	1957	Ghana's government has been plagued by rebellion and corruption.
	Kenya	Britain	1963	Kenya was ruled as a one-party state until 1992.
	Mauritania	France	1960	In a military coup, Mauritania's first president was overthrown.
	Mozambique	Portugal	1975	Mozambique suffers from famine and poverty due to civil war, a lack of food supplies and debt.
	Nigeria	Britain	1960	Since independence, Nigeria has been under almost constant military rule.
	Senegal	France	1960	Senegal was ruled as a virtual one-party government until the 1980s.
	Uganda	Britain	1962	A turbulent period led to over a million deaths.
	Zimbabwe	Britain	1980	Zimbabwe won independence after the black majority defeated the white minority. Tension continues.

SOURCE D: *African independence, adapted from* DK Pockets World History *by Philip Wilkinson (1996).*

Work

1 Copy out and complete the word grid below, using clues a–e. When you have correctly completed the grid, a word will be revealed (f). Write a sentence about the word in line f.
Clues:
a) Portuguese colony, independent in 1975.
b) ______ Africa: self-governing since 1910.
c) Formerly Rhodesia.
d) Former French colony.
e) New ______: a former British colony.

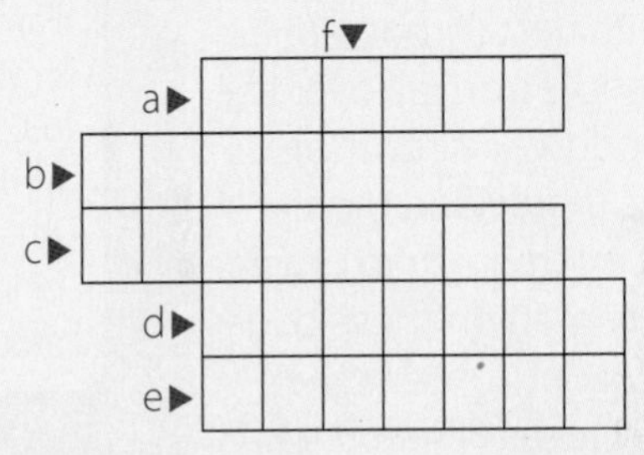

2 Explain what is meant by the term 'British Commonwealth'.

3 **a** In your own words, explain what challenges many African nations have faced since independence.
b Have **you** ever 'helped out' an African nation? Think carefully – there are lots of ways you may have done.

4 Many historians say that Britain lost much of its empire because of its involvement in two world wars. Do you agree with this view? Use the information on these four pages to support your answer.

7.3 How has immigration changed Britain?

Different groups and nationalities have been moving to Britain for hundreds of years. During the twentieth century, however, there was an increase in the amount of people from all over the world deciding to make their homes in this country. This **migration** had a dramatic effect on British society and way of life, changing everything from the music we listen to, to the way we speak and the food we eat. So just why did people decide to move to Britain? Where did they come from? And how were they treated when they got here?

Mission Objectives

- Explain where Britain's immigrant population moved from.
- Analyse how immigration has changed Britain.

Britain has attracted people from all over the world – but some areas have provided more immigrants than others. The map on these pages outlines some of the key areas where Britain's immigrant population came from.

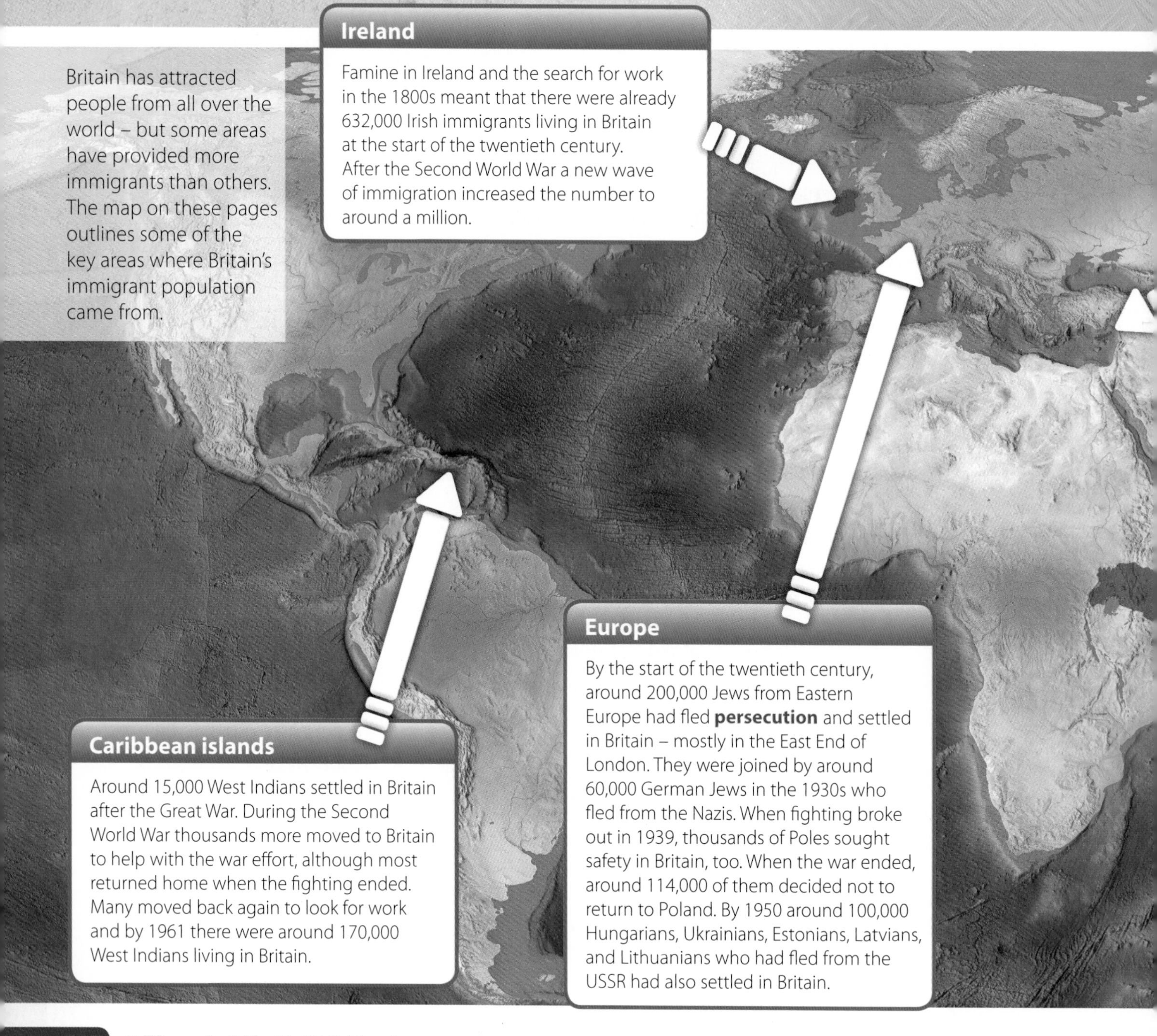

Ireland

Famine in Ireland and the search for work in the 1800s meant that there were already 632,000 Irish immigrants living in Britain at the start of the twentieth century. After the Second World War a new wave of immigration increased the number to around a million.

Caribbean islands

Around 15,000 West Indians settled in Britain after the Great War. During the Second World War thousands more moved to Britain to help with the war effort, although most returned home when the fighting ended. Many moved back again to look for work and by 1961 there were around 170,000 West Indians living in Britain.

Europe

By the start of the twentieth century, around 200,000 Jews from Eastern Europe had fled **persecution** and settled in Britain – mostly in the East End of London. They were joined by around 60,000 German Jews in the 1930s who fled from the Nazis. When fighting broke out in 1939, thousands of Poles sought safety in Britain, too. When the war ended, around 114,000 of them decided not to return to Poland. By 1950 around 100,000 Hungarians, Ukrainians, Estonians, Latvians, and Lithuanians who had fled from the USSR had also settled in Britain.

SOURCE A:
This poster was produced in the Second World War. It showed all the peoples of the British Empire – no matter what race, nationality or religion – working together under the same flag.

Wise Up Words

migration persecution

Hungry for More?

In recent years, due to the ease and low cost of travel, the number of people choosing to live and work in another country has greatly increased. This not only means people have been moving to Britain – it also means British people have started new lives abroad. See if you can find out about the people who have moved to Britain in recent years. And find out the number one destination for Brits moving abroad.

Work

1. a Make a list of reasons why different groups have moved to Britain.
   b In your opinion, which was the most common reason?
2. Can you make a link between immigration to Britain and the British Empire? Explain your answer.
3. Look at **Source A**. In your own words, describe the poster, including a sentence or two about the message of the poster.

Cyprus

Cyprus was very poor in the years following the Second World War and things got worse after Turkey invaded and divided the island in two. Around 70,000 Cypriots left to make their home in Britain.

India, Pakistan and Bangladesh

When 'British India' gained independence from Britain in 1947, it split into different countries: India and Pakistan. This partition of British India led to fighting and many thousands of people died as whole populations moved across the dividing lines. Some sought safety in the former 'mother country' – Britain. In 1955 there were around 10,000 immigrants from India and Pakistan living in Britain, hoping to improve their standard of living. By 1991 around 1.5 million people from the Indian subcontinent were living and working in Britain.

Kenya and Uganda

Many Asians from Kenya and Uganda came to Britain in the 1960s and 1970s. They had moved to Africa from India and Pakistan but now the governments in some African countries were driving them out. Around 44,000 Asians from Kenya and 26,000 from Uganda came to Britain at this time.

Hong Kong, Malaysia and Singapore

People from the Far East began to move to Britain throughout the 1950s and 1960s. Most came from the poorer areas of the British colony of Hong Kong, and by 1961 there were around 30,000 people from the Far East living in Britain. In 1997, Hong Kong stopped being a British colony and became part of China. Around 50,000 people from Hong Kong were given British passports at this time.

7.4 What was so special about the *Windrush*?

On 22 June 1948, a ship named the *Empire Windrush* landed at Tilbury docks in London. On board were 492 passengers – the vast majority of them men – who had come to live in Britain. It was an event that would change British society forever. So just what made these newcomers special, and what made them move to Britain? How were they treated? And how did they help to change life in Britain?

Mission Objectives

- Explain why some people from the British Empire decided to start new lives in Britain.
- Assess the significance of the *Empire Windrush*.
- Discover how the '*Windrush* generation' was treated in Britain.

Moving to the mother country

During the Second World War, Britain relied heavily on people from all over the British Empire to help with the war effort. The Caribbean islands, for example, supplied over 10,000 men for Britain's army, navy and air force. The men were proud of their role in helping Britain, but when the fighting ended most went back to their homes in Jamaica, Barbados and Trinidad. Life was very hard in the Caribbean at this time. Jamaica had been devastated by a hurricane in 1944, there was no tourist industry and the price of sugar – the Caribbean's most important export – was at an all-time low. For ambitious young men, it was clear that their future lay abroad – under the grey skies of Britain.

Why Britain?

In 1948, Parliament passed the British Nationality Act. This meant that all the people of the Empire – now called the Commonwealth – were given British passports and allowed to live and work in Britain. Many of these people had been brought up speaking English, been named after British heroes and educated to love Britain. Also, Britain was very short of workers after the war, so making the move seemed an attractive option.

Welcome, *Empire Windrush*?

In June 1948, the *Empire Windrush* became the first ship to bring immigrants into Britain after the war. The voyage made headlines in Britain before the ship had even docked. Thousands of immigrants from Europe and Ireland had been pouring into the country since the war had finished, but it was the arrival of one ship of English-speaking, Christian, British subjects that caused alarm. Newspapers were full of stories of the 'colour problem' that was heading towards Britain's shores and some MPs demanded that the ship was turned around. When the *Empire Windrush* finally docked, the smartly dressed West Indians smiled nervously at the journalists and one of them sang a song called 'London is the Place for Me'. Soon, they had all found jobs, and friends and relatives followed in search of work (see **Source B**). Although at this time immigrants still only made up a tiny proportion of the population, it was the beginning of a more **multicultural** Britain.

SOURCE A: *The first black immigrants to arrive in Britain after the war became known as the 'Windrush generation'.*

The British experience

Not all white Britons welcomed the new arrivals. Many West Indians found that the colour of their skin provoked hostile reactions. Some found it hard to get good jobs (even though they were well qualified) and decent housing (see **Sources C** and **D**). Yet, despite the discrimination, racial tension and obstacles such as low pay, many thousands of West Indians decided to make Britain their home. Some did go back to the West Indies, but most remained, determined to stay in spite of the difficulties they faced.

SOURCE B: *The NHS, London Transport, the British Hotels and Restaurants Association, and the British Transport Commission all encouraged people from the Caribbean to move to Britain.*

Wise Up Words

multicultural

SOURCE C: *Many black people faced prejudice and difficulty finding housing. This led to 'black areas' being created in most of Britain's big cities.*

'I knew a lot about Britain from schooldays, but it was a different picture when you came face-to-face with the facts. They tell you it is the "mother country", you're all welcome, you're all British. When you come here you realize you're a foreigner and that's all there is to it.'

◀ **SOURCE D:** *John Richards – one of the passengers on the* Empire Windrush.

'The second day in England I was offered five jobs. If someone want to leave, let them leave, but I have been here during the War fighting Nazi Germany and I came back and help build Britain. People said that we would not stay longer than one year; we are here, and I and my people are here to stay.'

▲ **SOURCE E:** *Sam King – one of the passengers on the* Empire Windrush.

'We appreciate of course that these people are human beings, but to bring coloured labour into the British countryside would be a most unwise and unfortunate act.'

▲ **SOURCE F:** *The General Secretary of the National Union of Agricultural Workers speaking in 1947.*

Work

1. a List reasons why people may have wanted to leave the Caribbean at the end of the Second World War.
   b List reasons why people from the Caribbean may have chosen to move to Britain.
   c Why might people from the Caribbean believe they had a right to live in Britain in the 1940s and 1950s?
2. Who were the '*Windrush* generation' and what was life like for them in the 1940s and 1950s?
3. Why do you think the *Empire Windrush* caused more alarm in the papers and in Parliament than immigration from Europe and Ireland? Explain your answer very carefully.
4. a What is meant by the word 'tolerant'?
   b Do you think Britain in the 1940s and 1950s was a very tolerant place? Explain your answer carefully.

7.5 Multicultural Britain

Although some in Britain were alarmed by the arrival of people of different religions, cultures and colours, it didn't stop these people building new lives and making their homes here. At first the immigrants were often treated like strange outsiders, but over the years they have become an important part of, and have made a large contribution to, British society and culture. In fact, it is hard to imagine what life in Britain would be like without the influence of immigration. So just what changes have immigrants made to British society? And does this mean that modern Britain is a tolerant place?

Mission Objectives

- Explain how immigration has affected life in Britain.

Cultural contribution

The sources on these pages outline how a variety of different people with different religions, languages and backgrounds in Britain has made an impact on the country.

SOURCE A: *John Lennon and Paul McCartney are the world's most successful singer-songwriters. They were born in Liverpool, but both had Irish grandparents who had moved to England in search of work.*

SOURCE B: *Singer-songwriter Emeli Sandé's Zambian father met Emeli's English mother when he moved to Sunderland.*

SOURCE C: *The Notting Hill Carnival in London is the second largest street festival in the world. It was started in 1964 by the area's large Caribbean community to celebrate their culture. It is now a major national event that attracts up to two million visitors from all backgrounds every year.*

SOURCE D: *Britain's sporting teams – especially England's – have benefitted from immigration for many years. Viv Anderson became the first black football player to represent England in 1978 and Paul Ince became the first to captain England in 1993. Both are the sons of West Indian immigrants. Since Anderson's debut, over 60 black football players have represented England.*

Hungry for More?

Many of Britain's greatest Olympians have been either immigrants or the descendants of immigrants. See if you can find out more about the achievements and backgrounds of Daley Thompson, Linford Christie, Kelly Holmes, Christine Ohuruogu, Amir Khan, and Mo Farah.

FACT!

Immigration has even influenced the English language. Look below at just a few everyday words that have been absorbed from other cultures:
Arabic: sofa, alcohol, sugar
Turkish: coffee, yoghurt
Gaelic: slogan, trousers
Hindi: bangle, shampoo, pyjama

Getting better

Many people see the National Health Service as one of Britain's greatest achievements. It means that everybody gets healthcare if they need it – not just if they can afford it. But it may not have been possible without the help of immigrants. In 2008, of the 243,770 doctors who worked for the NHS, 91,360 trained abroad before moving to work in British hospitals. Thirteen per cent of nurses were born outside the UK and, for the last ten years, half of all the other vital NHS positions have been filled by people who qualified abroad.

Hungry for More?

Many things that people consider to be 'typically British' are in fact the result of immigration to these islands. See if you can find out more about the origins of Marks and Spencer, Tesco, ice cream vans, and Punch and Judy shows.

A changing diet

Immigration has completely changed what people in Britain eat. In 1957 there were only 50 Chinese restaurants in the whole country. By 1970 there were over 4000, and now there is one in almost every town and village in the country. The food brought by immigrants from India, Pakistan and Bangladesh has been even more popular, and curry now rivals the Sunday roast and fish and chips as Britain's national dish. Chicken tikka masala is the country's best selling ready meal and 'going for a balti' has become a weekly event for millions of Britons. It is now such a part of life in Britain that a song called 'Vindaloo' became an anthem for the England football team!

SOURCE F: *Brick Lane in London houses many Indian restaurants.*

SOURCE E: *England's cricket team has long included many players of different racial backgrounds. In recent years they have been captained by Nasser Hussain (who was born in India to an Indian father and English mother) and Kevin Pietersen (who was born and raised in South Africa).*

Work

1 Write a sentence or two to explain what you think is meant by the term 'multicultural Britain'.

2 a Describe how immigration has affected British:
  • healthcare • diet • sport • music

  b For each category, explain if you think the effect of immigration has been positive or negative.

3 Immigration into Britain is a controversial subject. Many are in favour of it, but others think it should be stopped. Why do you think immigration is such a 'hot topic'?

8.1 The fifties

Life was tough in the first few years after the Second World War. Basic goods, such as meat, sugar and clothing, still had to be rationed and few luxuries were available. Even bread was rationed for a while. But, with careful government control, and loans from the USA, things began to improve. Thousands of houses were built for people whose homes had been bombed and there were plenty of jobs. By the early 1950s, Britain had recovered and some people were even calling it a 'golden age'. So what were the 1950s like? What were the new discoveries, ideas and inventions?

Mission Objectives

- Examine and assess significant changes, developments, inventions, and ideas in Britain in the 1950s.

Transport

- Car ownership more than doubled in the 1950s. By 1955 there were over three million car owners in Britain.
- The Mini was launched in 1959. It cost £496 (about the average yearly salary).
- Britain's first intercity motorway (the M1) was opened between Birmingham and London.
- In 1952, the first passenger jet aircraft took holidaymakers abroad. In the 1950s, around one million people holidayed abroad.

SOURCE A: *The Mini was designed by Alec Issigonis, a Greek immigrant who moved to Britain when he was 17.*

SOURCE B: *Elvis Presley performing in 1956. His television and stage appearances shocked many adults – and his wriggling hips earned him the nickname 'Elvis the Pelvis'. In total, Elvis has sold around 500 million records!*

Entertainment

- Younger people had more money and free time than ever before. A new type of fast and loud music from America became popular – rock 'n' roll. Elvis Presley and Buddy Holly were popular singers.
- Listening to music, dancing, reading, watching television, knitting, cinema visits, and board games (Monopoly, Snakes and Ladders) were popular pastimes. So too were sports such as football, cricket and boxing.
- There were 'crazes' for hula hoops, Lego and yo-yos in the late 1950s.

Technology

- Radio and gramophones were still popular, but the 'must-have' new item was the television. Millions bought a set to watch the live broadcast of the coronation of Queen Elizabeth II in June 1953.
- At first there was just one channel – the BBC – but ITV was introduced in 1955. Programmes were only in black and white!
- 33 per cent of households had a washing machine, 15 per cent had a fridge and freezer, and 10 per cent had a telephone. However, in 1950 around 20 per cent of homes had no electricity at all.
- The USSR launched the first satellite in 1957, and the first microchip was developed in 1958.

FACT!

'Post-war' is the name given to the time after a war. 'Post' is Latin for 'after'.

Work and home

- Most of the workforce was employed in 'primary' or 'secondary' jobs. 'Primary' means that workers obtain natural resources (e.g. miners or farmers). 'Secondary' means they make things with the natural resources (e.g. factory workers or food producers).
- Most people shopped at local shops in town centres. They would visit separate shops for bread (bakeries), vegetables (greengrocers) and so on.
- There were around three male workers for every female worker – many women stayed at home as 'housewives'. Around 10 per cent of female workers were in management positions.
- Large numbers of settlers came to Britain to work from countries in the British Empire – particularly Jamaica, India and Pakistan – but there were still only around a million people from other cultures living in Britain.

Politics and conflict

- Britain and France fought Egypt over control of the Suez Canal, which runs through Egypt in the Middle East.
- Soldiers from the US, Britain and other powers fought North Korean and Chinese forces in the Korean War.
- The Cold War continued – a time of threats and tension between the two global superpowers: America and the USSR.

Work

This chapter is a great opportunity to work in a small group (ideally five). Your challenge is to read through the next 12 pages and work out the answers to the following questions:

- What are the key changes and developments in transport, entertainment, technology, work and home life, and politics and conflict from the 1950s to the present day?
- When did these changes happen?
- Can you suggest reasons for these changes?

Next:

- In your group, divide the categories between you, so each person has a category.
- In no more than 50 words and a few pictures, make notes on your category.
- Keep your notes safe… and get ready to examine life in the 1960s on the following pages.

SOURCE C: *A boy and girl watching television in the front room in the 1950s.*

FACT!

Britain's population reached 50 million in 1952. At this time the population of the world was 2.5 billion.

What Happened When?

1950s

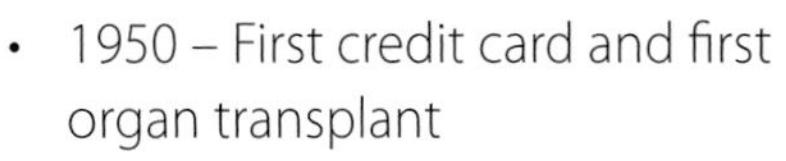

- 1950 – First credit card and first organ transplant
- 1952 – Polio vaccine developed
- 1953 – Structure of DNA discovered and Mount Everest conquered
- 1956 – Wireless television remote control introduced
- 1959 – Barbie doll went on sale

Most popular...

Key

- ♫ Bestselling music single
- Highest grossing film
- Bestselling car
- Most watched television programme

- ♫ 'Rock Around the Clock' by Bill Haley and His Comets
- *The Ten Commandments*
- Morris Minor
- Coronation of Queen Elizabeth II

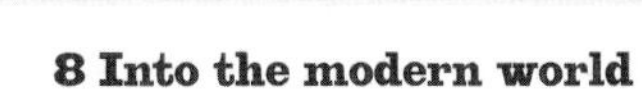

8.2 The sixties

The 1960s or 'the sixties' was a decade that began on Friday 1 January 1960 and ended on Wednesday 31 December 1969. The sixties saw television and motor cars become more popular than ever before. Women's skirts became shorter, men's hair became longer and a 'boy band' called the Beatles took the world by storm – John Lennon, a member of the group, even said that they were 'more popular than Jesus'. There were lots of jobs in the 1960s and young people had money to spend on music, entertainment and clothes. But what great events and inventions might you have seen in the sixties? How was life beginning to change?

Mission Objectives

- Examine and assess significant changes, developments, inventions, and ideas in Britain in the 1960s.

Transport

- By 1960 there were five million cars on Britain's roads, and by the middle of the decade around half of all UK households had access to at least one car.
- 95 per cent of cars sold in Britain were British-made.
- More motorways were made to link Britain's cities, and a national speed limit of 70mph was introduced in 1965.
- In 1966 the first InterCity train was used. It was powered by electricity (rather than steam or diesel), so was much quieter and cleaner. Concorde made its first test flight in 1969.
- In 1961 2.6 million people went on holiday abroad.

Technology

- 75 per cent of homes had a television. In 1964 BBC2 went on air and was the first channel to have colour (1967).
- Lasers, the audio cassette and video tape recorders first appeared.
- The first PC (personal computer) went on sale in 1965 – and the first public demonstration of the computer mouse, video conferencing and email soon followed.
- 1961 saw the first man in space (a Soviet named Yuri Gagarin) and in 1969 man walked on the moon (Americans Neil Armstrong and Buzz Aldrin).

FACT!

In 1960 Britain's population was around 53 million… and the world's population stood at three billion.

Entertainment

- The 1960s are sometimes called the 'Swinging Sixties' and are associated with the birth of pop music and fashions such as the miniskirt and flared trousers.
- Radio was still popular, but records sold millions of copies. In 1962 the Beatles, a 'boy band' from Liverpool, released their first single. This was the start of 'Beatlemania', a craze that swept the world and made the four lads into the biggest selling group in history.
- Millions of cinema tickets were sold, but television was the big hit of the 1960s. *Coronation Street* and *Doctor Who* first aired in this decade.

SOURCE A: *Beatles songs, such as 'Yesterday', are some of the most covered by other singers ever.*

Work and home

- Nearly all houses had electricity so fridges, freezers, television, and vacuum cleaners became more popular.
- By 1965, more than half the workforce was employed in service industries, rather than in manufacturing (making things). Service industries provide a service, like banking, teaching, healthcare, and tourism.
- Lots of new housing estates and high-rise tower blocks were built.
- The word 'teenager' began to be used for 13–19 year olds, and young people became very fashion-conscious!

SOURCE B: *Typical fashions of the 1960s.*

Mod
Smartly dressed, liked pop music, rode scooters

Hippy
Flowing clothing, experimented with drugs, anti-war

Rocker
Liked rock 'n' roll, wore leather jackets, rode motorbikes

Other popular trends
Tie-dye, flared jeans, miniskirt, 'mop-top' hair

Politics and conflict

- In the UK the death penalty was abolished, the Abortion Act made termination of pregnancy legal and the voting age was reduced from 21 to 18.
- The Civil Rights movement was at its height in America, calling for equal rights for black Americans. In 1964, the Civil Rights Act made racial discrimination illegal in the USA and in 1965 there were equal voting rights for black and white Americans.
- The Cold War continued between the USA and the USSR, and there were major conflicts in the Middle East and Vietnam.

What Happened When?

1960s

- 1962 – First James Bond film
- 1963 – US President John F. Kennedy assassinated
- 1965 – Miniskirt first appeared
- 1966 – England won football World Cup
- 1967 – First heart transplant
- 1968 – Martin Luther King Jr assassinated

Most popular...

- 'She Loves You' by the Beatles
- *The Sound of Music*
-  Austin 1100
-  1966 World Cup Final

Be a Top Historian

It is important that historians use the correct vocabulary. In this chapter you will have to use words associated with aspects of **change** (such as 'cause', 'effect', 'different', 'result'), words associated with **time** (such as 'decade', '1960s') and words associated with different **aspects of society** (such as 'industry', 'leisure', 'population', 'transport').

Work

In your group, each of you should continue adding to your notes on your chosen category. Think about:

- whether there were any big changes between the 1950s and 1960s. If so, in which categories did these changes take place?
- whether you can make any connections between the categories. For example, what changes in work and home life were caused by changes in technology?

8.3 The seventies

The 1970s or 'the seventies' was a decade that began on Thursday 1 January 1970 and ended on Monday 31 December 1979. The decade is well known for crazy, multi-coloured fashions and new types of music and technology. Jobs became harder to find because many factories closed down, and many British workers who still had jobs went on strike time and time again. But how were transport, technology, entertainment, and work and home life changing in the seventies? What were the big news stories in Britain and abroad?

Mission Objectives

- *Examine and assess significant changes, developments, inventions, and ideas in Britain in the 1970s.*

Transport

- There were now ten million cars on Britain's roads.
- Major developments in air travel, including the introduction of the Boeing 747 (Jumbo Jet) and Concorde (see **Source A**), meant that more passengers could travel faster to their holiday destinations than ever before. In 1970 over 5.7 million British people holidayed abroad.

SOURCE A: *Concorde was the first supersonic passenger jet, able to fly from Britain to the USA in under three hours. It first carried passengers in 1976 but was 'retired' in 2003 because of low passenger numbers and high costs.*

Glam rocker
Make-up, bright clothing, flares, platform boots, nail varnish. Music by T. Rex, David Bowie, Slade

Punk rocker
Mohican, ripped jeans, Dr. Martens, safety pins, offensive t-shirt. Music by the Sex Pistols, the Clash, the Ramones

SOURCE B: *Many 1970s fashions were bold and made a statement.*

Entertainment

- 91 per cent of families had a television, and all three television stations (BBC1, BBC2 and ITV) were in colour! Families could record programmes after the commercial production of the video cassette recorder.
- Skateboards, roller skates, stunt kites and space hoppers were popular toys.
- Glam rock and punk rock were the big new sounds in music (see **Source B**). Disco took the world by storm too. Young people flocked to 'discotheques' (nightclubs) to dance to this upbeat music with a strong rhythm.

FACT!

In 1971 the population of Britain was 54 million. In the 1970s thousands of families emigrated to Australia, New Zealand and South Africa. The world population reached 3.7 billion.

What Happened When?

- 1970 – The Beatles broke up
- 1971 – Britain's currency went decimal
- 1975 – Microsoft founded
- 1976 – Apple founded
- 1977 – Elvis Presley died, aged 42

SOURCE C: *Games for the Magnavox Odyssey included Simon Says and Shooting Gallery.*

Technology

- The Sony Walkman personal stereo first appeared in 1979, so music lovers could listen to tapes through headphones while on the move.
- In 1972 Magnavox released the first video game console, the Magnavox Odyssey, which came with a choice of 11 games (see **Source C**).
- Microwave ovens went on sale in the UK in 1974.

Work and home

- The Equal Pay Act of 1970 meant that men and women had to be paid the same for the same job. At this time around 17 per cent of people in management positions were female.
- The 1970s were known for strikes – by postal workers, lorry drivers and dustmen, for example. A miners' strike in 1972 devastated Britain's coal-powered electricity supply. Schools and offices closed down and the government introduced a 'three day week' to save electricity. After seven weeks, the government gave in and the miners won their pay rise.
- 64 per cent of homes now had a washing machine.
- Foreign nations began to produce goods cheaply and many British factories closed down. Unemployment reached 1.5 million in 1979.

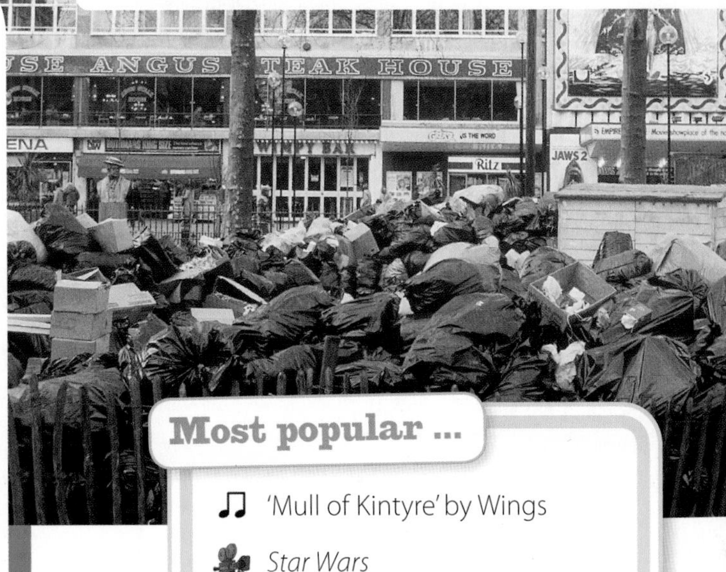

SOURCE D: *Rubbish piled up at Leicester Square in London, January 1979. This was known as the 'Winter of Discontent' because so many people went on strike – rubbish collectors, ambulance drivers and even television staff. ITV went 'off air' for 11 weeks!*

Most popular ...

- 'Mull of Kintyre' by Wings
- *Star Wars*
- Ford Cortina
- *Apollo 13* spacecraft ocean splashdown

Politics and conflict

- In 1973 Britain joined the European Economic Community (now the European Union), a group of European states that traded with each other.
- US troops came home from the Vietnam War in 1973, and the war eventually ended in 1975.
- In 1972 Palestinian terrorists attacked the Munich Olympic Games and killed 11 Israeli athletes.
- In 1979 British people elected their first female Prime Minister – Margaret Thatcher.

SOURCE E: *Margaret Thatcher entered Downing Street for the first time in 1979.*

Work

In your group, each of you should continue adding to your notes on your chosen category. Think about:

- whether there were any big changes between the 1960s and 1970s.
- whether you can make any connections between the categories. For example, what changes in transport were caused by changes in technology?

8.4 The eighties

The 1980s or 'the eighties' was a decade that began on Tuesday 1 January 1980 and ended on Sunday 31 December 1989. This was the decade of the BMX bike, the chunky mobile phone and the birth of CDs, cheaper games consoles and rap music. In this decade Britain had its first female Prime Minister, Margaret Thatcher. But how would you spend your time in the eighties? What impact was technology starting to have on your life? What were the big news events in Britain and around the world?

Mission Objectives

- Examine and assess significant changes, developments, inventions, and ideas in the 1980s.

Transport

- There were over 15 million cars on Britain's roads, and front seat belts were made compulsory in 1983.
- The Sinclair C5, a small battery-powered car, was launched in 1985; the company went bankrupt after ten months due to poor sales.
- Over 21 million Brits went on holiday abroad, over ten million of whom went by plane.

SOURCE A: *Formula 1 driver Ayrton Senna in a Sinclair C5 electric car in 1985. The company folded not long after this.*

FACT!

In 1981 Britain's population hit 56 million. The world population reached 4.5 billion in the 1980s.

Be a Top Historian

Top historians working at KS3 and A Level should be able to analyse change and continuity over large sweeps of time. They should consider developments in areas such as culture, science and technology, war, politics, and religion.

SOURCE B: *An early mobile phone. You had to carry the large external battery around with you!*

Technology

- By 1980 more than one million personal computers had been sold around the world.
- In 1982 the first CDs went on sale, and in 1984 the Apple Macintosh was launched (costing £4000 in today's money).
- In 1985 the Nintendo Entertainment System featuring the Super Mario brothers went on sale. Microsoft Windows was launched the same year.
- Mobile phones were introduced but were very large and expensive.
- In 1989 the World Wide Web was invented by British scientist Tim Berners-Lee.

Entertainment

- 95 per cent of families had a television. In 1982 there was another channel to watch – Channel 4. Britain's first satellite service – Sky TV – was launched in 1989.
- The Rubik's Cube, BMX bikes, Cabbage Patch dolls, and *Star Wars* toys were popular. Nintendo launched its 100 million-selling Game Boy in 1989.
- In 1984 musicians Bob Geldof and Midge Ure brought pop stars together to record the charity single 'Do They Know It's Christmas?' to raise money for an Ethiopian famine.
- The 1980s saw the rise of hip hop and rap music. Another music trend was the New Romantics, typified by bands such as Duran Duran and Adam and the Ants, who wore elaborate clothes and lots of make-up.

SOURCE C: *Adam and the Ants dressed as flamboyant pirates and had two drummers.*

What Happened When?

- 1980 – John Lennon (one of the Beatles) was assassinated
- 1981 – Many millions watched the televized wedding of Prince Charles and Lady Diana Spencer; new 'plague' identified as AIDS
- 1982 – Michael Jackson releases *Thriller*, the bestselling album of all time
- 1984 – Huge poison gas leak in Bhopal, India, kills nearly 4000 and injures 500,000
- 1985 – Television soap opera *EastEnders* starts
- 1986 – Space Shuttle *Challenger* explodes on takeoff
- 1987 – DNA evidence first used to convict criminals
- 1989 – Berlin Wall demolished; this boundary split the Soviet-controlled eastern part of Berlin from the western half

Work and home

- In 1982 over 50 per cent of homes had a telephone.
- Supermarkets began to move from town centres to out-of-town retail parks.
- Only 43 per cent of cars sold in Britain were British-made.
- In 1984 three million people were unemployed. Many had lost jobs because British factories closed down when cheaper foreign goods were imported. There was also increased automated manufacturing, so fewer workers were needed to operate equipment.

Most popular ...

E.T. The Extra-Terrestrial

'Do They Know It's Christmas?' by Band Aid

Ford Escort

EastEnders Christmas Day 1986 episode: Den serves divorce papers on Angie

Politics and conflict

- In 1982 Argentina invaded the Falklands, a group of islands in the South Atlantic Ocean governed by Britain. Britain and Argentina went to war for ten weeks until Argentina withdrew from the islands.
- In 1984 a major miners' strike against mine closures began, ending in 1985 with defeat for the miners.
- Conflict continued in Northern Ireland between those wanting to remain part of the UK and others who wanted an independent united Ireland.

Work

In your group, each of you should continue adding to your notes on your chosen category. Think about:

- whether there were any big changes between the 1970s and 1980s.
- whether you can make any connections between the categories. For example, what changes in work and home life were caused by changes in transport?

8.5 The nineties

The 1990s or 'the nineties' was a decade that began on Monday 1 January 1990 and ended on Friday 31 December 1999. The decade saw the end of the Cold War and the launch of the National Lottery and 24-hour shopping. Mobile phones became much smaller, cheaper and popular and the Internet began to change from something that a few 'experts' used to something that would play a key part in millions of people's lives. But what was life like in the nineties? And how was it changing?

Mission Objectives

- Examine and assess significant changes, developments, inventions, and ideas in the 1990s.

Transport

- There were around 20 million cars on Britain's roads by 1990 – and around 20 per cent of families had access to more than one car.
- Britain was linked to France in 1994 when the Channel Tunnel rail service began.
- In the 1990s around 20 million people took holidays abroad.

SOURCE A: *An engineer examines a section of the Channel Tunnel as it is constructed.*

Entertainment

- Watching television was one of the most common activities for all age groups in the UK.
- Spending time with family and friends, listening to music, shopping, reading, sport, and exercise remained popular. British bands such as Oasis, Blur and the Spice Girls made a big impact in the USA and Europe.
- Cinema trips increased in popularity after a decline in the 1980s.
- Home computers and games consoles were the 'must-have' goods of the decade.

SOURCE B: *The Spice Girls appeared at the 1997 Cannes Film Festival.*

FACT!

In 1991 Britain's population stood at 59 million, with almost 10 per cent being non-white or mixed race. By 1997 16 per cent were aged 65 or over and 7 per cent were over 75 – mainly because of medical improvements. The world population at this time was around 5.5 billion.

What Happened When?

1990s

- 1990 – Hubble telescope launched into space
- 1991 – South Africa ends racist Apartheid laws
- 1994 – Nelson Mandela elected president of South Africa
- 1997 – First Harry Potter novel published (*Harry Potter and the Philosopher's Stone*)
- 1999 – Euro currency introduced

Technology

- Mobile phones became smaller, cheaper and much more popular.
- In 1991 the World Wide Web was first made available to the public. Soon three million people in the UK were connected to the Internet, and by 1986 that figure had risen to ten million. By 1998 there were 130 million users worldwide.
- In 1994 Sony launched the first of its PlayStation consoles.
- The 1990s saw the popularity of digital cameras, satellite television, email, and text messaging (the first text was sent in 1992) soar. The Pentium processor, MP3 players and DVDs became available too.

SOURCE C: *A selection of technology on sale in the nineties.*

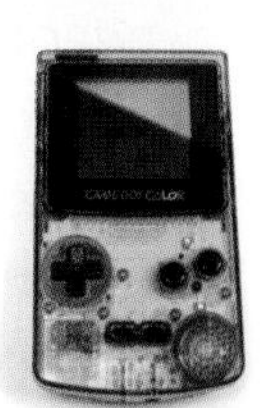

Work and home

- In 1993 12 million women were at work (and 15 million men). This was more than half of all women of working age (16–60) and 37 per cent of them were in management positions.
- 67 per cent of all workers were in the service industries such as teaching, healthcare, retail, banking, and tourism. Some jobs began to be moved abroad, such as in call centres.
- 56 per cent of employees worked with computers or automated equipment, and 12 per cent were self-employed.
- Virtually all homes had at least one television, washing machine and access to a phone (landline or mobile).
- Out-of-town shopping centres became popular – and 24-hour shopping and Sunday trading were introduced.

SOURCE D: *The fall of the Berlin Wall was one of the most iconic events of the 1990s.*

Politics and conflict

- In the late 1980s relations between the USSR and the USA began to improve. In 1989 some countries that were heavily influenced by the USSR (e.g. Czechoslovakia, Hungary and East Germany) began to reject Soviet control. In 1991 the USSR lost control of other areas. The system used to control these areas – communism – collapsed. The Cold War was over.
- In 1990 Iraq invaded Kuwait and the USA responded by sending in troops to fight Iraq in what became known as the Gulf War. Eventually, the Iraqis withdrew.
- On Good Friday (10 April) 1998 Irish Unionists and Nationalists finally came to an agreement. Similar to Wales and Scotland, Northern Ireland was to have an Assembly to run its daily affairs. This 'Good Friday Agreement' didn't solve all the problems, but it was a huge step towards peace.

Most popular ...

Titanic

'Candle in the Wind' by Elton John, rewritten after the death of Princess Diana in 1997

Ford Fiesta

Funeral of Diana, Princess of Wales

Work

In your group, each of you should continue adding to your notes on your chosen category. Think about:

- whether there were any big changes between the 1980s and 1990s.
- whether you can make any connections between the categories. For example, what changes in work and home life or entertainment were caused by changes in technology?

8.6 The noughties

The decade that began on Saturday 1 January 2000 and lasted until Thursday 31 December 2009 is known as the 2000s or 'the noughties'. These pages cover that decade… and beyond! The twenty-first century has seen a dramatic change in the way people live their lives. Since 1901 the population has grown from 41 million to over 64 million, which has led to ever-expanding towns and cities and increased pressure on services such as healthcare and power supplies. Advances in technology have also changed people's lives in all sorts of new ways – at home, at work and at school. So, how exactly have transport, entertainment, technology, work and home life, and politics and conflict changed since 2000?

Mission Objectives

- Examine and assess significant changes, developments, inventions, and ideas in the noughties.
- Create a presentation that draws together work from previous lessons.

Transport

- By 2000, there were over 25 million cars on Britain's roads, with 77 per cent of households owning at least one car.
- Traffic congestion has risen and some cities have introduced 'congestion charges' to try to reduce traffic. London introduced the scheme in 2003.
- In the 2000s, around 36 million British people took holidays abroad.
- Plans have been announced by a company called Virgin Galactic to offer tourist flights into space. A seat on the space flight could cost around £150,000.

SOURCE A: *A model of Virgin Galactic's spaceship.*

SOURCE B: *By 2013 social media website Facebook had a billion users. Many access it from their smartphones via a wireless Internet connection (wifi).*

Entertainment

- Virtually all homes have a television and there are a huge variety of channels to view and 'on demand' choices via satellite or broadband connections. The average UK citizen watches television for around 240 minutes a day, and it is the top leisure activity for eight out of ten people.
- Reading (via 'e-readers' as well as books), sport and exercise, shopping (now online, too), listening to music (now via media players such as iPods), cinema visits, and socializing with friends are very popular.
- The rise in the use of the Internet has led to the popularity of **social media** sites such as Facebook (founded in 2004) and Twitter (2006).

What Happened When? 2000s

- 2004 – The Boxing Day Tsunami killed at least 280,000 people in south-east Asia
- 2005 – London was chosen to host the 2012 Olympic and Paralympic Games
- 2007 – A financial crisis led to the closure of several banks and an increase in unemployment and business failures
- 2009 – Barack Obama became the first black President of the USA

FACT!

In 2008 Britain's population was 61 million. 12 per cent were aged over 85 and 1 in 12 were born overseas. At this time there were more pensioners in the UK than teenagers. The world's population hit six billion in 2000… and seven billion in 2011.

Technology

- In 2001 Apple launched the hugely successful iPod, a portable music player. This was followed by the iPhone, a smartphone, in 2007.
- In 2005, 50 per cent of people in the UK had Internet access at home. This increased to 67 per cent in 2008 and 83 per cent in 2013. By 2013 36 million adults (76 per cent) in the UK used the Internet every day, compared to 16 million in 2006.
- In 2008 around 70 per cent of adults owned a mobile phone, rising to 94 per cent by 2014.

Work and home

- In 2008 40 per cent of UK homes had a home computer (PC), but in recent years this figure has begun to drop as people move to the more portable smartphones and tablet computers.
- Out-of-town shopping centres and supermarkets are still very common, but a recent trend is online shopping. In 2014, 72 per cent of UK citizens said they bought goods and services online (compared to 53 per cent in 2008).
- All the washing machines, televisions, dishwashers, and mobile phone chargers in our homes mean that demand for electricity has increased dramatically – so too has the amount of polluting gases given off by the creation of this energy. In the last decade or so, the government has tried to use alternative sources of energy that create less pollution.
- In 2004 42 per cent of women who gave birth were unmarried and nearly one in four children live in one-parent families. Divorce rates remain high, with one in three marriages ending in divorce.
- In 2013, 29 per cent of households were made up of just one person.

Politics and conflict

- In 2001 terrorists attacked America, destroying the World Trade Center in New York. A 'War on Terror' began soon after when US-led forces invaded Afghanistan to search for terrorist bases.
- British soldiers began fighting in Iraq in 2003 as part of the 'War on Terror', although Iraq had no links to the World Trade Center attacks.
- In 2005 terrorists attacked tube trains and a bus in London, and in 2006 many people died in terrorist attacks in Mumbai, India.
- In 2005 Irish Nationalist group the IRA gave up its terror campaign and vowed to pursue peaceful methods to unite Ireland.

Wise Up Words

social media

SOURCE D: *A wind farm. Solar, tidal and wind power are becoming increasingly popular sources of renewable energy – although in 2014 these only met 4 per cent of the UK's demand.*

Most popular ...

♫ 'Evergreen' by Will Young

Only Fools and Horses Christmas Day episode 2001

Avatar

Ford Focus

Work

In your group, each of you should continue adding to your notes on your chosen category. Each member of your group should now have a full set of notes on one of the categories from the 1950s to the present day. In fact, as a group, you should now be experts on the way Britain (and the world) has changed since the 1950s.

Task

In your group, use all of your notes to create a presentation to highlight the key changes in each category from the 1950s to the present day. Think about:

- what the changes were
- when the changes happened
- reasons for the changes
- links between any of the changes; for example, did changes in one category lead to changes in another?
- which category changed the most... and the least.

Assessing Your Learning 3

Why will Margaret Thatcher be remembered in different ways?

In 1979 Margaret Thatcher became Britain's first ever female Prime Minister. She won three elections and remained Prime Minister until 1990, longer than any other twentieth-century British leader. But Thatcher was a very controversial figure. When she died in 2013 over 50,000 people lined the streets of London to pay their respects and throw white roses as her coffin passed by on its way to a service in St Paul's Cathedral… but later that week the song 'Ding-Dong! The Witch is Dead' from the film *The Wizard of Oz* reached Number 2 in the UK singles charts after people began downloading it to 'celebrate' her death! So why does Margaret Thatcher divide opinion?

This task focuses on the skill of what historians call **interpretation**. An interpretation is someone's version, opinion, or view, of something or someone. And different people can have different interpretations, or opinions, of all sorts of things… including people like Margaret Thatcher!

So, it is the job of top historians to:

- show *how* opinions or interpretations are different
- explain *why* they are different.

Study the sources about Margaret Thatcher below and then answer the questions that follow.

SOURCE A: *Margaret Thatcher was born in 1925 and died in 2013.*

David Cameron's viewpoint

'Margaret Thatcher didn't just lead our country – she saved our country. She took a country that was on its knees and made Britain stand tall again. We cannot deny that Thatcher divided opinion. For many of us, she was, and is, an inspiration. For others she was a force to be reckoned with. But if there is one thing that cuts through all of this – one thing that runs through everything she did – it was her lion-hearted love of this country.'

SOURCE A: *David Cameron made this short speech outside No. 10 Downing Street (the house of the British Prime Minister) shortly after Thatcher's death in 2013. He belongs to the same political party as Thatcher did and actually worked for her, in 1988, in one of his first jobs.*

David Douglass' viewpoint:

'I will not be shedding any tears over her. I wouldn't normally take comfort in anyone's death, but the woman shed no tears over our communities or the poverty she caused. An entire generation was thrown on the scrapheap, and sons and grandsons are still suffering now. Thatcher's legacy has been unemployment, crime, poverty, low levels of life expectancy, heroin addiction – the list goes on in places where she ripped the heart out of the community… a lot of people have no idea of the damage that woman inflicted on this country…'

SOURCE B: *David Douglass is a writer who worked as a coal miner in Durham and South Yorkshire. He was an important member of an organization called the National Union of Mineworkers that fought against the closing of coal mines by Margaret Thatcher's government in the 1980s.*

Be a Top Historian

It is important that top historians understand that a person's **interpretation (or opinion)** of someone or something will be based on their own personal views, ideas and attitudes. For example, a person's interpretation of an event could be influenced by their political beliefs or their nationality.

Task 1

Make notes on what impression of Margaret Thatcher each of the sources on page 160 gives you.

TOP TIP: Make at least two points about Thatcher (in your own words) from the source. Can you back up your point with a short quotation from the source?

Task 2

Write down the ways in which the view of Margaret Thatcher in **Source A** differs from that in **Source B**.

TOP TIP: Here, you are being asked to compare the sources and explain the differences between them. Think about what each person is saying about Thatcher.

Task 3

Suggest reasons why **Sources A** and **B** differ in their interpretations of Margaret Thatcher.

TOP TIP: This task asks you to think about WHY there seem to be two very different views about the same person. Here, you need to think about the two people who said these things about Thatcher... and the reasons why they might have different views!

Task 4

Write a short essay on why you think there are so many different opinions about people such as Margaret Thatcher. You should try to refer back to what you have learned in your History lessons about other controversial historical figures. You may also need to do some further research.

TOP TIP: You need to think about interpretations and viewpoints in general. Try to think of reasons why people who run countries, take nations into war, or make big political decisions divide people's opinions so much.

Hungry for More?

Find out more about Margaret Thatcher and write a mini biography.

Assessing your work

Good In a **good** essay, you would...	• describe different interpretations or opinions • identify and use some information from the two sources as examples to back up the points you've made • produce structured work.
Better In a **better** essay, you would...	• suggest some **reasons** for different interpretations • write mainly in your **own words**, but select and use information from the sources as examples to back up your work • produce work which is **carefully structured**.
Best In the **best** essay, you would...	• explain **how and why** different interpretations can be created or have arisen • write in your own words but carefully select and use information and **quotations** from the sources as examples to back up your points • produce work which is **clearly and carefully** written and structured.

9.1 The McDonald's story

Most people in Britain will have heard of a company called McDonald's. In fact, billions of people all over the world will have heard of McDonald's. Indeed, it is one of the global success stories of the twentieth century with more than 23,000 restaurants in 109 countries serving food and drink to 38 million customers daily!

Mission Objectives

- *Explain how and why McDonald's developed.*
- *Understand some of the arguments for and against a multinational company like McDonald's.*

McDonald's is what we call a **multinational** company – a huge moneymaking business that offers many products and services that are identical throughout the world. The rise in power and status of multinational companies such as McDonald's, Coca-Cola, Nike, and Disney is an example of what is known as **globalization**, a term used since the 1960s to refer to the spread of these brands all over the globe.

So how did McDonald's restaurants begin? What makes them so successful internationally? And is everyone happy about global success stories like McDonald's?

The beginning of a 'food empire'

McDonald's is a huge billion-dollar multinational restaurant chain and one of the world's most famous 'global brands'. There are restaurants all over the world willing to sell you a Big Mac or a Happy Meal, and McDonald's is a familiar sight in nearly every major city centre. Yet despite its size and popularity, McDonald's was only founded in the middle of the twentieth century by two brothers… neither of whom was called Ronald! The following cartoon outlines their success story:

1 In 1940 two brothers named Maurice and Richard McDonald opened a barbeque restaurant in California, USA. They sold all sorts of food… but felt they could make more money by opening a new type of restaurant.

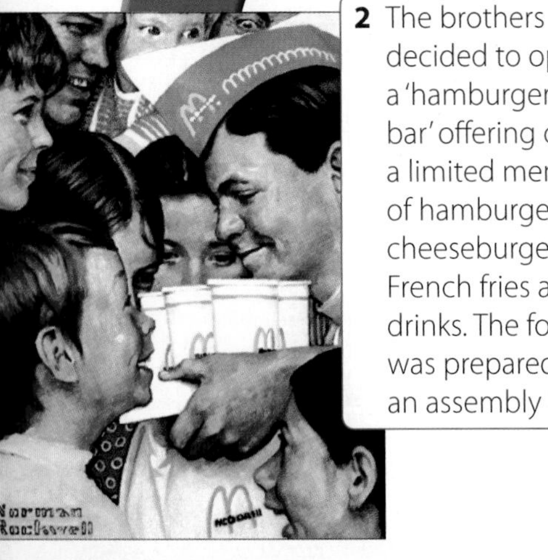

2 The brothers decided to open a 'hamburger bar' offering only a limited menu of hamburgers, cheeseburgers, French fries and drinks. The food was prepared on an assembly line.

3 The 'revamped' restaurant opened on 12 December 1948 and was soon making lots of money. Food from the limited menu was made quickly and sold cheaply.

4 In 1954 a salesman named Ray Kroc managed to persuade the brothers to buy eight of his milkshake machines. Whilst in the restaurant he was amazed at how the staff prepared food orders in seconds.

5 Kroc asked the brothers if he could open up a few other restaurants, each selling the same food and drink. Kroc would run the others, but they would share out the profits.

6 The brothers agreed and the first of the new restaurants opened near Chicago on 15 April 1955. It made lots of money… and by 1959 over 100 McDonald's restaurants had been opened all over America.

Not such a Happy Meal

Despite its worldwide success, McDonald's is not without its problems and controversy. In recent years it has come under attack from protesters who feel that it is just one big moneymaking organization that values profits above anything else. There have been criticisms over the treatment of workers, the amount of packaging used and concerns over how healthy its foods are.

McDonald's has also come under attack from environmentalists who claim that large areas of rainforest have been cut down to provide space for the millions of cows McDonald's needs to produce the beef for its burgers.

Global responsibility

On a more positive note, some argue that globalization has contributed to a growing sense of global responsibility. They say big multinational companies are now doing more than ever to combat developing-world poverty and conserve the environment by setting up projects in poorer countries and running their business in a more environmentally friendly way.

SOURCE A: *In recent years there have been anti-globalization riots that have targeted multinational companies such as McDonald's, Nike and Starbucks. Protesters are concerned that when these big companies make a profit, it is often at the expense of poorer countries who supply cheap labour and raw materials.*

7 Kroc wanted to open more restaurants all over the world… but the brothers weren't interested. In 1961 Kroc offered them $2.7 million to 'buy them out'. They accepted and Kroc took over the whole business!

8 In order to expand the business, Kroc introduced something known as **franchising**; anyone who wanted to open a McDonald's restaurant had to pay Kroc around $1000, and then 1.9 per cent of the profits of the restaurant. Kroc would pass 0.5 per cent on to the McDonald brothers.

9 The 'franchise method' proved very successful. By 1963 there were 500 restaurants, most of which were franchises.

Wise Up Words

franchising globalization multinational

Work

1 Write a sentence or two about the following terms:
- multinational
- globalization
- franchising

2 Write down reasons why you think global companies such as McDonald's have received:
   a criticism
   b praise.

3 Each of the following people have contributed in some way to the success of McDonald's:
- Maurice and Richard McDonald
- Ray Kroc

In your opinion, which one has contributed most to the success? Give reasons for your answer.

4 Each of the following dates are important in McDonald's history: 1959; 1955; 1963; 1974; 1948; 1954; 1961
   a Write each date on a separate line in chronological order.
   b Beside each date, write down what happened in that year.

10 Over the next few years McDonald's introduced many of the things that are now famous:

Ronald McDonald

Big Mac

Happy Meal

Egg McMuffin

Britain's first McDonald's restaurant opened in London in 1974 and now it is the largest food chain in the world, supplying food and drink to 50 million people a day in six continents.

9.2A What is 'terrorism'?

On the morning of 11 September 2001 19 terrorists hijacked four American passenger planes. After taking control, the hijackers flew two of the aircraft straight into the two tallest buildings in New York City – the twin towers of the World Trade Center – two skyscrapers containing thousands of office workers (see **Source A**). How did events unfold? And why did the attacks happen?

Mission Objectives

- Define the word terrorism and analyse how terrorists operate in today's world.
- Assess efforts to combat terrorism.

Further attacks

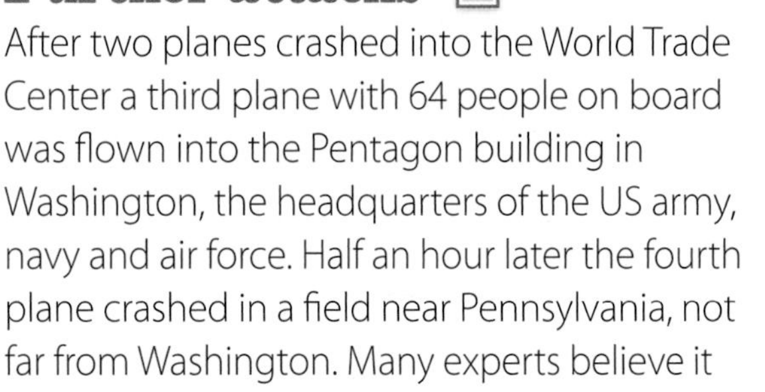

After two planes crashed into the World Trade Center a third plane with 64 people on board was flown into the Pentagon building in Washington, the headquarters of the US army, navy and air force. Half an hour later the fourth plane crashed in a field near Pennsylvania, not far from Washington. Many experts believe it was heading for the White House, the home of the US President. The fourth flight never made it because some of the 38 passengers fought with the hijackers to stop them reaching their target.

The US President, George W. Bush, was visiting a school when he heard of the first attacks. In a statement a few minutes later, he said, 'Today we have had a national tragedy. Two aeroplanes have crashed into the World Trade Center in an apparent terrorist attack on our country.'

THE Sun

DAY THAT CHANGED THE WORLD

Wednesday, September 12, 2001 30p www.thesun.co.uk

The ultimate crime of terrorism ... a huge ball of fire and smoke envelops the World Trade Center yesterday as a second hijacked airliner sma into the New York complex. Thousands are feared dead in the outrage, which struck at the heart of the free world, and ushered in a new age of

● SUICIDE HIJACKERS BLITZ AMERICA: SPECIAL EDITIO

SOURCE A: *The front page of the* Sun *newspaper from 12 September 2001. The photo shows the second plane hitting the World Trade Center.*

'Today our fellow citizens, our way of life, our very freedom came under attack in a series of deliberate and deadly terrorist attacks... Thousands of lives were suddenly ended by evil, despicable acts of terror... These acts of mass murder were intended to frighten our nation into chaos and retreat... Our military is powerful and it's prepared... The search is under way for those who are behind these evil acts. We will make no distinction between the terrorists who committed these acts and those who harbour them.'

▶ **SOURCE B:** *Part of President Bush's television statement, read out on the evening of 11 September 2001. What do you think the final line of his speech means?*

So what is terrorism?

Terrorism is the use of violence and intimidation for political reasons. Terrorists want to change the way governments and politicians behave by using threats, fear and bloodshed – in other words, terror. Terrorists don't usually represent a large proportion of the population so never get enough support for their ideas by normal peaceful methods. Instead, terrorists try to frighten people into behaving the way they want them to.

jihad terrorism

Why has the USA been targeted in recent years?

The attacks on the World Trade Center and the Pentagon in September 2001 were part of a series of attacks by one of the world's most famous terrorist groups, al-Qaeda. This mysterious group's members, who were led by a millionaire Saudi Arabian named Osama bin Laden, are all followers of Islam but have very strict, extremist beliefs that are different from most Muslims. They believe they are fighting a holy war, or **jihad**, against enemies of their religion.

SOURCE C: *The gaping hole in the side of the USS Cole, following an al-Qaeda suicide attack in October 2000. 17 American sailors were killed.*

The USA, in particular, is seen as one of al-Qaeda's greatest enemies. Other terror groups, with similar beliefs to al-Qaeda, have attacked American targets, too. They dislike the USA because they believe Americans interfere too much in the Middle East – an area including Kuwait, Iran, Iraq, Israel, Syria, Jordan, and Saudi Arabia. The Middle East is the source of around 60 per cent of the world's oil. In today's world, oil is essential, especially for transport. American cars, trucks and trains as well as homes and factories all need oil – as a result, the USA is very interested in what happens in this area.

For many years, the USA has kept battleships and built airbases in some Middle Eastern countries, most notably Saudi Arabia. Many countries find the American presence in the Middle East threatening, too. In recent years, terror groups (such as al-Qaeda) have targeted the USA because they believe they helped 'enemies of Islam', like Israeli Jews, during wars against Muslim nations in the Middle East. These terror groups want American influence out of the Middle East and are prepared to use terrorism to either frighten the USA into leaving or to anger America so much that it starts a holy war against all Muslim states. This, these groups hope, will end with final victory for Islam.

Why terrorism?

Terrorism has been used for many, many years to try to achieve a wide variety of different aims and objectives. Sometimes the terrorists have political reasons – they say they represent a group that wants to run their own country, for example – while other terrorists have religious reasons, like al-Qaeda. More often than not, though, terrorism is used for a mixture of religious and political reasons.

Work

1 Why do you think the terrorists might have been targeting:
- the World Trade Center
- the Pentagon
- the White House?

2 a In your own words, explain what is meant by the word 'terrorism'.
b What is a 'terrorist'?

3 Write a sentence or two to explain the following terms:
- extremist • jihad • al-Qaeda

4 a What do you think is meant by the term 'anti-American'?
b Why is al-Qaeda so anti-American?

9.2B What is 'terrorism'?

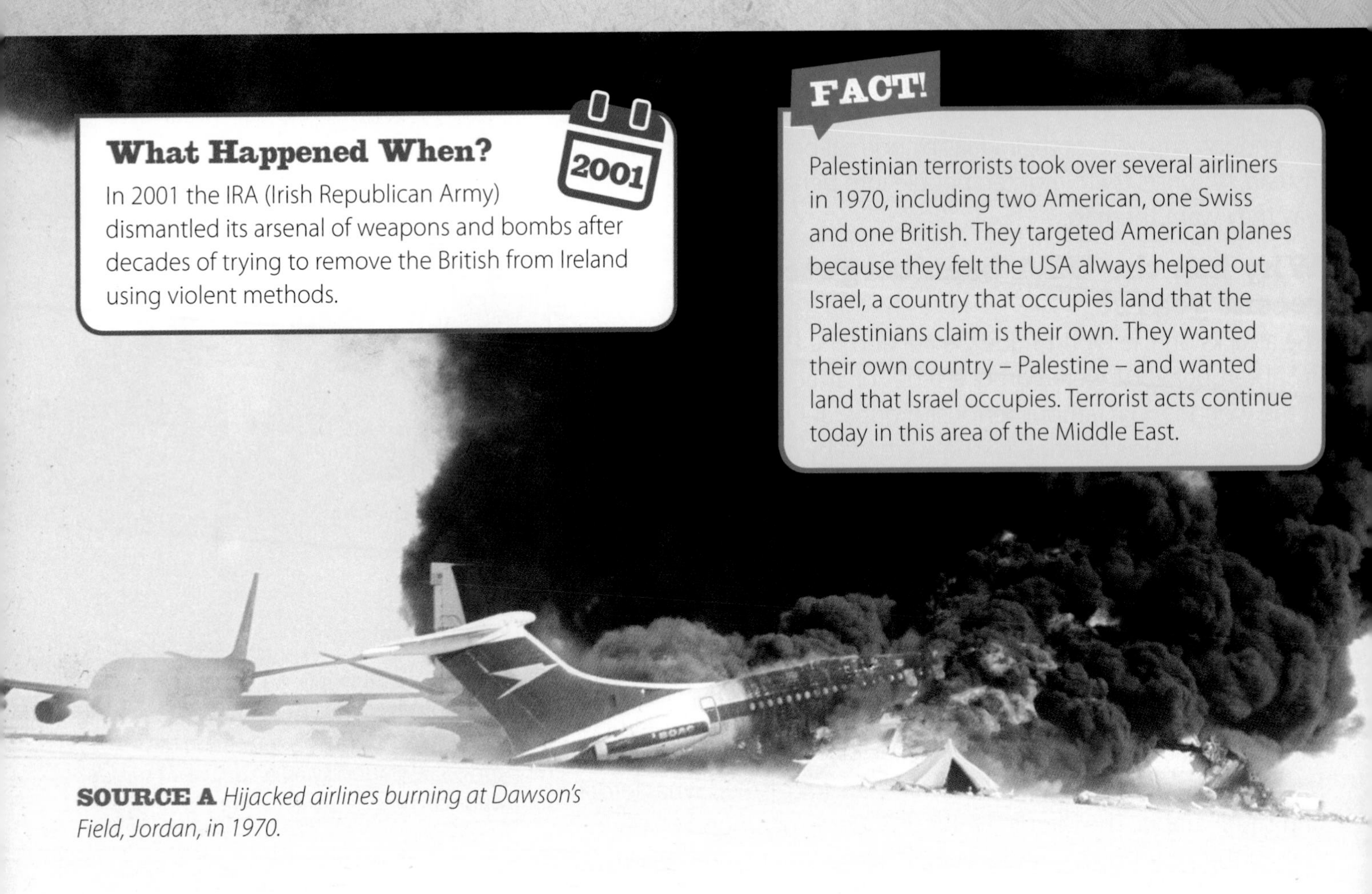

What Happened When?

2001

In 2001 the IRA (Irish Republican Army) dismantled its arsenal of weapons and bombs after decades of trying to remove the British from Ireland using violent methods.

FACT!

Palestinian terrorists took over several airliners in 1970, including two American, one Swiss and one British. They targeted American planes because they felt the USA always helped out Israel, a country that occupies land that the Palestinians claim is their own. They wanted their own country – Palestine – and wanted land that Israel occupies. Terrorist acts continue today in this area of the Middle East.

SOURCE A *Hijacked airlines burning at Dawson's Field, Jordan, in 1970.*

How do terrorists attack?

Terrorists use a variety of methods to cause death, destruction and disruption. They include:

Bombs Bombs can be hidden in busy places, on trains, buses, and even planes. A timer is usually used to set off the explosion when the bomber has left the area.

Car bombs A car or van packed with explosives is also a common terrorist weapon.

Chemical attack Poison gas can sometimes be used. In Tokyo, Japan, 12 people were killed in 1995 when the nerve gas sarin was released on the city's underground train system. In 2001 a killer disease called anthrax was used as a terror weapon in the USA. Anthrax bacteria, in the form of white powder, was sent through the US mail system.

Hijacking Terrorists can take control of boats, planes and buses. They use the passengers as hostages or use the vehicle as a weapon.

Letter bomb Explosives in an envelope or parcel that blow up when it is opened. This is a common method used by extreme animal rights groups.

Mortar bomb A bomb fired through a metal tube or pipe. It flies only a short distance (around 50–200 metres) but can be made cheaply. The IRA used mortar bombs to attack 10 Downing Street, the home of the Prime Minister, in 1991. The IRA were an Irish Nationalist group that wanted all British influence out of Ireland and were prepared to use terror tactics to achieve their aims.

Suicide bomb Explosives are attached to the bomber's body. They approach their target and explode the bomb. Palestinian terrorists are well known for this.

Can we stop them?

Stopping terrorists is not easy. Remember that their reasons for committing terrorist acts are just as established as our determination to stop them. However, many methods have been tried.

1 Hunt them down

This is hard to do. Many terrorists have remained hidden for many years, despite great efforts to find them. There are always more volunteers to take the place of any who are caught or captured.

2 Attack people who help terrorists

This is a commonly used method. In 2001 American troops, helped by other nations including Britain, invaded Afghanistan. The government there had allowed al-Qaeda to set up training bases for many years. This tactic makes it harder, but not impossible, for terrorist groups to operate.

3 Prevention

Security has been even stricter at airports since the 11 September attacks. In this country, the public have always been on their guard and asked to report any 'suspicious packages' to the police. Stations, city centres and any public places are very hard to guard all the time.

4 Negotiation

One answer is to involve the terrorists in discussions about their beliefs, concerns and activities. This has been tried several times, with some success. However, this is the most unpopular solution because to many it looks like the terrorists have won because their terrorist activities have got them what they want!

SOURCE B: *The remains of a London bus after the terrorist attacks on 7 July 2005. Three young men, members of al-Qaeda, blew themselves up on London tube trains, while a fourth exploded his bomb on this bus in Upper Woburn Place. In total, over 52 people were killed and 700 injured.*

Work

1 In your own words, explain the different methods used by terrorists to cause death, disruption and destruction.

2 Why have there been many years of conflict in the Middle East between Israelis and Palestinians?

3 a List each of the methods used to try to stop terrorists.
  b Which method do you think could be most effective in stopping terrorism? Give reasons for your answer.

9.3A What can Rebecca do that Laura couldn't?

The world we live in is always changing. Sometimes small changes, or inventions or discoveries, that might not seem very significant at the time can add up to large changes over a long period. For example, few people would have predicted the huge impact that the invention of the aeroplane or television would have had. But what impact would all this have had on two ordinary ladies like Laura and Rebecca?

Mission Objectives

- *Examine some of the key changes in British life from 1901.*
- *Judge how far Britain has changed since 1901.*

Step 1

Meet Laura, a lady living in 1901, around the time of Queen Victoria's death. Have a look at what life was like for Laura at the time.

Voting is for men... not women! In fact, it is very much a 'man's world' when it comes to politics and business. We are forbidden from doing certain jobs, too, and it is impossible for a woman to divorce her husband, no matter how badly he treats her!

In old age people are looked after by their families, or they use their savings or charity donations.

People communicate by talking to each other! And we write letters or use telegrams, which are short messages sent via telegraph and then typed and delivered by hand.

The average age of death for a woman is 56, and 53 for a man. It is much lower in very poor areas, though – in some parts of the East End of London it's 30!

One of the greatest luxuries would be a motor car! In 1901, there is only one car for every 900 people. And people save hard to buy things like a gramophone (to play music records), a piano, electric lighting or a new stove or 'cooker'.

The average couple have four children – but for every 1000 babies born, 125 will die before their first birthday.

School is compulsory up to the age of 12... and in the world of work there is a ratio of five male workers to every woman.

Britain is the most powerful nation on earth, ruling over more land, selling more goods and making more money than any other.

The most common causes of death are heart disease and illnesses that affect breathing, such as bronchitis and pneumonia.

In addition to sports such as football, cricket and horse racing, popular pastimes are cycling, indoor games (such as cards), trips to the theatre for variety shows... and evenings in the pub!

Step 2

Now you've met Laura and got to know her a little, study some of the key developments, discoveries and advances of the following century and beyond.

9.3B What can Rebecca do that Laura couldn't?

	Around 1901	The 1950s (halfway through the twentieth century)	Today
You would have to go to school from the age of five until...	 12 years old	 15 years old	 16 years old, and another two years in education
The main forms of communication were...	 Word of mouth, newspapers/magazines, telegrams, letters	 Word of mouth, newspapers/magazines, letters, radio, telephone	 Word of mouth, newspapers/magazines. TV, email, social media, telephone, radio, letters
This is how those in need might be looked after...	 Savings or charity	 Savings or small pension, some benefits and NHS	 Savings, pension and many benefits
The most common causes of death were...	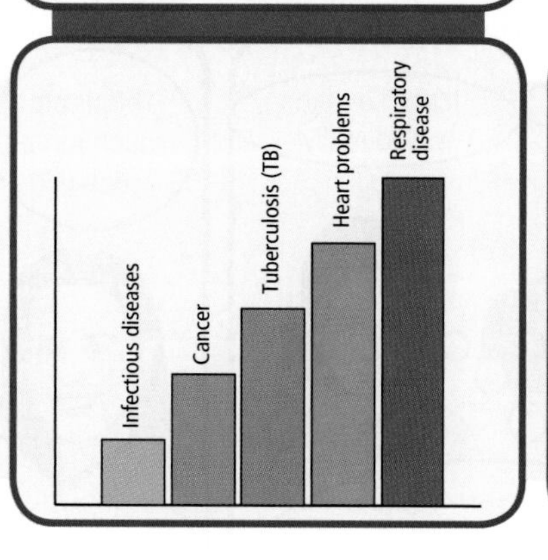	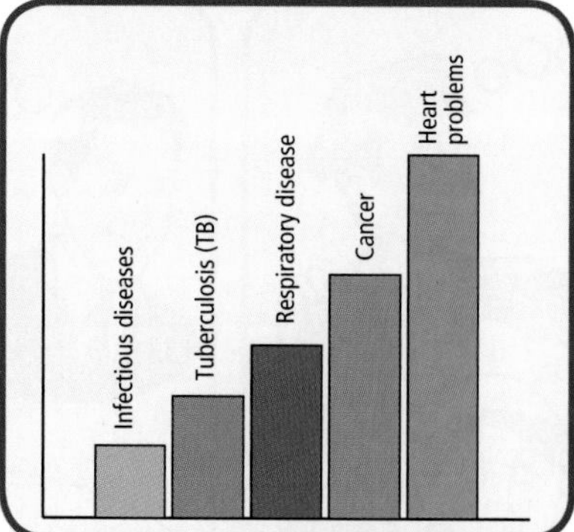	

SOURCE A: *A 2000 world ranking chart. This records Britain's position in the world (out of 192 countries) in several different categories.*

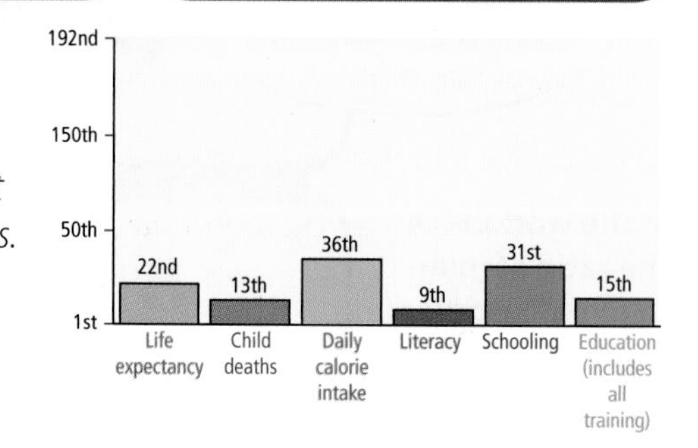

Step 3

Now it's time to meet Rebecca, a young lady who lives in today's modern world. Based on all the changes you've studied so far on these pages, think about the answers to the questions dotted around her. You might want to work with a partner or in a small group for this.

Be a Top Historian

GCSE

You will have noticed that during any one period of time, some things are changing and other things are staying the same (continuities). Understanding the **pace** of these changes is important too – knowing that some changes happen quickly and some happen slowly. You should be able to pick out areas of life where change happened rapidly and areas where change happened slowly between 1901 and today.

Is it a more 'caring' society that looks after vulnerable people?

Has education changed at all?

Have families and family life changed between 1901 and today?

How has the way people communicate with each other changed?

Has the motor car become popular?

How has the British Empire changed?

How has the way people spend their spare time changed?

Is Britain a healthier place?

How have women's rights changed?

What type of luxury goods do people desire today – and how are they different from the luxuries of 1901?

Work

1. a Draw two spider diagrams. One should be called 'Britain in 1901' and the other should be called 'Britain today'. Surround each spider diagram with facts and figures about Britain at these times.
   b Write a paragraph about the changes that took place in Britain between 1901 and today.
   c Of all the changes mentioned in your paragraph, which do you think was the most important? Give reasons for your choice. See if other people in the class agree with you.
   d When would you rather have lived: 1901 or today? Again, give reasons for your choice.
2. a A recent survey showed that 74 per cent of British people were happy with their lives and proud to be British. Why do you think so many people were proud to be British?
   b Are you proud of Britain or not? Give reasons.
   c Which of these words describe the country you would like to live in: free; caring; peaceful; safe; powerful; rich; fair; poor; equal; respected; religious; classless; clean?
   d Which of the words above do you think best describe Britain today – can you add some of your own?

Glossary

Alliance An agreement between countries to support each other in war
Anti-Semitism The hatred and persecution of Jews
Appeasement The policy of giving someone what they want in the hope that they will stop their demands
Area bombing Releasing bombs over a whole town or city
Armistice The ceasefire that ended the First World War on 11 November 1914
Arms race A competition between countries for superiority in the development and build-up of weapons
Assassinate To murder an important person for political or religious reasons
Assembly line A system using workers and machines in a factory to make goods in stages
Bayonet A long knife fitted to the end of a rifle
Blitz The German air raids on major British cities in 1940–1941
Blitzkrieg The intense German military campaign using tanks, aircraft and troops to try to bring about a swift victory
Bloc An alliance of countries with common interests
Bomber An aircraft designed to carry and drop bombs
British Commonwealth An organization of independent, free countries with close cultural, trade and sporting links to Britain and previously part of the British Empire
Brittle Hard but can break or shatter easily
Called up Being ordered to serve in the armed forces during wartime
Censor To delete sensitive information in a publication
Civilian A member of the public who is not part of the armed forces
Colonial Relating to land, people or ideas that are part of an empire such as the British Empire
Colony A country controlled by another country as part of its empire
Commemorate To recall and show respect for someone or something in a ceremony
Communism A political theory created by Karl Marx to make a society in which all property is publicly owned and each person works and is paid according to their abilities and needs
Concentration camp A prison camp where civilians and political prisoners were held by the Nazis under terrible conditions
Conscientious objector A person who believes that war is wrong and refuses to fight
Conscription The government policy of forcing men to join the armed forces in wartime
Court martial A military court for trying soldiers accused of breaking the rules
Cowardice Lack of courage
Currency The system of money used by a country
Death toll The number of people killed in war or a natural disaster
Democracy A system of government in which people vote to choose their politicians
Desertion Illegally leaving a military position without permission
Dictatorship A country governed by a dictator, who passes very strict laws
Dole Money goven to unemployed people by the government
Equality Being equal, especially in social position, rights and opportunities
Eugenics The scientific study of how to improve the human race
Euro The money system used by many countries in the European Union
Evacuation Being taken from places at risk during war, such as cities, to safer places, such as the countryside
Fascism An anti-democratic system of government developed by Mussolini in Italy and Hitler in Germany
Fighter A fast military aircraft designed for attacking other aircraft
Firestorm An intense fire caused by bombing in which strong air currents are drawn into the blaze, making it burn more fiercely
Foreign affairs Political matters connected with other countries
Franchising Permission given by a company to a business person to run a branch of that company and take a majority share of the profits
Führer German for 'leader', title used by Hitler as leader of Nazi Germany
Genocide The deliberate murder of a race of people
Gestapo The secret police in Nazi Germany
Ghetto A small, restricted area of a town where Jews were forced to live by the Nazis
Globalization The process by which businesses start operating on an international scale
Great Depression The period of high unemployment in the 1930s when many businesses failed
Hand grenade A small bomb thrown by hand
Hereditary A medical condition passed on from parents to their children
Holocaust The mass murder of Jews and other groups of people under the German Nazi regime during 1941–1945
Home front The civilian population of a nation whose armed forces are engaged in war abroad
Hull The bottom of a ship
Human rights The basic rights that it is generally considered all people should have, such as education, justice and freedom of speech
Hurricane The most common British fighter plane during the Second World War
Incendiary A bomb designed to start fires on the ground
Indoctrinate To brainwash someone to believe something without questioning it
Infantry Soldiers fighting on foot
IRA Irish Republican Army, which fought for Irish independence from Britain
Iron Curtain A term coined by Winston Churchill to describe an imaginary barrier between the communist countries of the Soviet bloc and the West after the Second World War
Jihad Islamic holy war against non-believers
Long-term cause An event or situation in the past that leads to an effect some time later

Luftwaffe The German air force until the end of the Second World War
Maiden The first attempt of its kind
Martyr A person who is prepared to die for their beliefs
Mass-produce To make goods in huge numbers, often for cheaper than before
Means Test An official check into a person's financial circumstances to work out if they qualify for state assistance
Migration Moving from one country to another in search of work and a new life
Multicultural Containing several cultural or ethnic groups within a society
Multinational A company operating in several countries
Munitions Military weapons, ammunition, equipment and stores
National Insurance Compulsory payments by employees and employers to provide state assistance for people who are sick, unemployed or retired
Nationalist A person who wants political independence for a country
Nationalize To transfer an industry such as coal mining from private to state ownership or control
No man's land The wasteland between the trenches of the Allied and German forces during the First World War controlled by neither side
Pals battalion A group of friends or co-workers who enlisted to fight in the First World War together
Pardon To remove the blame from someone wrongly accused of a crime, such as desertion in wartime
Partition The division of India into largely Muslim Pakistan and largely Hindu India in 1947
Patriotism Supporting your country, especially during wartime
Persecution Ill treatment of someone because of race or political or religious beliefs
Poverty The condition of being extremely poor
Precision bombing Carefully targeted bombing of specific locations such as docks, air bases and munitions factories
Propaganda False or misleading information used to spread a certain point of view
RAF Royal Air Force, the official air force of Britain
Rationing Officially limiting the amount of items such as food allowed to each person during wartime
Rearmament Restocking a country's supply of weapons and armed forces
Retreat Move back from a position
Security Council A permanent body of the United Nations seeking to maintain peace and security
Semi A house attached to another house on one side
Shell A bomb that is fired a long distance by artillery (heavy guns)
Shell shock A nervous condition suffered by some soldiers exposed to the noise and chaos of battle
Short-term cause An event or situation that leads to an immediate effect
Shrapnel Fragments of a bomb or shell that are thrown out when it explodes
Single market An association of countries trading with each other without restrictions or taxes
Social media Interaction among people in which they create and share information in virtual communities
Social security Financial help from the state for people with not enough or no money
SOS An international code signal of extreme distress, used especially by ships
Soviet The Russian word for council, used to describe communist Russia
Space race The competition between the USA and the USSR to explore space
Spitfire The most famous British fighter plane used in the Second World War
Stalemate A situation in which further progress by opposing sides in a war seems impossible
Sterilize To operate on someone to prevent future pregnancies
Strike To refuse to work as a form of organized protest often for better pay and conditions
Suffragette A campaigner for the right of women to vote who organized often-violent protests to press their cause
Suffragist A campaigner for the right of women to vote who used peaceful means of protest
Superpower One of the world's two most powerful nations in the Cold War period after the Second World War, the USA and the USSR
Swastika The crooked cross symbol used by the Nazi Party as their logo
Terrorism The use of violence and intimidation for political reasons
Transatlantic Crossing the Atlantic Ocean
Treaty A contract between countries
Trench foot A foot disease common among First World War troops who stood in cold and wet conditions for long periods
Triple Alliance The agreement between Germany, Austria-Hungary and Italy before the outbreak of the First World War
Triple Entente The agreement between Britain, France and Russia before the outbreak of the First World War
Unionist A person, especially a member of a Northern Ireland political party, who is in favour of the union of Northern Ireland with Britain
Viceroy A ruler who leads a colony on behalf of a monarch
Welfare state A system whereby the state protects the health and well-being of its citizens with free healthcare, pensions and other benefits.
Western Front The area in Northern France and Belgium where British, French and Belgian forces fought Germany in the First World War
Zeppelin A large German airship used during the First World War for reconnaissance and bombing

Index

NOTES TO HELP YOU USE THIS INDEX:

Kings, queens and other royals are listed by their first name, so look for 'Edward VII' and not 'King Edward VII'. All other people are listed by their surname, so look for 'Churchill, Winston' and not 'Winston Churchill'. Any dates or time periods included in this index can be found at the start of the index and are in date order.

A

B

C

D

E

F

G

H

OXFORD
UNIVERSITY PRESS

Great Clarendon Street, Oxford, OX2 6DP, United Kingdom

Oxford University Press is a department of the University of Oxford. It furthers the University's objective of excellence in research, scholarship, and education by publishing worldwide. Oxford is a registered trade mark of Oxford University Press in the UK and in certain other countries

First published in 2015

British Library Cataloguing in Publication Data
Data available

978-0-19-839321-4

10 9 8 7 6 5 4

Paper used in the production of this book is a natural, recyclable product made from wood grown in sustainable forests.
The manufacturing process conforms to the environmental regulations of the country of origin.

Printed in Hong Kong by Sheck Wah Tong Printing Press Ltd.

Acknowledgements

Artwork by Martin Sanders, Moreno Chiacchiera, QBS Media, Rudolf Farkas and Oxford University Press.

Full image acknowledgements can be found at www.oxfordsecondary.co.uk/acknowledgements

We are grateful for permission to reprint extracts from the following in this book:

Vera Brittain: *Testament of Youth: An Autobiographical Study of the Years 1900-1925* (Gollancz 1933/Penguin 1989), reprinted by permission of Mark Bostridge and T J Brittain-Catlin, literary executors for the Estate of Vera Brittain 1970.

Josh Brooman: *The Great War: The First World War 1914-1918* (20th Century History, Longman, 1985, and *Hitler's Germany: Germany 1933-1945* (20th Century History, Longman, 1985), reprinted by permission of the publishers, Pearson Education.

Winston Churchill: 'Blood, toil, tears, and sweat', 13 May 1940, House of Commons; 'Wars are not won by evacuations', 4 June 1940, House of Commons; and ' Never give in', 29 Oct 1941, Harrow School; copyright © Winston S Churchill, reprinted by permission of Curtis Brown, London, on behalf of the Estate of Sir Winston Churchill.

Daily Express editorial: 'Why do we let this man cast a shadow over our war dead?, *Daily Express*, 6 Nov 1998, reprinted by permission of Express Newspapers.

George Haig (Earl Haig) interviewed on BBC News, 30 June 2006, reprinted by permission of the BBC.

Max Hastings: *Finest Years: Churchill as Warlord 1940-45* (HarperPress, 2009), copyright © Max Hastings 2009, reprinted by permission of HarperCollins Publishers Ltd.

Nick Higham: 'Dunkirk: The Propaganda War', BBC News, 2 June 2000, reprinted by permission of Nick Higham and of the BBC.

Ian Hislop: commentary on *Not Forgotten: Soldiers of Empire*, Channel 4, November 2009, reprinted by permission of Casarotto Ramsay & Associates Ltd on behalf of Ian Hislop.

Tom Hopkinson: *Of This Our Time - A journalist's story 1905-1950* (Hutchinson, 1982), copyright © Tom Hopkinson 1982, reprinted by permission of Sheil Land Associates Ltd.

Sean Lang: *The Second World War: Conflict and Co-operation* (CUP, 1993), copyright © Cambridge University Press, reprinted by permission of Cambridge University Press.

Caroline Lang: interview with Anita Bowers in Keep Smiling Through: Women in the Second World War (CUP, 1989), reprinted by permission of Cambridge University Press.

J A R Marriott: The English in India: a Problem of Politics (Clarendon Press, 1932), reprinted by permission of Oxford University Press.

Phil Plait (aka The Bad Astronomer): 'Fox TV and the Apollo Moon Hoax', 13 Feb 2001, posted at www.badastronomy.com, reprinted by permission of the author.

Gary Sheffield: 'The Western Front: Lions led by donkeys?', BBC History website, 3 Oct 2011, reprinted by permission of the author.

Dan Snow: 'Viewpoint: Ten Big Myths about World War One debunked', *BBC News Magazine*, 25 Feb 2014, reprinted by permission of United Agents (www.unitedagents.co.uk) on behalf of Dan Snow and of the BBC.

S Warburton: *Hindsight*, Vol 8, April 1998, Philip Allan Magazines, reprinted by permission of Philip Allan for Hodder Education.

Steven Waugh: *Essential Modern World History* (Nelson Thornes, 2001), reprinted by permission of the publishers, Oxford University Press.

We have made every effort to trace and contact all copyright holders before publication, but if notified of any errors or omissions, the publisher will be happy to rectify these at the earliest opportunity.

From the author, Aaron Wilkes: The author wishes to once again thank the fantastic team at OUP for all their hard work, enthusiasm and support. Special thanks must also go to Sarah Flynn, my publisher, and Becky DeLozier, my editor. They have been part of every stage of this process and have always been on hand to encourage me, give advice and make brilliantly practical suggestions. I must also acknowledge my wife, Emma, and two other blossoming historians who share my life, my daughters Hannah and Eleanor. Their love, patience and kind words have been a constant inspiration.

The publishers would like to thank the following people for offering their contribution in the development of this book and related components:

James Ball, for writing parts of the Second Editions of the books in this series.

Patrick Taylor, Director of Teaching at Chenderit School, for literacy consultancy.

Jerome Freeman, Educational Consultant, for assessment consultancy.